CONFLICT AND CORRESPONDENCE

CONFLUENCIAS

Series Editors
Susie S. Porter
UNIVERSITY OF UTAH

María L. O. Muñoz
SUSQUEHANNA UNIVERSITY

Diana Montaño
WASHINGTON UNIVERSITY IN ST. LOUIS

Conflict and Correspondence

Belonging and Urban
Community in Guadalajara,
Mexico, 1939–1947

JASON H. DORMADY

University of Nebraska Press
Lincoln

Portions of chapter 3 were previously published in "God, Cleanliness, and the City: Local Uses of Hygiene and Anticlerical Language in Religious Conflict—Guadalajara, Mexico, 1939–1942," *Latin Americanist* 64, no. 4 (2020): 393–422. Copyright © 2020 by the Southeastern Council of Latin American Studies. Used by permission of the University of North Carolina Press. www.uncpress.org.

♾

For customers in the EU with safety/GPSR concerns, contact: gpsr@mare-nostrum.co.uk
Mare Nostrum Group BV
Mauritskade 21D
1091 GC Amsterdam
The Netherlands

Library of Congress Control Number: 2025006457

Designed and set in Bulmer MT Std by Lacey Losh.

For Jacob Finley
Thank you for your excellent timing

For Rebecca Maureen Dormady, 1963–2020

Contents

Illustrations

Acknowledgments

First, I thank Emily Casillas at the University of Nebraska Press for her patience and professional guidance as I moved this project from presentation to monograph. Similarly, I appreciate the hard work and attention to detail of independent copyeditor Maureen C. Bemko. Next, I should recognize that working at a teaching-centered institution while engaging in research requires support and resources from administrators and effective union representation. I would like to thank former deans Stacey Robertson, Todd Shiver, and Jill Hernandez, as well as the leadership team of the United Faculty of Central (and the collective bargaining agreement) for sabbatical leave and the small but important research support at Central Washington University (CWU). Similarly, I express my appreciation of the CWU International Studies and Programs Advisory Committee for funding to present preliminary research and get feedback on the material in this book. Without the hard work of MA student research assistants McKenzie (Max) Graham, Lilian Alcazar-Oseguera, and Henry Jennings in helping me create and organize the database of tens of thousands of names gleaned from archival sources, this project would still be in draft stages. Karen "Angie" Hill and later Kristy Magdlin provided the logistical support for research, writing, and travel.

I am grateful to the librarians and archivists in Guadalajara and Mexico City who made this research possible. Mayra Susana González Jaime at the Archivo de Instrumentos Públicos del Estado de Jalisco offered great advice as I worked through stacks of notary books. Most important, the now-retired José Manuel Ramos López, who directed the historical documents collection at the Archivo Histórico Municipal de Guadalajara (AHMG), spent hundreds of hours hauling indexes, boxes, and blueprints to the reference area, unearthing uncataloged documents, and telling me stories about the city and its neighborhoods. Also at the AHMG, Irma González Medina, in the library and book collection, served as an instrumental guide for helping me find secondary material. In addition, I share my immense gratitude to Robert Curley Álvarez of the Universidad de Guadalajara for introductions and access to resources in Guadalajara and at the UdeG that made my time in the city productive.

Professional organizations that create inviting and comfortable places to present and get feedback have helped this project grow from its earliest iterations. In particular, I thank the many organizers of the Rocky Mountain Council of Latin American Studies and the Southeastern Council of Latin American Studies for their hard work to create spaces of exchange. The feedback and encouragement from particular colleagues have helped immensely in those settings: thank you to scholars Heather Chiero, Christina Jiménez, Sandra Mendiola, Mónica Ricketts, and Donald F. Stevens.

Great thanks also go out to those who read parts or all of the manuscript, but any errors in this work are mine alone and do not reflect the efforts and input of my long-suffering colleagues. In my home department at Central Washington University, Professors Chong Eun Ahn, Roxanne Easley, Josué Estrada, Lacy Ferrell, Jason Knirck, and Marilyn Levine all provided valuable insight as part of our department research and writing circle. Sarah L. Cline, professor emerita at UC Santa Barbara and my former dissertation advisor and current friend and colleague, applied her usual vigor to improve the many mechanical and conceptual weaknesses. I am extremely grateful for the network of scholars who willingly dedicated their time to reading this work at various stages: Rafaela Acevedo-Field, Catherine Colwell, David Dalton, Paul Gillingham, Hanni Jalil, Rebecca Janzen, Andrae Marak, Kathleen McIntyre, Nicole Pacino, Gretchen Pierce, and Benjamin Smith. I want to offer particular thanks to Robert Weis at the University of Northern Colorado for not only his suggestions but also his encouragement. I also thank the peer reviewers who read the manuscript and made tough but fair suggestions and comments that transformed and improved the book.

Research on this book happened at some of the best and worst times of life. Literal and figurative survival would not have been possible without the support of members of our local communities in Guadalajara and Ellensburg, Washington. Particular thanks go out to our adopted family in Guadalajara's Barrio Naciones Unidas for kids' activities, holiday parties, and dinner invitations that brought added joy to daily life. Special thanks also go out to the Rendón and Arcila families for late-night trips around Guadalajara to all of the best food spots and for the eternally memorable Chancla Jos. When I returned to Ellensburg from Mexico burned and unable to walk, the help of the Ailshie, Breckon, Dixon, Pollock, Robinson, Schilling, and Walker families helped our transition home and brought light at a dark time.

Most important, the immense willingness of Carol, Isaac, Oliver, Helen, and Jacob Dormady in supporting and enduring the process of teaching, research, and writing is and has been admirable. Special thanks go out to Carol for her honest responses to impenetrable passages and in letting me talk through the conundrums, puzzles, and roadblocks associated with this project. I fully owe her credit for being the first to encourage me to explore more deeply the documents regarding women as property owners. To Isaac, Oliver, Helen, and Jacob, who watched with us as we lost so many family members and friends to COVID-19 and other illnesses from 2020 to 2025, I extend my admiration for your resilience and gratitude for your love toward one another.

CONFLICT AND CORRESPONDENCE

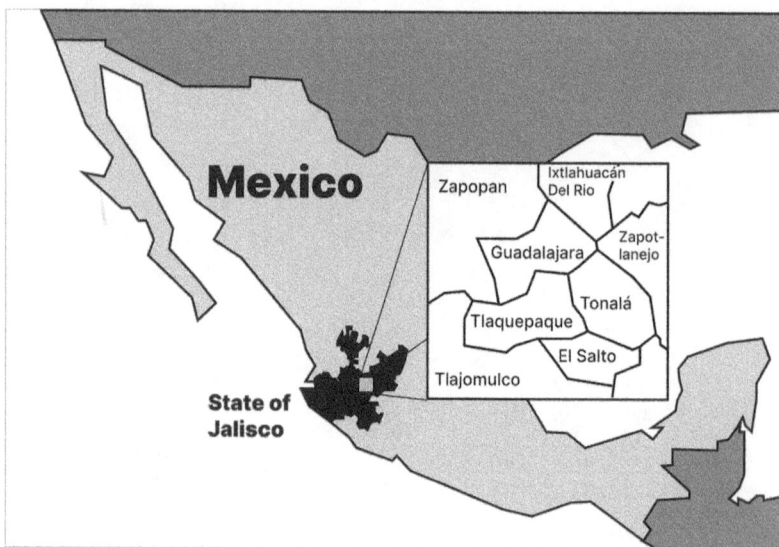

FIG. 1. The state of Jalisco and the present-day boundaries of Guadalajara and surrounding *municipios*. Map by the author.

Introduction

Indulge me for a moment of historical imagination.

It is 1940. You are fifty years old. Born in Guadalajara, you raised your children in the city center as your parents did you and their parents before them. During the upheavals of revolution and religious violence, the rhythm of life in the city brought you comfort. The smell from the corner bakery, the familiar feel of paving stones on avenida Colón, the steady ecclesiastical calendar rhythms, and the calming clerical influence during the Catholic Mass—these all brought you a sense of ease in times of change. But now things have gone too far. Between 1920 and 1940, the city grew by over one hundred thousand people. Familiar streets are being torn up for water lines that never materialize or that bring only illness when they do. You have had to change your route to church because the city bus made your former path too dangerous. The bakery is gone, replaced by a mechanic's shop, whose cars spill out onto the street along with the employees' foul language. Even when you travel to nearby Tonalá to visit your cousins, you can't escape the chaos: what used to be the great haciendas are now rows of small houses. What happened to your city? You feel angry, disoriented, and on edge.

And if you will, a second moment from a different perspective.

The year is still 1940. You are fifteen years old, and you just arrived in Guadalajara for the first time from a rancho in Michoacán. Your sister says she can find you work in the shop of a family she cleans for, and so you left your mother at home and came to the city. When you climbed down from the truck you hitched a ride with, the first thing you notice is a smell of exhaust—not the exhaust from an occasional passing car but a constant, pervasive stink of diesel and gasoline fumes that choke you. All around you, trucks or horse carts are removing goods from the market to close the day. You have never seen such a variety of items and in such quantities. Stepping forward to get a better view, a motorcycle nearly hits you, the rider shouting an obscenity. On the corner you hear laughing and music that draw you toward some open doors. You recognize the sound of a trumpet and drums, but even though you love this new music it doesn't sound quite right. Looking past the beautiful men and women dancing and drinking, you see a box that the music comes from. No musicians! What is going on here? As you start to step in, a hand lands on your shoulder and then a voice speaks: "Your Savior and Redeemer searches for you. Don't get lost in there, my child." You turn to see a woman pulling a tiny cart of sweets with one hand and carrying a book with a cross on it in the other. Who is this person? What does she mean? What is this music? You can't decide if you have landed in paradise or in purgatory. A sudden longing for your family wells up inside of you. How will you ever fit in here?

The transformation of Guadalajara, Mexico, by 1939 stunned both natives to the city and new arrivals. The city's population increased by 75 percent between 1920 and 1940 (143,000 to roughly 250,000) and by just over an additional 60 percent in the next ten years, reaching an estimated 403,000 inhabitants by 1950. Guadalajara is unique in that this growth represents a rate that is double the rest of Mexico in that same decade.[1] As the city changed around its longtime residents and as incoming migrants arrived, how could either group keep from feeling alienated, isolated, and divorced from the community around them?

The answer to that question is my argument in this work: petitions and correspondence to the city government allowed women, men, residents, domestic migrants, international immigrants, the rich, and the poor to find a sense of belonging in a rapidly changing urban community. As they expressed their desires and definitions of community through correspondence with city leaders, they went beyond simply requesting goods and services. The petitioning process allowed residents a way to socially and physically orient themselves in a new city. While this process naturally put residents in conflict with one another, as well as with city officials, participating in conflict to define the good life contributed to a sense of belonging in the changing city.

Residents used petitions and letters to municipal officials in sensate, moral, recreational, spiritual, and gendered ways with the aim of creating livable community and avoiding the disorientation experienced as a result of urban transformation. First, the petitioners and letter writers curated and communicated about the city sensoryscape to better fit their own economic or cultural contexts and lifestyles. Second, various parties attempted to set the moral and/or ludic boundaries for city life—two impetuses that often worked against each other. Additionally, religious residents interpreted local and national laws in unconventional or unintended ways to attack ideological adversaries and defend sacred space to declare their belonging during a time of religious transition. And finally, many women seized opportunities in property ownership or commerce during this era of rapid expansion to support themselves and networks of other women as active builders of Guadalajara. In the context of infrastructure failures, tight housing markets, and a dramatic aesthetic transition, petitions on these topics reinforced to residents and (they hoped) city officials their belonging to the community. As such, this is a history based primarily on evidence from correspondence archives, and it focuses on ordinary people expressing themselves in their own words.

Correspondence directed at city, state, or federal officials occurred in the additional context of a government loudly proclaiming an active revolutionary movement. Residents living the Mexican Revolution's consequences within a transforming city in the 1940s had to ask themselves what they could do to make the 1910 revolution work for them without inciting the ire of its political leaders. Like the residents of Morelia, Michoacán, the people of Guadalajara interacted with city government to establish their "rights, responsibilities, and contributions" to the city.[2] However, gaining a sense of belonging in urban society goes beyond the transaction between people and government for goods and services; it encompasses more than the legal citizenship denied to most of Guadalajara's residents by virtue of their gender, immigration status, or age.

Correspondence between residents of Guadalajara and the city government demonstrates not only how *tapatíos* (the nickname for people from Guadalajara) perceived the city around them but also how they imagined life in the revolutionary city.[3] These letters and petitions also reveal how residents defined their membership in the wider community. This revelation happens on two levels: it directly discusses the demands of residents crafting petitions, and it also helps readers learn about the lives of residents against whom petitions are directed. As Guadalajara city life fragmented, traditional corporate relationships shattered, new alliances emerged after decades of conflict, and as even the physical space around them was transformed, how could residents find any sense of belonging?[4] *Tapatío* visions for shaping urban space and creating a sense of place rarely reconciled comfortably with one another and at times took completely opposing positions. For example, the fetid stench of tanneries and the decay found in their runoff was a horror for most people in western Mexico but served as the smell of profit and employment for others.[5] Amid fragmentation, residents began the process of finding this sense of belonging through petitions. These grassroots narratives defined what the good life meant for them, how the city space should be engaged through the senses, and how city regulations could be marshaled to best respond to the petitioner's vision of a new city.

Naturally, the different approaches to defining the sense of place as well as ordering the city's physical space bred conflict, but in conflict *tapatíos* could find belonging in community. This sense of inclusion grew through conflict as both a ritual and a narrative of belonging, even when the outcome of conflict may have fallen short of expectations. In these pages I examine the significance of the act and the process of conflict itself and emphasize that disagreements are important for creating urban community and a sense of belonging to that community. In this approach, I bypass centering the results of resident demands and instead focus on the process of petitioning and conflict itself as a creator of community. Conflict and petitions reinforced petitioners' views of their place in city life. Petitioning individuals could find belonging, no matter their individual identity, through correspondence and conflict because the processes signified a ritual of proclaiming one's belonging to the community. Rather than sitting to the side and keeping their mouths shut, residents proactively expressed their widely varied views of city life in line with their sensibilities.

The Framework: What Does Belonging Mean?

Mexicans interpreted the 1910 revolution's consequences through the outward expression of community formation, even if it rarely rose to the level of "utopian tomfoolery."[6] Particularly after 1940, when the revolution-as-radical-change is considered finished by most historians, the revolutionary rhetoric and consequences had not evaporated.[7] Mexicans harnessed revolutionary language to shape the world around them in the face of incredible bureaucratic or other systemic limitations. Following that line of reasoning, the present work considers the correspondence of a variety of residents as a way to read their interpretation of rebuilding Mexico at the community level as the lived experience of revolution that came after the armed phase of the revolution. Each chapter explores a wide range of people who argue over water bills, raise families, solicit sex, attend mass, fight with neighbors, dance into the night, build networks of support, drive their rivals out of business, or cleanse their places of worship. Through these varied actions, residents of all types found a sense of belonging by telling themselves the story of their position in the city and expressing it to civic leaders. But what is "belonging"?

Reinforcing their position in the community to themselves and to political leaders in this "mosaic" city through petitions matches well with the psychological and sociological idea of belonging.[8] Consequently, I have chosen to use for my theoretical framework the concept of belonging in new settings, an approach used by sociologist Floya Anthias. Mental health researchers define belonging as a subjective but deeply important sense of "personal involvement in a system or environment" that splits into two important areas. Individuals who find belonging because they feel needed or accepted demonstrate one form of belonging. The other group comprises those who gain a sense of belonging because something about themselves "complements the system or environment" that they are in.[9] Anthias's work focuses on how immigrants find a sense of belonging in their new receiving societies and reinforce it through narratives they share within their social circles. In other words, she examines how migrants establish a sense of belonging to a wider community in their receiving country through telling stories about themselves and their place in their new society.[10] In examining belonging, Anthias considers how people exercise agency to develop "coping strategies and negotiation of belonging in transnational spaces" and how these strategies help them "assess their needs and life projects."[11] I have adapted this concept to Guadalajara by showing how residents found a sense of belonging to a new city community because either the city had changed around them (long-term residents) or they had recently moved to the city (new arrivals). Instead of transnational spaces, the focus here is belonging in transitional spaces established by residents telling stories about themselves in those spaces.

How does one create a story about a community and its members' place in it? According to Anthias, residents in an area create what are called narratives of belonging—stories people tell themselves and others to establish their relationship to each other and to the physical space around them. Anthias states that these collective tales circulate among associates and the wider community and help people to understand the actions they must take to fit in with others around them. "At the same time," Anthias states, "these stories are ways in which we try to order and organize our experiences in terms of certain conventional norms or rules. These relate to the type of narration that is deemed appropriate in a particular context and in relation to a particular audience—imagined or real."[12] The subjects in this book used petitions and correspondence to generate and reinforce narratives of belonging or, in other words, stories about how they fit into the growth, tradition, and revolutionary trajectory of Guadalajara, Mexico.

In using this framework from Anthias, I examine strategies of how residents sought to cultivate a sense of belonging in the wider urban community by penning narratives of their desires for themselves and civic leaders that went beyond the particular street or neighborhood where they lived. As local histories, MA theses, PhD dissertations, and a seemingly endless stream of journal articles and books show, every neighborhood and even street in Guadalajara built its own local identity. For example, Valentina Napolitano's ethnography explores how residents in Guadalajara's Colonia Polanco engaged in "belonging to and identifying with a particular space" through physical acts such as homeownership, home décor, and domestic space organization.[13] By contrast, *Conflict and Correspondence* is set in a larger scale. This study of letters and petitions engages with a body of archival resources to explore the idea of belonging to the wider urban community beyond the neighborhood. The sources used here reference the city broadly and examine how people engage in an attempt to "synthesize diverse histories and culture and, thereby, provide civic meaning for an otherwise incoherent urban world."[14] For a city filling with rural migrants, for a population with a range of classes, and in the face of growing urban anonymity, cultivating a sense of belonging through correspondence and the conflict inherent in petitions became a strategy for many residents.[15]

Why is this work examining belonging so important for communities? Traditional urban centers face the challenge of finding ways of helping residents feel a sense of belonging. Unlike utopian societies (intentional communities), most cities lack a charismatic leader, shared ideology, or universal kinship ties to bind them together. They also dissolve with less ease than intentional communal societies, whose internal conflicts or differentiation in goals might slowly or quickly disassemble the community and the legitimacy it relied on.[16] Simply put, people in cities are stuck with each other, and they have to figure out why and how to live together without the illusion they can do so by eliminating all conflict. Placed in new communities by migration or faced with a changing community, how do city residents establish who they are, who their people are, and where they fit in the world? What makes new residents of São Paulo feel like they belong to a larger community of *paulistas*? How do suburban residents in an area annexed to a larger city come to feel they share a community with their former neighbors in another entity? If we accept Benedict Anderson's idea that community is imagined, how do we get to that point where people can imagine themselves as part of (or belonging to) a community that is fragmented, divided, and in the process of explosive growth? Established residents and new residents of Guadalajara all imagined themselves as part of a broader community by engaging in the petitioning process that helped them see themselves as attaining insider status in a community of *tapatíos*. They created for themselves, for their neighbors, and for city leaders their own narratives of belonging, and they did so through the circulation of petitions.

Belonging to a wider city community is challenging compared to living in other units of social organization. Villages, small towns, and neighborhoods allow for consistent interaction and the maintenance of social ties that establish belonging. The grand emotional narratives, artifacts, and distortion or manipulation of history at the nation-state scale are difficult to produce in urban situations where the up-close realities of day-to-day life often preclude the delusions that may lurk in abstract notions of patriotism.[17] Nevertheless, the *patria chica*, or local identity, is foundational in the Ibero-heritage world and is often useful for imagining the historical realities of a city's residents.[18]

In Guadalajara, religious institutions, public festivals, shared physical spaces, climate, weather events, illness (and responses to it), external political forces, and networks (work, kin, parish, etc.) functioned reasonably well to generally bind the residents together at some level for nearly three centuries. Nevertheless, by the time Mexico declared its independence in 1821, Guadalajara had already attracted migrants from all around Mexico.[19] Steady but not overwhelming increase over the next century strained traditional ties and networks. Growing class divides with decreasing network reciprocity had further eroded senses of community by the late nineteenth century as the city prospered under the dictatorship of Porfirio Díaz (1876–1911).[20] And as Catholic thinkers had feared, the increase in religious liberty and the growing number of Protestants in the city in the late nineteenth century introduced more ideological divides.[21] Secular, Catholic, and Protestant senses of civic life—with a multitude of variations within each of those categories—emerged alongside cultural divisions, reduced daily shared physical space, and decreased ritual space, all of which challenged the sense of community.[22]

One might be tempted to identify the Mexican Revolution of 1910, the reforms that followed, and various state formation projects as ample tools for unifying the ever-increasing population. However, the vast scholarship on the subject often underscores the fissures, faults, and failures of state-building strategies of revolutionary projects.[23] As the Cristero War's (1926–29) jarring violence demonstrates, the Catholic rejection of the secular vision advanced by the Constitution of 1917 exemplifies the document's inability to unite the nation. Subsequent outbreaks of religious violence such as lynching public school teachers or brutal assaults on Protestants by Catholics and the harassment and jailing of Catholics by government officials created further divisions. For smaller civic units in Mexico, communities united around "a hegemonic cultural, political, or religious identity" to stand against threats to the order of that community through violence.[24] However, in larger units, such close, intense ties elude residents, while violence poses a greater threat to social order. In Guadalajara, domestic migrants from rural areas brought with them recent memories of fighting on both sides of a bloody religious conflict, which together undermined opportunities for a sense of greater community belonging through the Catholic Church.[25] By 1939 Mexico had emerged from a disorienting national revolution, a destructive regional religious war, and a world-wide economic depression, only to find itself playing a key economic role for the Allies in their global war. Simply surviving and attending to the needs of individuals and families could be overwhelming. Added issues of class, sexuality, gender, language, or simple life habits further divided a city of migrants. How could one find a sense of belonging amid such challenges?

Daniel Kemmis, a politician and scholar of community building, has argued that residents of any area need to move beyond viewing community life as a matter of individual survival. Instead, people should see community as a collective experience of using shared resources as the key to place making and community building with minimal conflict.[26] In short, can you share space and resources without falling into violence? In a city such as Guadalajara, there existed nearly limitless opportunities to engage in rituals, acts, and narratives centered on arguing over limited resources in shared space. Petitions from individuals, groups of neighbors, associated businesses, and congregations served as both rituals (the act of petitioning) and narratives (the petition content) of belonging. Certainly on one level petitions functioned to establish citizenship in a political context outside of direct electoral politics.[27] However, engaging in petitions also allowed *tapatíos* to establish their membership in community beyond their neighborhood as a ritual act. What that could mean for each individual or group might vary according to context or timing.

Take, for example, the following two divergent descriptions of Guadalajara. First, we have its many monikers and the way that travel authors expanded on the images those names conjured up: Pearl of the West, City of Flowers, City of Roses, Bride of Jalisco, Sultan of the West, City of Churches, the Mexican Dresden (or Florence or Athens). Guadalajara has many titles, and all of these nicknames encourage the image of a polished city, church spires climbing into blue skies in which the sun shines brightly on intricate stonework, whitewashed buildings accented with beautiful women leaning from wrought iron balconies to bestow a rose on a passing *charro* as the perfume of innumerable flowers hangs heavily in the air. Of Guadalajara, travel guide author Reau Campbell penned in his 1899 *Campbell's New Revised Complete Guide and Descriptive Book of Mexico* that "it is one of the most charming, most fascinating places in the world in every way."[28] In 1910 travel guide author T. Philip Terry wrote, "After the Mexican Capital it is unquestionably the most orderly, the handsomest and most attractive city of the Mexican Republic."[29] And now let us consider a different description: a petition from five women and five men living in the north of Guadalajara beyond the Hospital Civil and near the boundary between the Hidalgo and Libertad sectors.[30] These neighbors reported to officials in July 1939 that a stream polluted with the waste from tanneries brought stench and filth to the neighborhood. The horrific conditions near the water discouraged police patrols, and the area became a site of crime and "immoral behavior." Piles of garbage, rotting animal corpses, and industrial waste accumulated in the area, rendering the stream "a direct danger to the health of our families and to society in general."[31]

These contrasting descriptions provide readers with different perspectives, though the second better indicates the challenges residents faced in a rapidly transforming urban area. In reflecting on these two ways of viewing the same city, one might be tempted to think of Guadalajara in the traditional manner of Daniel Vázquez's "two cities." Yet residents from all social stations and occupations sent correspondence to public officials detailing similar concerns about human health, infrastructure, property management, networking, and other issues of city life. But residents who called for infrastructure improvements or argued with their neighbors did more than establish citizenship or reckon with political rights.[32] When neighbors shared these actions of petitioning and conflict, they reinforced a social concept of self, their relationship to an immediate circle of participants, and a greater sense of social belonging in the wider community that created a narrative for both them and city leaders. The expression of concerns about the noise from a park, the width of a sidewalk, or the look of a house is a larger act of belonging. What do I mean by that?

While Kemmis hopes that people recognizing that they share resources will lead to conversation, cooperation, and conflict reduction, I consider

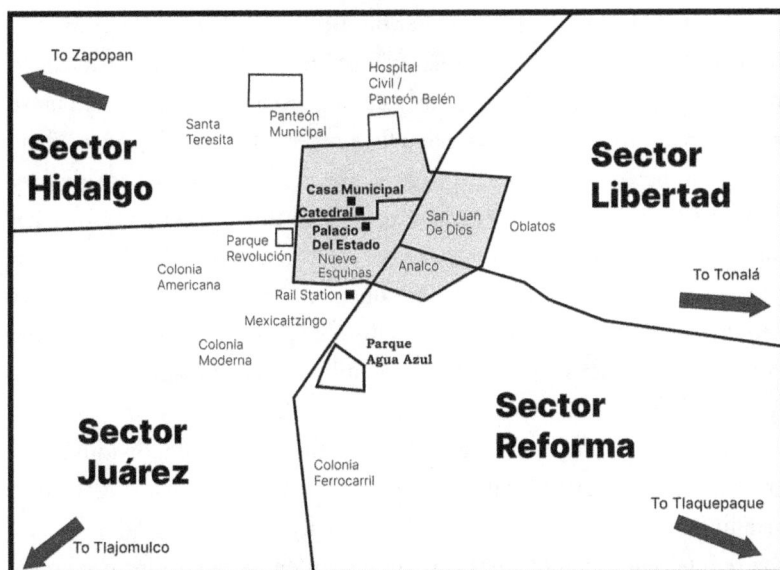

To Zapopan

Sector
Hidalgo

Santa
Teresita

Panteón
Municipal

Hospital
Civil /
Panteón Belén

Casa Municipal
Catedral ■
Palacio ■
Del Estado
Nueve
Esquinas

San Juan
De Dios

Oblatos

Parque
Revolución

Colonia
Americana

Analco

Rail Station ■

Mexicaltzingo

Colonia
Moderna

Parque
Agua Azul

Colonia
Ferrocarril

Sector
Libertad

To Tonalá

Sector
Reforma

To Tlaquepaque

Sector
Juárez

To Tlajomulco

FIG. 2. Guadalajara city center in 1942, the city's four administrative sectors created in 1928, and important neighborhoods that lie beyond the city center. The gray area of the map represents the colonial-era core of the city. The Nueve Esquinas area marks the early colonial-era southern entrance to the city that by 1942 was considered part of the city center. Map by the author.

this view of urban community excessively optimistic. Conflict between residents is the most consistent, unifying factor of urban residential life. The acts of petition and conflict established that "a reciprocity exists between the way one identifies with place and the physical character of that place itself, between the conceptualization of a civic identity along political, social, and cultural lines, and the materials, structures, and spaces of the city itself."[33] Writing petitions created a narrative and served as a ritual act by people that helped them orient themselves to their place and in their space as both individuals and as groups.

This approach to conflict as a form of community cohesion differs from scholarship that looks at coalitions built by residents on the same side of conflicts and that focuses on identity. For example, scholar Josefina Elizabeth Villa Pérez examines conflict in midcentury Tijuana over tourist versus residential space and the city's reputation.[34] She describes a social cohesion between those who banded together on the same side of an issue in civic clubs to form "a collective belonging that identified them as Mexican."[35] While these are areas crucial to understanding urban life, in this work I move in a different direction and argue that the process of petitioning allowed the authors to better imagine their place in the city, no matter what side they took in the argument, what results came from those arguments, or what identity process they might have undergone as individuals. Focusing on processes of belonging allows me to consider a wider range of petitioners and their work to orient themselves in the changing city and to avoid some of the pitfalls of focusing on Mexican identity. On the limitations of identity, Anthias is once again more instructive.

Anthias has argued that issues relative to the identity of individuals and groups are so important that we run the unfortunate risk of losing the true meaning of those issues by relying too broadly on the term "identity." As she points out, much of what is written on identity comes from scholars discussing how another scholar gets the concepts of identity incorrect. Even when they arrive at the idea of multilayered identity, they still run the risk of intimating "that identity might be a possessive property of individuals rather than a process."[36] For this reason, Anthias draws on the concept of belonging to understand immigrant experiences in transnational spaces instead of making an argument about identity. Because I want to avoid falling into this trap of erroneously defining *tapatío* identity or the stickier *mexicanidad* (Mexican identity), this book discusses the ways that residents imagined their belonging in the city where they wanted to live, as stated in their correspondence, and does not focus on identity.

Additionally, the sense of belonging as used here transcends the limitations of citizenship as well as those of identity. As Paul Gillingham argues, "Citizenship . . . by definition coldly excludes at the same time as it warmly includes, and women, slaves, indigenous peoples, peasants, the poor, and the illiterate are just some of the groups that Latin Americans have at times defined out of the body politic."[37] Even descriptions of the psychological rather than legal aspects of citizenship are limiting in that citizenship requires a "crucial test" of "social integration"—the idea that disparate groups accept one another as "a unified society, especially when this is pursued as a deliberate policy" or where individuals assimilate "into the group."[38]

Acceptance and assimilation are perhaps present on the petitions and letters reviewed for this work, but questions arise: unified with whom and assimilated into what? There is no single social integration or assimilation in Guadalajara that can adequately define the lives of residents as reflected in their letters and petitions. Accepting the city as a space of conflict, nuance, and difference allows us to understand how so many people with conflicting interests could find differing senses of belonging in the city.

In this way, *Conflict and Correspondence* joins the ranks of other books from scholars considering the lives of average Mexicans. Examples of works that extensively use petitions to examine a particular topic include William E. French's *A Peaceful and Working People* (decency and labor in Chihuahua), Ingrid Bleynat's *Vendors' Capitalism* (markets and conditions in Mexico City), Sandra C. Mendiola's *Street Democracy* (vendors and market rights in Puebla), Rocio Gomez's *Silver Veins, Dusty Lungs* (environmental, health, and decency concerns in Zacatecas), and Christina M. Jiménez's *Making an Urban Public* (political rights and citizenship responsibility). This work most complements Jiménez's in that her approach also considers the larger meaning of petitions. The present book finds confirmatory agreement with Jiménez in that the discourse of "rights, responsibilities, and contributions" in Morelia, Michoacán, is repeatable in other Mexican cities (though that is not my focus here).[39] It departs significantly in other areas, particularly in discussing the role of women in property and business beyond political movements, the examination of conflict and belonging, resident manipulation of the petition process (falsification, forgery, repurposing), and considering petitions as commentary on the lives of people being petitioned against (the subjects of complaint petitions, such as rowdy neighbors, sex workers, rambunctious youth, etc.).

Correspondence and Petitions as Rituals and Narratives of Belonging

Even though several state and local archives as well as digitized collections form the basis for my findings, the primary body of material used for this investigation comes from the correspondence collection at the Archivo Histórico Municipal de Guadalajara. The *correspondencia* archive contains tens of thousands of documents, searchable only by using the original *índices de correspondencia* (index books) kept by municipal clerks who cataloged correspondence by author and topic as it arrived. These communications might include letters to various city offices from federal or state entities, communications between city offices regarding projects or problems, registrations for licenses for a myriad of fee-based permissions, official correspondence from other city governments, queries about Guadalajara from around the globe (mostly from the United States), inquiries from Mexicans around the nation (frequently looking for missing relatives), but the correspondence mostly comprises communications from residents regarding city issues.

The organization of letters from residents lends itself to creating a trail (often incomplete) of discussions between multiple parties. For example, a letter or petition sent to the municipal president's office might be filed with subsequent responses placed on top of the first communication, creating a conversation thread that covers weeks, months, or (in rare cases) years. This arrangement has the danger of creating a collection that privileges the views and actions of politicians, administrators, and functionaries. However, at the center of nearly every file is the original communication containing the voice of one or more average residents. These might be letters from individuals, or they might be petitions from groups of neighbors not yet officially organized under the ruling party before 1947. Both letters and petitions served similar functions legally, though petitions might have carried more weight for both the number of residents involved and for the revolutionary emphasis on neighborhood associations. This conversation on paper is a result of constitutional Article 8 (in both 1857 and 1917), which guarantees the right of petition and requires that the official to whom the petition is directed respond quickly.

This study centers correspondence creators and the neighbors they target with their petitions instead of the bureaucrats receiving the letters. In 1990 Daniel Vázquez wrote that Guadalajara contained two types of people: "the known people" from wealthy neighborhoods and the "anonymous masses."[40] The correspondence archive puts names to thousands of typically anonymous city residents and preserves a fraction of their stories. At times their desires are preserved in fully formed letters they drafted themselves or for which they had an amanuensis, while at other times it is simply the appearance of their name on a petition (signed or perhaps with a simple fingerprint to indicate participation). Because petitions come from all classes, ethnicities, races, genders, religions, and walks of life, I reject too strict of an interpretation of Vázquez's concept of "two cities" and posit that the petitioning process itself made all residents part of a single (though layered) city. Vázquez argues that "the physical reflection is the material expression in [the] space of social relationships," meaning that, for him, rich and poor neighborhoods reflect two different Guadalajaras.[41] I understand and am sympathetic to that view because class creates dramatically different lives in Mexico, as it does in most places in the world. However, petitions and the petitioning process are also a physical manifestation of a social practice in which residents—whether rich or poor—all participated. The desire of all parties to shape the shared physical space places residents in the same community, and their expression of those desires underscores their belonging to that community. Visions of the good life in the city often crossed class boundaries. We are as likely to see letters from poor residents of tenements complaining about their neighbor's debauchery as we are to see the same kind of letters from a rich neighborhood. Petitions are an act of participation, but the story they weave on the page is also a narrative of location and a technology of belonging where *tapatíos* tried "to order and organize [their] experiences in terms of certain conventions and norms or rules."[42]

The petitions enter into the world of ritual, both in terms of their long heritage in Iberian society and in the stylized introductions.[43] Much like the declaration of a religious creed or rite of passage, the act of petitioning affirmed for both the sender and the receiver their membership in the larger community beyond constitutional definitions of citizenship. From individuals, the petitions often begin with the declaration of name, nation of origin, age of accountability, and often (for women) marital status. A letter from Margarita Flores Venegas from 1943 serves as a representative example. When this "*señorita*" believed that the police had failed to quickly investigate Enrique Nava's murder, she wrote to the police with a copy for J. Jesús Landeros (1943–44), the municipal president. She states her full name and follows that with a string of adjectives: *mexicana, soltera, mayor de edad, vecina de esta ciudad,* and *señalando como domicilio en el numero 37 de la calle Jarauta* (Mexican, unmarried, legally of age, a neighbor of this city, and resident of no. 37 calle Jarauta).[44] Nationality, gender, marital status, status to participate in public issues, and location in the city in the working-class neighborhood of Oblatos on calle Jarauta all signified to the police and the municipal president her position in society and her needs.

Groups of neighbors addressed their own set of identifying markers. Neighbors writing to the city established their relationship to status and property early on, declaring themselves *"vecinos de esta ciudad con residencia"* (*vecinos* of this city and residents of) followed by their neighborhood or address. These statements alerted city officials to their status as *vecinos*, or residents with valid opinions on city life, and then their class by virtue of the naming of the area where they lived, thus alerting city leaders to their relative class status. These introductions of residents are more common when not all participants are property owners, however, and they frequently came with a declaration of class indicating their exemption from income tax in the areas of commerce, agriculture, gambling, industry, subsoil extraction, pay, salary, professions, arts, entertainment, and other areas (a tax of less than 2,000 pesos a year in most businesses).[45] For group petitions when all of the petitioners own property or businesses, letters often begin with "we that write you, property owners of" (*los que subscribimos, propietarios de*), followed by their addresses.

Other group petitions indicate relationships such as membership in a religious congregation or working at a particular job. Work status might be indicated simply by a mention that the petitioners are workers (*trabajadores*), or it might appear as an indication that the petitioners work in a particular industry or profession, such as the three hundred employees who wrote to complain because they lost overtime due to a change in city overtime pay laws.[46] While some petitions did come from organized labor or renters' unions, the vast majority of petitions from the time period under review did not come from labor unions. Nearly all group petitions of any kind came with names signed and with and at least some names with fingerprints next to them for those not able to sign for themselves. Residents may have drafted some of these letters themselves, but there also existed the common practice of using a paid scribe known as an amanuensis (at times in Mexico referred to as an *evangelista*) to help draft letters. These scribes also helped people construct the necessary language to navigate bureaucratic channels. The literacy rate in Jalisco of 47.5 percent in 1940 (a figure that had reached 60.1 percent by 1950) virtually guarantees that some petitioners used an amanuensis.[47] Still, while the use of an amanuensis might undermine the idea of urban residents as lay bureaucrats of a sort, since the *evangelista* might craft the necessary language, it does not lessen cooperative literacy or the shared construction of belonging inherent in these community approaches.[48] The value of petitions goes beyond the simple use of bureaucratic language.

In the process of identifying their relationship to city authorities, community members explicitly established their position, using class and gender markers nested in spatial, linguistic, and productive descriptors. Both Iberian tradition and informal liberal training in civics and constitutional rights dictated the medium of communication through letters with signatures and produced the loose and informal ritual found in each. Writing (or dictating) and expressing their desires for the physical and conceptual space itself reified abstract concepts of belonging. For this reason, even letters and petitions that failed to follow the linguistic or format rituals of establishing verbal relationships are valuable: simply sitting down to write a letter to authorities or going to an amanuensis confirmed to city residents who they were and how they felt about where they lived. For historians of midcentury Guadalajara, few sources remain (or even existed to start with) with the same depth or breadth of social commentary from the public as correspondence archives.

The letters in the correspondence archive also allow readers to imagine the community that *tapatíos* of the 1940s hoped to build with the help of city administrators, but there are limitations. Petitions at this time are naturally of limited use for analysis of state formation because their point of view lacks insider knowledge of political systems, politicians, and bureaucrats. By extension, correspondence contains few threads that explore the full scope of any given issue. Though original petitions or a transcript created by a clerk are common, few materials accompany most petitions. The city might acknowledge the letter's reception, and on occasion the folder may contain various replies from different city entities as they tried to solve the problem. In very rare cases, a city official might issue a final letter with an overview of how the problem got resolved.

In addition, the authors' intentions can be difficult to ascertain from letters. In cases where a resolution to a situation is identified, there is no definite way to indicate that the resolution came as a part of policy and investigation of a complaint or if it resulted from corruption and bribery. For example, when Sara Aceves González wrote officials in April 1942 that she could no longer afford to retrieve her disabled son from the police station after yet another episode of his being taken into custody, the city responded that they had no record of his ever having been detained.[49] For the city, the case seemed resolved, but for readers the situation is cloudier. Did the police shake down a disabled man and his elderly mother for money? Had the city simply lost the records? Did the city have the records but choose to cover up the arrests when challenged? We cannot know for sure. Similarly, when inspectors arrived at a saloon about which neighbors had complained of noise violations and alleged prostitution and the inspectors reported that no such issues existed, what are we to think? Did the establishment's owners change their ways in the face of community pressure before the inspector arrived? Did the saloon owner bribe the inspector? Did neighbors exaggerate the issue or did they have other reasons to sabotage their neighbors that they did not share with city officials? Similarly, when vendors complained that sellers previously expelled from a market suddenly returned to their old places, are we seeing the result of people cleared by an investigation or did connections and bribes influence the precinct chief or the market administration to allow their return?[50] Extant documents leave immense space for speculation, but they do provide an opportunity to hear the voices of poor and working-class *tapatíos* and how they describe the city, how they wanted to be perceived, how they thought municipal officials would want them to act or think, what they imagined the city could be, and where they positioned themselves in both the contemporaneous and future city.

In 1989 Daniel Vázquez wrote that *tapatíos* themselves needed to be engaged in the work of improving the city: "even though we are few, if we put forth the effort, get organized, take action, and we aren't indifferent—if we love the city we can contribute to its improvement and not its destruction and not let others destroy it, either."[51] Every letter or petition carries with it a certain amount of affection for the city, implied in the residents' desire to contribute to its improvement. As William E. French does with his book

The Heart in the Glass Jar, I examine these letters because they are crafted "by everyday people" and inform every aspect of this book.[52] I intentionally privilege letters and their democratizing technology over other sources, such as biographies and oral histories about the upper classes, who are Vázquez's "known people." While future projects may expand on ideas in this work, this book asks what we can learn from a broad spectrum of society as its ordinary members communicate their comments, requests, and often their personal stories in their own words. We learn in the following pages how everyday residents thought of their urban lives and attempted to innovate during a time of plentiful revolutionary rhetoric but limited resources.

Jane Jacobs challenged the world of mid-twentieth-century urban planning when she wrote of creating a dense, diverse, mixed-use urban environment that hinged on human contact. For Jacobs, the city danced in a vast performance of "intricate" and improvised interactions (what she called a sidewalk ballet) that played out on various "stages" throughout a city.[53] Her vision of the city is at once beautiful and messy, pragmatic and fanciful. In considering Guadalajara, however, and petitions from residents for this book, I start with Jacobs's artistic approach to the city but shift the metaphor. Instead of ballet, in which dancers work out both rigid and improvised choreography on a stage created by stagehands whom the audience never sees, I offer that improvisational performance art is a better conceptual approach. Residents of Guadalajara are not merely dancing on a stage built for them by an all-powerful state, but they engaged in a mass-participatory exercise to define both conceptual place and physical space. In the case of Guadalajara, performers built multiple venues to create a performance art mosaic. We can also still retain Jacobs's concept of improvisation but perhaps not in the same way Jacobs intended. As city officials either defined what modern city life should be or looked away in neglect, the residents responded with the first rule of improvisation theater: say yes to the general premise and then move the conversation forward in the direction you want it to move (known as the concept of "Yes, and . . .").

In examining petitions, we are able to see *tapatío* intellectual innovation and creativity in using or influencing the tools of government to accomplish residents' goals that differed dramatically from those of city leaders. Written into petitions are also the reflected hopes, worldviews, aspirations, and the remnants of daily lives of people who left few other documents. Even more deeply hidden between petition lines we find the views, actions, and desires of those whom petitioners complain about.

Periodization, 1939–47

This study examines the period of urban growth in Guadalajara from 1939 to 1947, an era that various chroniclers and historians have seldom covered despite indicating its importance in city history. While the nine-year period has the convenience of beginning one year before and ending a year after the term of President Manuel Ávila Camacho (1940–46) and roughly concurrent with economic growth during World War II (which for Mexico lasted from 1942 to 1945), it also represents a particular moment for Guadalajara. Noted Guadalajara engineer, politician, and academic Jorge Matute Remus called it "the most interesting in the history of Guadalajara by virtue of being a clear dividing line of what came before and what came after."[54]

During the municipal presidency (1922) and governorship (1923–26) of José Guadalupe Zuno, a series of urban infrastructure and housing reforms sought to provide shelter for Guadalajara residents. However, after 1926 there emerged a piecemeal approach to development policy, formulated by a constantly rotating roster of municipal presidents and governors, with five state governors in 1931 alone. Even when the state governor's office stabilized in 1939 under Silvano Barba González (1939–43), the city saw a decrease in access to resources for large public works that year and into 1940. Spending on social improvement for the whole state remained flat during this era. Barba González had come to power as a Cardenista governor whose vocal support of socialist education and the ideals of Lázaro Cárdenas (1934–40) put him at odds with the new, more conservative administration of Manuel Ávila Camacho (1940–46). It also did not help that many in the Guadalajara middle classes had openly supported Ávila Camacho's opponent in the 1940 elections, General Juan Andreu Almazán.[55] President Ávila Camacho did not try to co-opt those with political differences but instead chose to consolidate support from those he agreed with and to marginalize those with whom he disagreed.[56] The constant tension with the federal government left Jalisco outside the presidential orbit of power and ended with

Barba González exiled from Jalisco in 1943.[57] General Marcelino García Barragán (1943–47) followed as governor, and he faced similar divisions with the Ávila Camacho administration when the governor backed candidates not supported by the ruling party. García Barragán also traded barbs over federal distribution of *bracero* work contracts to Jalisco residents (which he as governor opposed).[58] This political misalignment between Jalisco and the federal government came at an unfortunate moment and made it unique compared to other cities, such as Puebla, Mexico City, and Monterrey, that had access to more federal resources and on a more consistent basis.

The year 1939 marked a tipping point, when Guadalajara could no longer develop sufficient infrastructure (housing, water, sewer, transportation, and electricity) to support population growth. From 1920 to 1940, Guadalajara's population nearly doubled, from 143,000 to 250,000 residents. It grew an additional 60 percent between 1940 and 1950.[59] The *Gaceta Municipal* declared in 1939 that "there is a fever for construction of homes in Guadalajara. There isn't a street, direction, new or old neighborhood, or four corners of the city where you don't see the hustle of construction workers building new homes or rebuilding existing ones."[60] Such growth catapulted Guadalajara into place as Mexico's second-largest city, bypassing the city of Puebla. This era started a population growth juggernaut driven by rural and small-city migration to Guadalajara that lasted several decades.[61] From this point forward Guadalajara transitioned into a metropolis of "unusual growth due to national industrialization."[62] State authorities explicitly announced their intention to exploit the economic window offered by World War II to improve industrialization in Jalisco, with a focus on Guadalajara in particular.[63] Scholar Jesús Arroyo Alejandre has declared that "from the forties, the city of Guadalajara began to experience rapid demographic growth attributable—in great part—to migration."[64] Unlike cities such as Paris or New York, internal migration rather than international immigration primarily drove the growth of Guadalajara as a "second city."[65] Economic growth and a decline in violence in the 1930s after first Cristero War (1926–29) created a sense of possibility. For example, migrants sought home ownership when the city opened up thirty-two new housing developments (known as *fraccionamientos*). Private developers created these construction projects mostly for the working class. Consequently, few housing developments saw city enforcement of building codes such as required connections to municipal services or quality construction standards. And even had there been any code enforcement, only a very few rules existed in the late 1930s and early 1940s at the state or city level.[66]

Few planning laws before 1939 addressed urban growth in Jalisco; the first went on the books in 1933, under Governor Sebastián Allende (1932–35), attempting to regularize street, water, and sewer installation. In 1935 Governor Everardo Topete (1935–39) modified that law to call for planning at the municipal level by recognizing prioritization of urban challenges and calling for more citizen input.[67] Prior to 1946, urban planning in Guadalajara and Jalisco usually generated "technical and administrative advances that had later results," but years passed before they became "more precise in terms of concepts, methodology, and an adequate information infrastructure" for making major improvements.[68] In short, big growth inspired big plans for expanding municipal services and infrastructure—plans that came to fruition only in future decades. The increasing pace of urbanization could not happen without harming city planning and the ability to deliver goods and services.[69]

We can also see that the lack of resources during this era is reflected in the inability to maintain even municipal properties. City-owned lots could not connect to water or sewer services, and municipal buildings experienced crumbling roofs and deteriorating walls.[70] When Jalisco's director of engineering and sanitation asked for a Guadalajara water system plan in 1942, the city responded that they had no such plans.[71] In another case, in 1944, the director of public works begged for the building of a municipal forge to make the tools and materials for water and sewer projects because he could not afford to purchase them.[72] Taking note of this inability to deliver quality planning, goods, and services, scholars of government and development of Guadalajara have called the 1940s "spontaneous, lacking in infrastructure and any control to limit the actions of developers" and a time of "few resources to create a plan of urbanization," along with the associated ability of developers to "dodge their responsibilities to connect to public services."[73] What that meant for average city dwellers makes for grim reading: neighbors living at the intersection of calles Lerdo de Tejada and Veracruz describe "tanks of potable water for the city" in which were "floating . . . all manner of filth," while local residents used the area around the tanks as a place to relieve themselves. Additionally, pigs and chickens lived in pens just under a meter from the tanks' edges.[74]

Facing that inability to deliver quality urban development, the state government of Jalisco mandated that city leaders create the Comisión de Planeación, Urbanización y Obras Públicas del Municipio de Guadalajara (Commission on Planning, Urbanization, and Public Works). By May 1939 the city had complied in creating the commission, and it began choosing representatives from among civil and architectural engineers. The new commission ignored a 1935 law prohibiting city commissions from including representatives from private groups, and it brought in two representatives each from the Cámara Nacional de Comercio e Industria de Guadalajara (National Chamber of Commerce and Industry) and the Cámara de Propietarios (Chamber of Property Owners). These groups represented commercial businesses and private landowners, respectively.

In July 1939 the planning commission held a citywide meeting at the Universidad de Guadalajara, with invitations to engineering students and faculty who devised a plan to improve city water and sewer infrastructure. The plan collapsed when participating business and property owners realized that the projects required 1.4 million pesos in new taxes (roughly US$159 million as of this writing). Instead, they urged the city to reduce the project's scope, spread the costs among all city residents, draw from the treasury, and borrow more money. And where would the city find lenders? The Cámara Nacional de Comercio e Industria de Guadalajara offered to facilitate a series of loans.[75] These loans guaranteed that its member banks would profit from the public works. Guadalajara's political leadership had attempted a private-public partnership financed by a combination of city funds, taxes, state resources, and federal funds, but instead they found themselves blocked in their ambition by business and property owners' desire to profit from improvements.

A second attempt came in 1943 with Jalisco congressional decree 4882, which created the Consejo de Colaboración Municipal de Guadalajara (Guadalajara Council for Municipal Collaboration) to improve infrastructure. Negotiated with Guadalajara's municipal president J. Jesús Landeros and the Cámara de Comercio (Chamber of Commerce), it engaged in some

ZAPOPAN

COLONIA SEATTLE

ZOQUIPAN

ATEMAJAC

EL

Rio de Atemajac

Barranca del Profundo

PRESA DE LA CAMPANA

PRESA DE ZOQUIPAN

Los Colomos

SECTOR HIDALGO

Barranca Ancha

Roble Obrego

Campo de Polo

Coordenadas Geográficas del Observatorio Astronómico:
Latitud Norte: 20°40'36"
Longitud W de G: 6°33'32.5"
Altitud: 1583.15 m.   POSTE ASTRONOMICO

OBSERVATORIO

Campo de Polo

SECTOR JUAREZ

VNIVERSIDAD DE GVADALAJARA
INSTITUTO DE GEOGRAFIA
PLANO DE LA CIVDAD Y VALLE DE GVADALAJARA
LEVANTADO POR LA DIRECCION DE GEOGRAFIA,
MET. E HIDROL. DE LA SRIA DE AGRICULTURA
CON LA COOPERACION DEL INSTITUTO DE GEO
GRAFIA DE LA VNIVERSIDAD DE GVADALAJA
RA EN EL AÑO DE 1942

EL RECTOR DE LA VNIVERSIDAD   EL DIRECTOR DEL INSTITUTO

ESCALA = 1:10 000

ESCALA GRAFICA

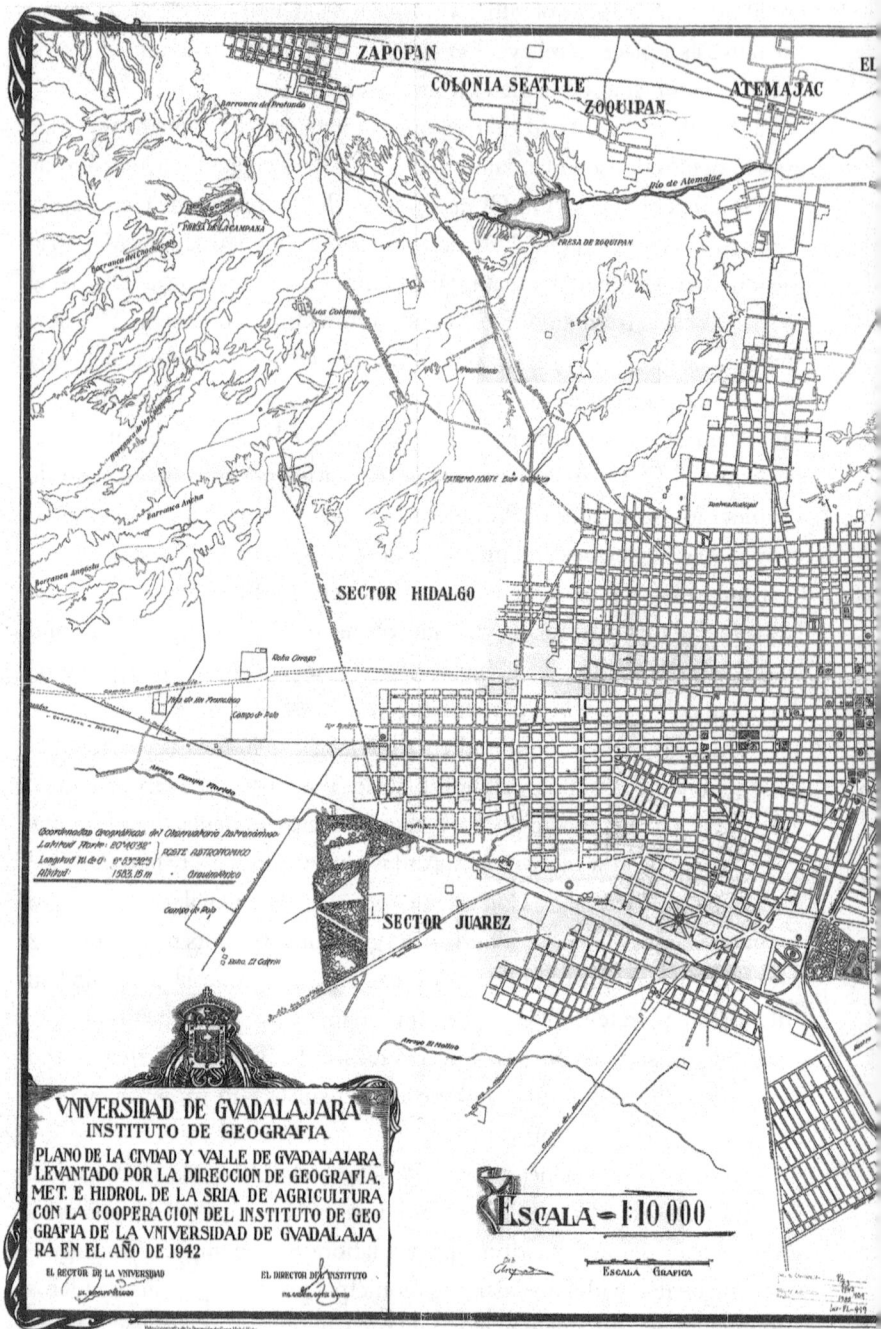

FIG. 3. City plan of Guadalajara created in 1942 by the University of Guadalajara. By 1947 nearly all the empty areas to the west, east, and south had been filled with new construction. PL 7.3 1942 409. Courtesy of the Archivo Histórico de Jalisco.

HUENTITAN EL ALTO

PRESA RANCHONUEVO

PRESA DEL AGUA DELGADA

PRESA DE LA CANTERA

PRESA DE LA PIEDRACHA

PRESITA DE LA PUERTA DE LOS BANCOS

PRESA DEL COLUMBIO

S

PRESITA DE LA BOMBA

PRESA MOLINO DEL CHOCOLATE

PRESA LOS PARAISOS

SECTOR LIBERTAD

EL PARQUE DE LA PLANTA
PRESA DE OBLATOS

PRESA DE LOS CAÑOS

SAN ANDRES

SECTOR REFORMA

PARQUE SAN RAFAEL

TLAQUEPAQUE

TABLA EXPLICATIVA

DIGNOS CONVENCIONALES
Construido
En Proyecto

small road and water projects, though with little success beyond paving the way for a reconciliation between municipal leaders and private capital and helping to unify elite visions for the city for the first time since 1910.[76] It also followed a pattern of shifting the burden of development to residents through their financial or even labor participation in the work of paving roads and installing sewer and drainage projects.[77] To pay for the projects, the city levied fees on residents of areas where the work would take place and thus on those who would benefit most directly from the improvements. At times the city even purchased materials and left them in place for residents to do the installation work themselves.[78]

The city leadership attempted some works in cooperation with the federal government, but between 1939 and 1947 unpaid bills stacked up as either the city or the federal government variously failed to meet their obligations.[79] For eight years the city attempted different strategies and laws to cobble together water and drainage systems for a city center whose infrastructure increasingly failed under the figurative and literal weight of people and cars. The city also faced an ever-expanding municipal periphery with little regulation or guidance. Daniel Vázquez points out that at this moment when the city struggled, it experienced immense growth in small industry, an explosion in the subdivision of private land into housing, and a growing movement in the city to attempt to beautify and "give it the same stature as other cities."[80]

This study ends in 1947, when the increasingly powerful consolidating central state apparatus and its mask of the Partido Revolucionario Institucional (PRI, founded in 1946) brought Mexico under new levels of control.[81] By 1947 city leaders increasingly were ignoring requests in letters and petitions from residents because they did not come from formal *juntas vecinales*, or neighborhood associations within the party structure, and clerks increasingly cataloged residents' letters and petitions with no response at all.[82] Additionally, in 1947 the constant changes in leadership ended at the state level, where governors now served for six years instead of four or fewer. These governors—particularly Jesús González Gallo (1947–53)—looked toward a reinvigorated private-public partnership to improve infrastructure.[83] The cumulative effects of the Ávila Camacho years and the postwar PRI consolidation weakened the effectiveness of local creativity and responses from outside of the party's wide reach. Certainly, concerns about population growth and crumbling infrastructure continued, but increasingly an array of inspectors and police, followed by unrestrained engineers and their bulldozers, dealt with those issues.

Additionally, the city gradually became part of a larger municipal zone integrated into a broader Mexican economic plan.[84] In 1947 Governor González Gallo promoted the idea that Guadalajara possessed links to a wider urban zone of adjacent *municipios*. As city growth devoured orchards, small farms, haciendas, and grazing land to run up to (and across) the limits of neighboring towns, regulations such as the Ley para el Mejoramiento Urbano de Guadalajara, Tlaquepaque, Zapopan y Chapala (Law of Urban Improvement, for the areas specified) and the second Ley del Consejo de Colaboración (Law of Advisement and Collaboration) created links between Guadalajara and the towns of Zapopan, Tlaquepaque, and Chapala.[85] Over the course of fifty years this process led to the 2009 creation of the Área Metropolitana de Guadalajara (AMG, or Guadalajara Metropolitan Zone, now the Zona Metropolitana de Guadalajara, or ZMG). The ZMG is just one of several dozen Mexican unified metropolitan zones, created after 2005, that severed the term "urban" from the political unit of an individual "city."[86]

What, then, is the purpose of looking at this era of mild chaos between 1939 and 1947, often passed over quickly by some scholars?[87] Just as daily life in Guadalajara was no "sweet kiss of its women . . . who remain in the patios of their homes" (as one chronicler described the city), neither was life a type of waking nightmare for most residents.[88] One person's chaos—mild or otherwise—is often another person's opportunity. This study examines the correspondence of Guadalajara's residents to the city's leadership, with special attention to the petitions of neighbors not officially organized into formal political or union organizations. These letters reveal a citizenry actively engaged in attempting to shape their city and expressing their desire to create a livable, attractive space for themselves and visitors. However, the meanings of both "livable" and "attractive" caused debate, and it is this process of debate that instilled belonging. Rather than focus on the work of engineers, politicians powerful after 1947, or unions influential in the years before 1939, this study instead focuses on the women and men of Guadalajara who not only contributed their sweat and toil to build the city but also spilled considerable ink expressing their perception of city life and desires for what it might be during a window of opportunity before the state fully consolidated power.

This concentrated period of analysis differs significantly from some excellent recent English-language works on life in regional Mexican cities. Studies such as Lisa Pinley Covert's *San Miguel de Allende* (2017), Christina Jiménez's *Making an Urban Public* (2019), and Rocio Gomez's *Silver Veins, Dusty Lungs* (2020) all choose sweeping, decades-long terms over which to examine the cities they cover (San Miguel Allende, Morelia, and Zacatecas, respectively). With my limited scope of inquiry (1939–47) in a time that is neither the radically engaged world of Cardenismo nor the nation dominated by the PRI, I make no pretensions that this is a history for all of Mexico or even all of Guadalajara. Additionally, this work occupies the middle ground between the sweeping spatial analyses of Gomez's broad environmental history with dozens of different players in both rural and city spaces and that of Sandra Mendiola's powerful *Street Democracy* (2017), which focuses on a specific segment of urban society (market vendors) in limited areas of Puebla in the late twentieth century. But like Mendiola, I am actively working to de-center the politicians and engineers who for generations have drawn attention. The chapters that follow emphasize the human ways residents engaged with faith, anger, joy, pragmatism, innovation, pleasure, disgust, concern, and love in the context of a changing city and their quest to build community there.

Chapter Overview

The chapters in this work function as complementary stand-alone discussions about Guadalajara and how residents found a sense of belonging there. Modeled loosely after Mauricio Tenorio Trillo's *I Speak of the City*, the chapters each offer an opportunity to explore the varied experiences of urban space and place.[89] Using this approach, I created a work whose organization is designed to support a layered argument in chapters that stand alone. Taken together, these chapters contribute to the broad concept that petitioning and conflict created both a narrative and a ritual of belonging.

Petitioning and writing letters reinforced residents' perceptions of city life and their relationship to their community. The work draws attention to the varied desires of average residents, particularly women who did not have full rights as political citizens at the time. Each chapter makes its own intervention in the historiography, as discussed in this chapter overview. The volume's sections may stand alone, but when considered together they address the broader question of how *tapatíos* responded to the challenges of urban growth in the late 1930s through most of the 1940s and located themselves in that process via sensate, moral, merry, holy, and gendered ways.

In chapter 1, "A Battle of the Senses," I address residents' sensory reactions to their city, particularly those of touch, sound, sight, and smell. This is a rarely used tool by historians of Mexican cities and of residents' perceptions of their community experience. Establishing a sense of belonging in a space requires a level of comfort for the senses, or at least patience with discomfort. Beyond the considerations of political or economic interpretations, Guadalajara is a city felt, heard, seen, and smelled. U.S. and European histories engage the use of senses more frequently than histories of Mexico, where the approach is rarely used beyond discussions of music or the scent of death.[90] With urban expansion, *tapatíos* responded to an array of sensory stimuli that blossomed in the world around them. For example, a growing city meant crowds of unsupervised children playing in public areas, street paving, and the slow replacement of carts by automobiles with their internal combustion engines. Life in the city is the real, physical interaction with the space residents inhabit. This chapter also argues that petitions tell only a portion of the story. Offenses against the senses decried by one group often fail to account for the needs, pleasure, or profit that cities provided for those causing the sensory offense. It is through these conflicts over the senses that residents issue letters and petitions (or become subjects of the complaint) that reinforce their narrative of what a community should be and how each signatory or subject belongs in that community.

Chapter 2, "Morality and Merriment," extends the exploration of belonging beyond the physical realm into the conceptual. This chapter showcases citizen attempts to activate the city's leadership on their behalf using ideas of morality, liberalism, and revolutionary reform. The sense of place for many working-class and upper-class *tapatíos* in the 1940s remained rooted in perceptions of family and neighborhood that together preserved the purity of children, women, and honest fathers. City residents faced situations where law enforcement and city inspectors could not shield families from the moral peril of unclean spaces. Petitions and correspondence from neighborhoods around the city had to find creative ways of motivating city leaders to respond to their calls for help. In many cases neighbors banded together, often under the leadership of women, still lacking full constitutional rights. While the morality referenced in these letters had aspects of nineteenth-century liberalism, we also see Catholic tradition as well as the language of family and state espoused by revolutionary leaders. And even though petitions and letters broach the topic of morality in areas one might expect, like witchcraft, necromancy, brothels, saloons, and extramarital sex, it also appears in questions of housing and infrastructure as *tapatíos* used a rhetoric of morality to preserve whatever particular vision of city life they imagined.

However, in chapter 2 I also expand an argument from chapter 1 and pull back from the excessive emphasis on liberalism triumphant in urban spaces to focus on petition-targeted people whose lives illustrate the limitations of moralizing reformers. For every petition decrying boisterous cantina scenes, a cantina full of people demonstrate that they saw the city as an opportunity for recreation, entertainment, self-medication (a concept not widely discussed by historians of drink in midcentury Mexico), and pleasure. Whether people were relocating permanently from elsewhere in Mexico or temporarily traveling through, Guadalajara offered an escape from work and boredom, an escape sought by those whose notion of the good life did not align with that of their socially "respectable" neighbors. Similar to colonial New Spain, where people engaged in bodily and celebratory "daily resistance to exploitation and survival strategies of extreme poverty" through pleasure seeking, the targets of petitions in modern Mexico found a range of experiences from joy to self-medication as markers of belonging in urban life.[91] This chapter goes beyond petitions as a conversation between government and citizen or conflict between factions and instead considers the lives of those against whom the petitions are leveled.

The vision of what a city could be went beyond the secular space. In chapter 3, "Divine Hygiene," we transition into an exploration of belonging for those focused on the spiritual. I explore in this chapter a Guadalajara whose religious populations stood at a crossroads. Not only had the church-state relationship shifted significantly away from fierce conflict and toward accommodating Catholicism after 1940, but we also find a Guadalajara with a burgeoning Protestant population. With direct, state-sponsored anticlericalism generally off the table and replaced with mild administrative controls, urban Catholics and Protestants found creative ways to protect or cleanse the sacred spaces of their city. Each side attempted to use health and hygiene laws to purge (or at least attempt to purge) spaces of any foes of their own congregations (both external and internal). Catholics and Protestants used the rhetoric of hygiene and anticlericalism to mobilize city officials on their behalf in inter- and intracongregational disputes. While the state used the concept of hygiene to order the physical and political world, religious groups co-opted that language to order and arrange their respective spiritual worlds. Consequently, religious residents legitimated the state through their use of reform language while simultaneously turning the tools of secularism toward religious ends. The petitions and letters of Catholic residents reinforced their views of city life as linked to a larger sacred mission for Catholics. For non-Catholics, correspondence solidified their sense of belonging to a greater revolutionary urban project linked to their own divine destiny. As of this writing, no other work addresses the use of state health and hygiene laws by churches to engage in church-on-church conflict or the religious use of the revolutionary state to order their sacred space.

In the sources on the sensate, moral, merry, and holy experiences of urban life, the voices of women clearly appeared in Guadalajara's correspondence archive. While Mexico's rulers denied women the rights of voting and clear constitutional citizenship, their place in the public sphere is evident as they developed and managed property and businesses in Guadalajara. In chapter 4, "Concrete Requests," we see women from all classes who used property ownership and management to prove their positions as good residents and secure their own fortunes and those of their families. From building networks of women entrepreneurs, taking on the city to get basic services, or engaging their capital and land to provide shelter and expand the city, women proved vital to the growth of Guadalajara. This localized revolutionary citizenship becomes more important in consideration of Mexico's 1917 Constitution and the rights that accrued to city (*municipio*, or municipal) government, as "Article 115 guaranteed the political and economic autonomy of municipalities for the first time, thus affirming citizen rights."[92] In a constitution that granted women no federal citizenship rights, their participation in municipal life allowed them space in a "system of power" in which they "seized opportunity or created it."[93] In short, they found participatory belonging in a wider community. The topic of women as urban property holders in the colonial and prerevolutionary era is well covered in the historical literature.[94] Instead, this chapter represents an aspect of revolutionary women rarely if ever explored in urban areas before the 1970s and 1980s, when women became more associated with large commercial corporations in Mexico. The chapter also intervenes in the historiography with its discussion of women in modern Mexico using property and businesses as intentional networks of financial support for other women beyond political or syndical networks.[95]

As we come to 1947 and the conclusion of this book, certainly not all the trends discussed herein would disappear. By 1947 Guadalajara had emerged as a city that depended more on state and federal directives dominated by the cult of engineers. Such characters were common in twentieth-century Mexico, where people who often "carried out top-down state and corporate designs" never really attempted to account for "the crucial importance of working closely with local people within their cultures."[96] This transformation appears in the municipal correspondence archive, where it is apparent that the letters of protest or requests for aid continued, but responses became scarce if those requests lacked legitimization from the ruling party. Technocrats and their bureaucracy also began to make citizen participation in the making of urban space less relevant to government plans. Engineers have wielded an outsized role in Mexico, a nation obsessed with progress and modernization since the eighteenth century.[97]

By the late 1940s, engineers had removed many colonial and nineteenth-century buildings on the north side of avenida Benito Juárez to widen the city's key east/west axis for automobiles. They followed this act by reorienting the heart of Guadalajara to center on the cathedral instead of the central plaza (the Plaza de Armas) as nearly all cities in Spanish America had done since the sixteenth century. As one author puts it, they "crucified" the city by gutting the colonial center and replacing it with a giant "Cross of Plazas" where churches and palaces had once stood.[98] Catholic-leaning politicians and engineers ushered Guadalajara into a new phase of existence in which centralization created gargantuan projects, all with little regard for local residents.

For the people featured in this work, it is likely that they would not have recognized the city that sprang up around them in the following decades. This is true of course of residents in the 1920s, the 1890s, or the 1850s. In their own time and context, urban residents seek to build and shape the physical space around them as well as imbue the location with a sense of "felt value."[99] This process necessarily brings them into conflict with a host of factors, such as economic trends, political movements, climate, weather, pests, illness, or objectionable neighbors with their own visions of the good life. To be in community is to be in conflict, and these disagreements did not indicate a detachment from society but rather a signal of belonging. *Tapatíos* expressed their desires for that "felt value" in these letters and petitions to their city, and this work explores some of those desires and contexts as they unfolded in one period of revolutionary Mexico.

1   A Battle of the Senses

¡Guadalajara! ¡Guadalajara!

Anyone who has heard mariachi music knows the opening lines of José (Pepe) Guízar Morfín's 1937 song "Guadalajara," perhaps the single largest promotional tool for the city's brand. Performed by vocalists such as Lucha Reyes, Placido Domingo, Vicente Fernández, and Mariachi Vargas, the song is a staple of mariachi groups in any setting. It also appears in the catalog of Nat King Cole, who made two albums in Spanish (recording his version of "Guadalajara" in 1962), and Elvis Presley, who performed the song with his Mississippi-tinged Spanish vocals in the 1963 film *Fun in Acapulco*. As of this writing, "Guadalajara" has provided the soundtrack to the world's imagination of Mexico for nearly a century.

When Pepe Guízar wrote the song, Guadalajara surged into its new status as the second-largest city in Mexico ahead of Puebla, but the sensory-centered lyrics indicated little about the experience of a busy, crowded urban landscape. The first line of this unofficial city anthem declares that Guadalajara has a *provinciana* soul, offering the double meaning of its having an essence that is steadfastly local as well as in counterpoint to the nation's capital, Mexico City.[1] It then refers to smells, such as an early rose, fresh earth, and aromatic foods. All the senses swirl together as Guízar describes listening to music or smelling the aroma of pottery jars holding the cool sweetness of pineapple *tepache* (the pottery of the region has its own scent that it makes when damp). Sensual moments of physical contact happen on moonlit nights at Lake Chapala to the south and on rainy hilltops among the trees to the north. Prayers and ringing church bells round out the sensory trip through Guízar's Guadalajara. By the end of the 1930s, the ideal city laid out in those lush verses and the reality of life had generated contradictory pictures.

Four years after the first release of "Guadalajara," the *regidores* (city council members) of Guadalajara in charge of public cleaning issued advisories to the community through the press. What they described in the autumn of 1941 is not the city found in song but the reflection of a desire to be the city of Pepe Guízar's imagination. Perhaps hoping to attain the scent of early roses and damp earth instead of piles of trash and heaps of night soil, this series of announcements required *tapatíos* to improve their property upkeep. The list of tasks included both reminders of existing policies and new ideas alike: water should not run into the streets; trash needed containment; all properties required perimeter walls or a tall fence on all sides; all façades must be painted; sidewalks should be repaired; and all grass or verge needed to be cleared from streets, curbs, and sidewalks. *Tapatíos* shouldered both the labor and the cost of the upkeep.[2] Such notices of course served as just one element in a long chain of municipal campaigns to keep the streets, sidewalks, and buildings clean and in good repair. While this link certainly had its roots in hygiene, by the 1940s the experience for both residents and visitors was increasingly entering public discussions of seeing, smelling, feeling, and hearing Guadalajara. Either directly or indirectly, the municipal public guidance established sensory expectations for experiencing Guadalajara that had links to the hygienic and physical experience of the city. In a way, this linking was truly a revolutionary act.

The Mexican Revolution of 1910 offered to bring the benefits of elite Porfirian society—particularly hygiene—to the wider population.[3] While some Mexicans did pursue the lofty goals of structural reform and chased dreams of social revolution (both secular and religious), many more had rejected the presidency of Porfirio Díaz (1876–1911) over mundane but ultimately important issues such as the goods and services provided by government. Under Díaz, reliable water supplies, fire control, paved roads, law enforcement, public sanitation, and a host of other services unevenly appeared in Mexican cities despite widespread demand.[4] Indeed, some members of society judged the regime by its own modernization claims and condemned Díaz and his advisors for failing to more widely and evenly achieve their goals.[5] While some segments of society, such as cowboys or displaced agri-culturalists, rebelled in response to the regime's heavy hand, others rebelled because that same hand failed to carry a broom and a dustpan and thereby create a land of "hard work, hygiene, sobriety, and progress."[6] For these revolutionaries, issues such as public health marked Mexico as a progressive, civilized society.[7] In this regard, the mundane *regidores* urging clean streets metaphorically sought their place in the revolutionary pantheon next to Pancho Villa and Emiliano Zapata—but mounted on garbage trucks instead of horses. For example, Mexico City boasted its Museo de Higiene (Museum of Hygiene) that touted the advances of the 1910 revolution and that by 1942 had requested presidential support to expand from its smaller space "due to the enormous quantity of visitors" and the massive size of the exhibit collections.[8]

This chapter, however, is not about elected officials and bureaucrats but average Mexicans who lived and interpreted with their senses the revolutionary actions of politicians and their expansive networks. Avoiding a state-centered approach, this chapter steps around another trap: the triumph of urban liberalism. After an initial reading of resident petitions, accepting liberalism's interpretation of the senses in Mexico is understandable. The demands of *varios vecinos* (or assorted neighbors, as they often refer to themselves in the documents) seeking their ideal living situation shine through the dense text of most petitions. But we have to ask not only what the people are petitioning for or against but also *whom* and *how*. Petitions from one set of neighbors attacked fellow residents whose sensibilities did not align with those of either the revolutionary state or the petitioners' imagined city. Some residents petitioned for restricted automobile movement, opening space for natural light through removal of commercial stalls, and spotlessly tidy routes of travel for pedestrians. These formal written petitions came in response to other more symbolic, physical manifestations of place making and belonging made by those being petitioned against. People targeted by petitions lodged their own petitions via action, not text on paper. They made their declarations with jukeboxes at full volume, swearing as they worked, leaving puddles of rancid oil, or scattering broken glass, and they signed with animal carcasses and the piles of human feces left in empty lots. The story of the senses in Guadalajara is not just that of formal written petitions demanding an idyllic liberal city and the city bureaucracy struggling to meet those demands.

What we see in the following pages is a tiered and complex sensoryscape that city residents contested at every turn. The process of this conflict acted as a ritual of belonging, and the narratives of that ritual expressed in petitions (written or acted out) carried the story of both types of authors. As defined in the introduction, a sense of belonging helps individuals establish "personal involvement in a system or environment" by either helping people feel needed or accepted or by proclaiming that their way of being "complements the system or environment" they are in.[9] In this regard, petitions relative to the senses helped residents in both ways. First, such petitions sent to city officials often stressed residents' defense of sensory perceptions established by those same officials: residents felt needed in the struggle to save the city from the trials of growth and change. Similarly, petitioning helped them narrate to themselves and to city officials that their sensory interpretation of the city complemented the system laid out by the political leadership. Still, residents had widely varying ways of interpreting the city with their senses.

One view held by some *tapatíos* was a longing for a city more akin to the colonial or early nineteenth-century period, featuring streets abuzz with peddlers and wooden stalls (known as *puestos*) whose owners called out to pedestrians. In this myth of a golden past, the narrow, dimly lit streets gave relief from the scorching sun, the air held the odor of bake shops and bodily human scents, while residents moved about without potentially murderous automobiles and their attendant roaring, honking, and gear grinding. Other city residents imagined the liberal city of sterile streets and sidewalks. Scrubbed free of human smells, the ordered work of profit defined for the senses a space of individual economic self-fulfillment taking place mostly indoors, unless otherwise necessary. Upon leaving their places of commerce, respectable citizens took to clean, safe, and well-constructed sidewalks bordering well-designed streets with orderly traffic. Such clashes of perception took place in multiple cities around Mexico, particularly in the nation's capital.[10] This liberal approach to the city matches the vision of Jane Jacobs, who writes that "sidewalks, their bordering uses, and their users, are active participants in the drama of civilization versus barbarism in cities. To keep the city safe is a fundamental task of a city's streets and its sidewalks."[11] Additionally, liberals desired a modern city in good taste when it had restrictions on the excesses of mechanical noise and effluent and where respectable residents could meet their needs in tidy, indoor shops. Finally, there is the aspirational modern global city that some inhabitants envisioned. Free from past limitations or the myopic vision of traditionalist elites, this would be the city of the future, or at least a city that could look like all the other notable world cities of the future. Here, the reality of industry, cutting-edge architectural design, and mechanical triumph dominate every aspect of visual, olfactory, tactile, and auditory sensoryscapes. A stream of buses and trucks meant labor at work, and the clang and crash of industry are just capital going about its fecund business of profit. None of these concepts about the city as imagined by petitioners or city leaders existed in a neat chronological order or even without significant conceptual crossover. Instead, these letters and petitions portray the sensoryscape of Guadalajara as a city of layered experiences of place.

Engaging in a discussion of how people bodily perceive the city goes beyond simply a "literary device to spice narrative."[12] Few can deny that "sensory experiences are central to the design of urban built environments."[13] And it is through the senses in their cultural context that we interpret and construct most of our sense of place. Through the interaction of taste, touch, smell, sight, and sound, people take in the "plethora of sensorial stimuli . . . from the built environment to fix their position psychologically, emotionally and physically in the world."[14] The building of this sensorial experience informs how humans inhabit a space fully and not just survive in the place they live. Senses and the way we discuss and process them are culturally determined products. Through the senses we communicate with the world, making it "present as a familiar setting of our life."[15] Through our senses, we bodily embed a feeling of belonging in our physical and emotional being.

This experience, however, is not accomplished through the effort of a single sense or even a single individual. The creation of the context that interprets senses in a wider cultural conversation (as well as the subsequent communication of the sensory experience) happens in a collective setting on two levels. First, the senses themselves work together to create an experience "collectively patterned to shape people's understanding of and interaction with the world."[16] But those experiencing the senses themselves engage in a communal action that shapes a feeling of place. What follows in this chapter is not only the lived experience of the senses in Guadalajara but also the negotiation and creation of narratives of belonging (physically perceived) to create the bodily stories *tapatíos* told themselves about who they are or desired to be.[17] Through the senses, we establish where and how we are, but in talking about those senses we reinforce and share who we are. One way residents modified urban space came through their work to shape the sensory experience, approving or disapproving of various experiences of sight, sound, scent, and touch. When they engaged in the process of discussing their sensory experiences with each other and telling their story through letters and petitions, they further contributed to a construction of place and their position in it.

Seeing the City

Tourism guidebooks established visual expectations of Guadalajara for travelers and indicated that they would find a "a stately, dignified, friendly, ably-governed, antique-modern, Spanish-Moorish, Mexican *metrópoli* . . . on a gentle, hill-environed slope overlooking the fine Atemajac valley, on the [west] side of the Great Central Plateau, in the beautiful Zona Occidental."[18] *Terry's Guide* describes a city of lustrous shine revealing the nature of one of its nicknames: Pearl of the West. The reputation of the city also lured Mexican travelers from around the nation, particularly newlyweds honeymooning amid the city's famed flowers, romantic balconies, and curving colonial Mozarabic architecture.[19] Said architect Garrett Van Pelt of Guadalajara in 1926, "Your immediate and lasting impression will be of a clean, well-ordered city."[20]

For *tapatíos*, the experience of city life extended to considerations beyond simple visual aesthetics, though enjoyment of physical space informed their views of Guadalajara. However, issues extended to other areas, such as workspace, safety, navigation, or culturally appropriate spectacle. Many saw the city as a "visually appreciated entity" that brought to life memories or created new ones, situated people in a context, interpreted an aesthetic that created individual identity, and helped people navigate their environment for everyday issues of work, play, health, and safety.[21] Defining the ideal visual interpretation of those issues, however, proved a challenge as *tapatíos* grappled with issues of political and social control in the city.[22]

Modernizing the center of Guadalajara to include new styles of architecture and wider streets for automobiles caused consternation among a selection of both downtown residents and business owners. Beyond the *"mal aspecto,"* or poor appearance, traffic and construction also did significant damage to lighting and lighting infrastructure.[23] When Luz Santamaría de Nachtigal faced new construction at the intersection of calles Hidalgo and Pedro Loza at the city's center, she condemned the lack of protections from dirt, dust, noise, and destruction as a lack of "civilization" facing existing residents. More important, as construction destroyed the electrical cables to her business without warning, she worried primarily about her inability to catch the attention of pedestrians because her illuminated signs lost power. She described that event as an "assault on the rights of people without the slightest concern for others."[24] A clash of modernizations appeared daily on the streets and sidewalks of Guadalajara between consistent, attractive lighting on one hand and expanded transportation infrastructure for mechanized mobility on the other.

For others, the war on the civilized city of light came from cars, trucks, and buses. When a roadster smashed into a special decorative streetlight that María Cruz Vda. de Acero had installed in front of her home, she wrote to the city to complain about the loss of light and the damage from the car. Worse, the transit authorities had carried off the special decorative light post and had not returned it. For the widow Cruz de Acero, lighting her property went hand in hand with creating an attractive and civilized city. While the letter doesn't give great detail about the crash, the incident wasn't a singular event. As reflected in the newspaper *El Informador* and city files, motor vehicles constantly destroyed public lighting. Widened streets allowed faster traffic, and by 1947 bus drivers, drunk drivers, or people who simply lost control of their vehicles were regularly crashing into light poles. With a fine of as much as 700 pesos per accident for the destruction of lampposts, the battle between cars and public lighting proved costly for all parties.[25] Cars, however, only headed up the list of offenders; drunken soldiers who smashed public lighting and cadres of youths playing soccer became the subjects of numerous complaints about their damaging the visual quality of city neighborhoods.[26]

A visual sense of place also affected those with shops and businesses along city streets, and their concerns went beyond artificial lighting. The city center of Guadalajara before 1940 included a hodge-podge of colonial-era government buildings, arcades with small shops, markets, several large retailers in Belle Époque–inspired buildings, narrow streets, and residences both grand and humble. To conduct daily commerce, business owners inside buildings demanded adequate natural light from street-facing windows. In January 1947 the city ordered that owners of stalls give up their positions in the streets of working-class areas to the south and east of the San Juan de Dios market. In addition to attempting to force merchants to rent space inside the city-regulated market (the memo made a pointed comment that forty stall spaces needed renters), the city also responded to the complaints of residents. The "obstruction of the view and of the light for adjacent properties" appears as a key concern. This marks a distinct change from just five years earlier, when the city resisted similar complaints by residents who wanted to move street stalls out of the area to another neighborhood. In 1942 city administrators had viewed wooden street stalls as a natural (though contested) part of the city and moved them from area to area when conflicts arose or when renovations necessitated their relocation.[27] From the city's point of view, as long as a vendor's stand did not block traffic (pedestrian or automobile) and vendors kept their space neat and clean, paid their fees, and did not unfairly compete with a storefront business by selling the same items, vendors in wooden stalls had little to worry about. Regarding the stalls' physical appearance, the city only demanded vaguely that they "stay in good repair so as to not act as a detriment to the visual aesthetic [*ornato*] of the city."[28] For Guadalajara, the complaint that stalls blocked light or constituted eyesores fueled tension between stall owners and storefront businesses.

Concern about the visual qualities of the city was not limited to different kinds of business owners. The widow Rosario Ochoa de González Guerra rebuked the municipal president in August 1942 for the lack of garbage collection and street cleaning in her neighborhood. Community members simply threw their trash at the intersection of calles Pavo and López Cotilla, a narrow intersection just a block from the new Parque Revolución and the main thoroughfare of avenida Juárez. She couched her complaint in terms that appealed to an aesthetic of Guadalajara as a shining city, "desiring to contribute to the good presentation of our beloved Pearl of the West." When her initial letter went unanswered, she followed up with another, pointing to the approaching Independence Day celebrations scheduled for September. This celebration required a "pleasing decoration" for Guadalajara as the "second capital of our beloved Mexico."[29] González Guerra attempted to appeal to love for the *patria chica* as well as the larger narrative of celebratory nationalism.[30] Her declaration of unity with the nation and the city could be a strategic play to get what she needed. It might be a declaration of her true feelings of patriotism. It could even be both.

An additional concern that extends from sight is that of security. While some historians focus on the use of light by reformers to expose working-class doings in the dark and control them, workers also saw improved lighting as a source of protection.[31] Artificial lighting transformed the world's urban spaces, revealing obstacles to safe navigation and stripping anonymity from criminals. That letters regarding the pairing of light and security peppered the Guadalajara city offices is no surprise. Government entities strove to limit violence at the same time public lighting began to appear all over the city. The state wielded the powers of both public lighting and policing in an attempt to dominate urban spaces. When Leonor de Rivas led her neighbors at the intersection of calles Camarena and Langloix in petitioning the city in 1939, she protested both the lack of light and the thin police presence in the neighborhood—"*un solo gendarme* [one single officer]"—in the area.[32] Robbery and the acts of "villainous people" using the "absolute lack of light" as a cover for their crimes caused grief to area families, according to Rivas. Even in what the petitioners called a *barriada*, or peripheral neighborhood, residents expected the artificial light and police protection that would keep them safe.[33]

Ten blocks south of Camarena and Langloix, the workers at La Marsellesa, a factory making blankets and duvets, joined with the factory owners in 1942 to demand more light. The workers, they said, were being "bothered and attacked [*molestado y atropellado*] by individuals who take advantage of the darkness" cast by the railroad warehouses in the area. Considering the textile industry and its record of employing women, it is more than likely that rape and sexual assault also plagued the area.[34] The sensory experience of darkness threatened the physical, mental, and financial safety of workers. For working women and men, darkness signified city officials' failure to provide infrastructure and security, as well as opportunity for criminals.[35] Criminals are also city residents, and they found dark areas a beneficial hunting ground for their predations.

Visuality also involved issues of morality and class beyond the material concerns of economic opportunity, business aesthetics, and safety. The visual spectacle of death and the disposal of bodies also concerned some members of society. When Eduardo Collignon attended the funeral of one of his employees, a disturbing sight upset the funeral attendees at the municipal cemetery of Mezquitán. Not far from the burial, workers busily disinterred the bodies of people whose families had buried their relatives in temporary plots. A member of Guadalajara's high society from one of its prominent Porfirian-era French business families, Collignon described it as "a scene that could not have been more repulsive." Like elites in his class from earlier eras described by Jonathan Weber, the "disgusting spectacle" of bodily decay and the potential for spreading disease caused his anxiety.[36] Collignon urged the city to take measures to avoid these kinds of visible activities that are "repugnant and dangerous to health." He offered a solution by asking that disinterment take place early in the morning if no graveside services concurrently took place. Finally, he discussed an additional concern: he urged that night guards watch over the cemetery to stop the "profaning of tombs and the mutilation of cadavers" (though he offered no additional details or evidence of such crimes).[37] Collignon thus eagerly pushed for the cessation of less-than-gentle daylight exhumations of corpses that offended his visual senses while calling for guards to prevent the nocturnal desecration of others.

Collignon objected to the disinterment and rough treatment of the bodies of those who could not afford to purchase permanent plots because the sight of it disturbed visitors, not because the grisly processing of the long dead offended him. According to Collignon, such disinterment and disposal in a common grave should not happen when decent people might witness it, but that did not mean it should not happen. By contrast, for those with permanent tombs, Collignon asked that the city work to prevent the mutilation of corpses in the dark of night and to maintain the cemetery and graves by day. Like the nineteenth-century elites of his family heritage, Collignon worked to "hide or eliminate the unclean aspects of the city."[38] Issues of hygiene aside, the elite concerns about the visible processing of death outweighed respect for the dead—respect that could only be purchased and did not come with mere residency in the city or by virtue of having been a human being.[39] Such concerns about spectacle and death as well as the potential for spreading disease constantly concerned elites from the Bourbon Reform period through the Porfiriato.[40]

From the sight of death to the rays of afternoon sun in a shop window, visual perception helped people feel comfortable in the city. While the sight of looted corpses or of broken lights offended some, for others their work or entertainment hinged on such behaviors (as discussed more thoroughly in chapter 2). Sight is a sense that dominates how many perceive the world around them. Examining that sense opens our discussion to the differing ways people attempted to establish belonging in the city through describing their interpretation of both visual pleasure or the often related visible aspects of commerce. Every petition created a narrative of belonging wherein the authors reinforced how they complemented the goals of city leaders. In this regard, we now turn to the sense of sound and its consistent, similar use.

Hearing the City

To stand silently and listen to the urban landscape reveals much about the city. Is there the sound of wind in trees? Does the roar of a bus bounce off flat surfaces or is that dull sound actually the hum of an electric tram absorbed by cloth hanging in a market or clothes drying on balconies? Are peddlers calling out? Does the crackle of food cooking in grease at a *puesto* cover the shrieking of children playing nearby? Are there shouts of distress or playfulness (or both) occurring? What machines punctuate the audio space? Form, function, location, pleasure, disruption, population, happiness, and any number of other city characteristics are assessable through the medium of sound. The interplay of sound, too, gives us layers of urban experience. Is there a droning sound whose constancy is as ever-present as the physical street itself? As one moves, do sounds cut out suddenly, marking the passage into a new city section? What about absences, such as when a sound suddenly stops or its reverberations continue after the initial eruption that first caused the sound ends?[41] Or perhaps there is a layered wall of sounds that come at once, rendering the original sources unidentifiable and creating a new audio location that distinguishes an urban geography for the listener.[42] All of these expressions are sounds for some and noise for others, and they marked a battle for the audioscape of Guadalajara.[43] Although the use of sound does not rise to the level of "insidious manipulation" or sonic resistance in most of the cases covered here, it nevertheless marks a battlefield over such issues as one's belonging in the city, the use of space, the definition of place, and acts of belonging through petitioning about sound and sound creators.[44]

More than just their taste in music divided *tapatíos* in the way they imagined the good life through sound. Live music associated with establishments of dubious reputations and the new ability to use electricity to amplify music divided residents on the meaning of urban life. For María Guadalupe Vda. de Jiménez, the former proved a challenge to the hotel on calle Ferrocarril that she inherited at the death of her husband. While her hotel rooms (though they had more in common with a boardinghouse setup) occupied the top floor of a building, on the bottom floor could be found two cantinas: La Alhambra and La California.[45] In addition to the scandalous behaviors that drove away her customers, she grew most distraught at the establishments being "open night and day without interruption, and . . . every night there are jazz performances." Because her hotel and the attached cantinas stood in front of the rail station just south of downtown Guadalajara, she assured the city in her letter of complaint that the cantinas' visibility served as a "detriment to the good name of the city."[46] For Jiménez, it is either unfathomable or unwelcome that visitors disembarking at the train station might visit Guadalajara for jazz and other possible associated entertainments. Nevertheless, for both locals and visitors, the availability of alcohol and jazz with the accompanying sounds of human sociality and levity defined their recreational city experience. Jazz had not yet entered its "golden age" in Mexico (the 1950s and 1960s), but its popularity beginning in the 1920s reached into Guadalajara and became associated with the desired universal, cosmopolitan, and modernization of Mexican nationalist developmentalism. Despite opposition from sectors such as Acción Católica Mexicana (ACM, Mexican Catholic Action) or Mexican communists, jazz drove the establishment of a wave of new dance halls and cabarets.[47] Secular music was not the only music that drew the ire of *tapatíos*, and scandal in music could take multiple forms.

As working-class people in Guadalajara explored alternatives to Catholicism and joined Pentecostal churches, the enthusiastic preaching and singing irritated neighbors. In 1939 the non-Catholic Luz del Mundo church pointedly retreated from the center of the city because of complaints from their Catholic neighbors about the singing and loud preaching. Pentecostal-inspired churches found it difficult to engage in "singing and praying with all their strength" while neighbors harangued them.[48] During Mexico's postwar economic boom, when the national leadership urged the citizenry to focus on its "fecund and creative labor," the neighbors used the language of disturbing productivity as a strategic attempt to alienate sounds associated with behaviors they abhorred.[49] Nevertheless, the sounds of Pentecostal churches signaled an opportunity for residents seeking religious lives outside of Catholicism. For Pentecostals, engaging with music that could be heard throughout the neighborhood created within their worship space "a familiar religious cultural home."[50] As targets of angry petitions, these religious dissenters made their own counterclaim on the sensory space by using song as a ritual of belonging.

Though musical performance could scandalize certain residents and mean sociability and devotion for others, some *tapatíos* simply worked to preserve live music in Guadalajara altogether. In March 1942 the Unión Filarmónica Jalisciense (Jalisco Musicians Union) pleaded with city leaders to defend the role of musicians in the city. By issuing licenses for "mechanical musical apparatuses with speakers in commercial establishments," the musicians argued, the city had placed performing musicians in a position of great risk to their livelihoods. "[Those businesses] where our associates were working and that have received licenses," the musicians wrote, "have ceased to be sources of employment."[51] This communication to the city reflects a long-running concern of musicians in Mexico as various mechanical devices, from player pianos to radio, saturated society. For example, in 1930 the Sindicato de Filarmónicos de Torreón (Musicians Union of Torreón) succeeded in imposing a tax on pianolas, phonographs, and "all classes of mechanical instruments" in restaurants and bars as a way to protect musicians' livelihoods.[52] In Jalisco in 1932, Governor Juan de Dios Robledo (1931–32) passed along letters from the Confederación Obrera de Jalisco (Workers Union of Jalisco) to the state congress demanding the state regulate mechanical music apparatuses.[53] And so it went, year after year, with unions, government, and a selection of city residents demanding regulations or controls on musical devices in the city.[54] For a short time, musicians even scored a victory; in 1934 the city occasionally restricted licenses on new musical devices in commercial establishments.[55] On the other hand, restaurants, cafés, and bars, as well as their patrons, showed no sign of retreating from their use of recorded, amplified music, and the city itself had an interest in the use of mechanical music-making devices: just as it required businesses to obtain a permit to sell alcohol or even tortillas, the city licensed the use of musical apparatuses and profited from their use.[56]

In 1932 the city issued a proclamation on noise regulation "due to the many complaints the municipal president has received because of the many annoyances thrust onto the neighborhoods of the city center." The draconian rules limited music in commercial businesses to three hours a day (from noon to 1 p.m. and from 5:30 to 7:30 p.m.). Similarly, musicians who performed before public audiences faced the same limitations, as well as an additional requirement that they fill out applications to perform. The new rules limited church bells to thirty seconds, with the exception of civic holidays and national celebrations (though public complaints about church bells at late-night hours continued well after 1932).[57] Violators faced fines of between 10 and 100 pesos.[58] To nobody's surprise, such regulations proved impossible to enforce. By 1944 *El Informador* was complaining about the "intolerable" and constant sound of music made by jukeboxes (*sinfanolas*).[59] While Mexico's elite debated the merits of what styles or kinds of music should be broadcast from the mechanical miracle of radios (introduced to Guadalajara in 1924), *tapatíos* still debated the role that music should play in the urban soundscape.[60] Indeed, for some the possibility of speakers installed in parks presented an opportunity: on days that the state band could not perform in the city center's Plaza de Armas, the owner of a record store offered to install speakers and a record player so that the public could still enjoy music.[61] Even as the technology evolved, community members reinforced the role that music played in creating community life.[62] The speaker installation soon took place, though not to provide music. On August 27, 1947, Governor Jesús González Gallo ordered the city to wire public buildings, plazas, and markets with speakers so that a September 1, 1947, speech from President Miguel Alemán could be broadcast to the public. The ruling party's voice—not mechanically reproduced music—was earmarked to unite the community.[63]

Perhaps surprisingly, fewer complaints came in from the public regarding the mechanical and human noises generated by business and industry. The sound of labor as well as audio advertising offended some members of society, though the small number of complaints in the archive is probably representative of the limited public concern on those matters. While some saw the city as one that should reside in peace, the sound of labor or the advertising of goods and services meant profit and a livelihood for many drawn to the city as migrants. Cities have of course never been fully silent places, particularly when vendors alert passersby to available wares or services.

Traditionally, ambulatory peddlers (with carts, animals, or even bicycles by the late nineteenth century) and stall vendors attracted business with their voices or a symphony of instruments such as bells, horns, whistles (steam, instrumental, or human), or drums and other percussion devices. Increasingly in the postrevolutionary period, peddlers (now using motorized vehicles), stall and market vendors, and businesses in fixed shops all engaged in mechanical magnification of their voices. Electric loudspeakers, megaphones, repetitious jingles, and narrations of products flowed freely from shops in every city sector. For business owners and perhaps more than a few customers, the sounds they made represented opportunity and the variety of goods, services, and diversions of city life. Indeed, the idea of silence in a city carries with it a sinister edge, implying an imposed quiet based on control and hierarchies of power rather than the practical, audible flow of daily life.[64]

Still, for a few, the barrage of advertising ran against their vision of the good life in the city. The popular imagined city soundscape may revel in church bells and mariachi, but it does not celebrate the rumble of a truck operated by a scrap dealer calling for customers to bring out their old mattresses or, similarly, loudspeakers in front of a record shop.[65] For example, when resident Carlos Tapia Robles issued his list of noise complaints to the city in January 1947, he included the noise of loudspeakers issuing from businesses and the cries of peddlers.[66] Record stores that played beyond noise-limiting curfews also drove neighbors to distraction.[67]

More common, however, were complaints about the noise caused by the proximity of small industries to residential buildings in the city center, where 70 percent of residents lived and where small industries and commercial enterprises abutted residences.[68] Neighbors complained about both machinery sounds as well as the salty language of workers. For many, the productive "hum" of industry in the urban audioscape signaled income and modernity in both the working and the capital classes.[69] However, others adhered to contemporary critiques of sound as "disorder" and an assault on citizens attempting to get the rest needed for productivity.[70] For example, to Amalia Mireles and ten other neighbors in calle Hidalgo, the small shoe manufactory of Juan Zarquín stirred their ire for numerous reasons. Among them was the constant hammering of machinery at night, as well as other noises such as swearing, shouting, and drinking "that at times drives one into the street so as to not have their morals offended."[71] "Zarquín" appears to have been Juan Zarkin Icikowich, born in Lithuania and a member of Guadalajara's Jewish community and respectable society (judging by the family's frequent appearance in the society pages).[72] Zarkin represents an interesting case in which the record does not register the dispatch of an inspector to see if the business violated noise laws; instead, city officials forwarded to Zarkin a copy of the petition from his neighbors, making it entirely possible that Zarkin himself agreed with their assessment of noise in the neighborhood where he himself lived. By 1949 his shoe factory, called Bota Cow-Boy, had relocated south and east to calle Gigantes in Sector Reforma in a neighborhood of working-class residents and newly arrived rural migrants. Presumably his business and employees better fit the expectations for the soundscape on calle Gigantes.[73]

In the case of neighbors located in a Mexicaltzingo *vecindad*, their shared wall with a machine shop that operated twenty-four hours a day brought no end of agony. The noise reverberating through the walls, as well as the physical shaking and smoke from the engines that turned the lathes, "bother[ed] to the extreme."[74] Hundreds of small businesses (though mostly in Sectors Hidalgo and Reforma) just like the Mexicaltzingo machine shop produced humming, rattling, banging, and pumping noises that punctuated the soundscape throughout the city. Engines used in the downtown area ranged from 3.5 horsepower motors (about the strength of a modern-day gasoline-powered lawnmower) in a chocolate and coffee grinder's shop to tanneries and textile producers whose boilers and generators had ten times the power.[75] Though the city periphery attracted large industry, the center hosted hundreds of small producers, whom politicians often urged to work there.[76] This small industry meant consumer goods for local markets and a certain level of prosperity for producers and owners, but the audio toll on the population is evident in the letters from *tapatíos*.

City noises bothered some residents because of what the sounds represented and not just for the physical sensation they caused. For example, Diego Villalobos decried the radios in stalls, honking vehicles, firecrackers, airplanes in the sky, and church bells, and he wrote a letter to the municipal president saying, "Don't you think it is time you put an end to this lack of organization and discipline, which we need for the ordered march of civilization?"[77] For others, the noise of musicians, radios, advertising, engines, and boilers signaled exactly what they had come to the city in search of: profit and pleasure. Noise signaled the height of civilization for some and the drumbeat of decline for others. For either cohort, expressing their views on sound as a sort of declaration of civilization or barbarism helped them locate themselves in society. By defending certain noises and attacking others, residents affirmed that they lived in line with their perception of what city officials envisioned for society. For others who simply led their lives with little regard for their neighbors or city officials, the sounds or noises they produced represented the possibilities of revolutionary society. Either way, their petitions and actions help readers in the present understand how residents at that time interpreted their urban experience through the senses.

The City of Flowers and Carcasses

As with sound, the sense of scent can carry both figurative and physical meanings for different people. While sound becomes a noise for those whom it bothers, smells may become an odor or a stink perhaps physically unbearable for those who experience certain smells in a negative manner. According to scholars of sense, "Smell is cultural, hence a social and historical phenomenon." How we talk about smell carries values and tells us how societies interact with the world around them, giving us a different tool for the analysis of humanity.[78] Smell and the value placed on it is not a product of just individual likes and dislikes but is constructed as part of "shared culture" because "society associates certain values, for example, the smell of cleanliness, the meaning of a warm tortilla, or fresh bread." No smell has universal or definite meaning.[79] So important is smell that it even plays a key role in our mental health by helping us orient ourselves in our physical world and by providing pleasure, warning us of pain, or triggering memories.[80] Smell's link between the physical and the mental renders the contextual meaning of smells or alternative interpretations of those smells difficult to imagine for readers reared in the late twentieth and early twenty-first centuries' regulation of bodily and other naturally occurring scents. In his historiographic overview of senses and history, Mark M. Smith points out that "what was rank and fetid to, say, a tenth-century Viking's nostrils is not recoverable today, not the least because that world . . . has evaporated."[81] Readers in the present can never fully appreciate the past's sensory context, though they can be aware of their modern sensory biases. This context even has class implications. In reflecting on the divide between the middle or upper classes and the working class, George Orwell opined that the most effective tool in creating class divides is a focus on the visceral feeling that "the lower classes smell." The creation of "physical repulsion," he adds, does the initial hard work of creating a dislike and disgust for working and poor classes. Quoting Somerset Maugham, he writes, "The matutinal tub divides the classes more effectively than birth, wealth, or education."[82]

Smell as a focus of eighteenth- and nineteenth-century liberal reformers helped create the context of scent as a reflection of health and safety in Mexican cities. Standing water, human waste, animal carcasses, rotting vegetable matter, unbathed human bodies, and all manner of human-created or natural smells vexed reformers because they associated odors with the origin of disease.[83] Literature, language, and laws link smell to gender and sexuality, with desirability, reproductive potential, and sexual purity all having links to scent: even the crude Spanish word for sex workers (*puta*) is linked to the same root from which we get the word "putrid."[84] In modern cities, zoning laws attempt to isolate scents in particular spaces where residents or travelers can expect particular smells associated with the industrial, the private, and the public.[85]

Understandably, satisfying the aspirations of reformers in all zones of a city proved difficult around the world. Cities, as Ivan Illich wrote, have not always been places that required washing, and the "odorless utopia" is a relatively recent phenomenon.[86] Transitioning from smelly to odorless overnight or even over centuries seems an impossible task. In the case of Guadalajara, both the wealthy class's reluctance to contribute the necessary taxes and the massive influx of rural, working-class people restricted the efforts of urban reformers to create effective infrastructure.[87] How does one regulate scent in a constantly evolving space filled with people whose social contexts connote a variety of values on smell? In this regard, the various petitions on scent (or odors) allowed incredible flexibility for a range of residents to reinforce to themselves and (they hoped) to the city leadership that their interpretation of scent signaled their belonging to the wider city community.

Related to the previously discussed issue of sound, the proliferation of small businesses and industrial facilities bothered many residents. For *tapatíos* in Colonia Moderna, the presence of La Marsellesa, the factory that produced bedspreads, created a situation where the stench made living in the area unbearable. Upon inspection, the city discovered that La Marsellesa had repositories of dyes on the property that caused the smell, as well as an extremely short chimney that spewed ash and soot onto the homes of its neighbors.[88] Similar complaints came from neighbors who saw a new casting workshop appear in the middle of their neighborhood; they soon found their homes filled with smoke.[89] In the case of the bedspread factory, inspectors ordered the dyes removed from the residential area and the installation of a taller chimney to carry the smoke away from the area. For the foundry, the inspectors said that the ovens ran only one or two days a week and that smoke entered homes exclusively on windy days; the city therefore ordered no changes for the workshop.

Residents experienced the employment benefits of small industry, but they also suffered the sensorial effects of smoke and stench. For city officials, the reality of their pro-industry position often collided with their training of residents to reject practices that resulted in the creation of unhealthy or unbearable odors. In large part, this represents one challenge for industrial cities: officials tolerated the odors of industry until they became an immediate physical danger, while hygienic regulation and reform targeted smells from living organisms. City officials deemed it unnecessary to regulate the non-life-threatening smells of production in the face of their ambitions to industrialize the city.[90] For example, neighborhoods near the Productos de Maíz (Maize Products Company) plant at the intersection of calles Inglaterra and Cinco de Mayo received no action at all after they complained of the stench of "foul waste" from the plant. They said the smell became "unbearable and pose[d] a serious danger to the health of passengers on the buses" on the street "and especially us . . . with established homes and offices in the area."[91] The city and nation's productive growth could not halt for small things like smell.

Issues related to the smellscape created by stall vendors also vexed fellow vendors. For example, in March 1947 María Isabel Sánchez pleaded with the municipal president to help her find relief from a neighboring vendor's smelly "smoke that penetrates my freshly made candies." The accused vendor was "a young, single woman with an apparatus that transforms corn" into a puffed, toasted snack. Sánchez's regular clients found the machine's smell so terrible that they refused to return to the area. Upon inspection, the city discovered that the young woman and her puffed and toasted corn machine irritated other vendors. The inspectors suggested she move from the area, but not for stinking up the air. Instead, they shut her down for operating without a license, placing the stall too close to other vendors (stalls had to be at least one meter and fifty centimeters apart), and impeding the flow of foot traffic.[92] Much like the inconvenience of industrial fumes, the smell of cooking—no matter how annoying or potentially ruinous in the case of María Isabel Sánchez—required toleration unless it impinged on navigation and licensing fees.

While industrial or small-scale issues of scent and their collision with profit faced some residents, a far larger struggle took place over the intersection of scents created by other people. Garbage, water, sewer, and animals (dead and alive) all generated the largest number of letters and petitions to the city over concerns of both smell and health. Esteban Muñoz lodged a complaint to the municipal president in 1943 because of a series of failed letters to the director of hygiene coordination. Due to pens of hogs and chickens on avenida Colón, the area smelled of animal waste. Muñoz asked the municipal president to suggest tips on dealing with flies. He acerbically added that since it was impossible to remove the pens of hogs and chickens from the street and that since all inspectors that came to this neighborhood had broken noses that couldn't smell anything, his only recourse was to get suggestions from officials for dealing with the flies. In a more serious tone, he ended by demanding that the city send somebody "honorable" to enforce the laws.[93]

Similarly, in Sector Hidalgo, in the city's northwest, Carmen González M. told officials that on the corner of calles 29 and 30, an empty lot had become a place for people to dump garbage "as well as dead animals, and burning them with the garbage produces unbearable odors for this entire neighborhood."[94] Notably, González M. does not provide a petition from a selection of other neighbors to support her complaint. Are they the ones responsible for the garbage and dead animals? Is the area a simple, convenient location to dispose of garbage and bodies, as some might have previously done while living in the countryside? Whatever the concern, the city responded not to the smell but instead to the possible health risks, and they classified the unplotted area "a focus of infection and a danger to the residents in the immediate vicinity."[95]

Empty lots used as places for disposal and incineration are one reason that lots had to be bordered by walls under city regulations. While Mexican officials had spent decades haranguing residents on the finer points of modern trash disposal, the cost, inconvenience, and lack of infrastructure made it impossible for average people to comply. People like Carmen González M. envisioned the city as a place that discreetly disposed of waste without residents having to smell it. However, even when infrastructure for the disposal of waste existed, residents still made alternate choices that dismayed their neighbors. At the intersection of calles Independencia Sur and Catalán, neighbors complained of a large box always full of garbage and reported that it had become "a public bathroom and bedroom of a drunk." They followed up with an additional comment that plants being watered on residential balconies dripped on the box, soaking the garbage and increasing the smell. They begged to have the box removed because it had become an "*asco*" (point of disgust) for families in the area, and they feared that "now that it is hot [March] sickness could fall on us because it smells very bad and makes the street look terrible."[96]

The neighbors drafting this petition not only suffered from the presence of odors but also potentially ascribed the health threat to either older medical notions (e.g., miasmic air) or even folk notions of bad air (*mal aire*) causing illness in the same way that previously cited examples do. However, it is not too far-fetched to consider that petitioners might also interpret issues of germs in the air through the lens of city officials' guidance to *tapatíos* regarding illness such as influenza.[97] Additionally, as we will see in chapters 2 and 3, residents assigned moral weight to the odors coming from the box and linked the sanctity of the Mexican family to the quality of the scent in the street. These sorts of issues may have had some roots in health and hygiene, but health policy is also social control. The concept of stench in public spaces provided a way for some residents to attempt to control behavior that tarnished (in the plaintiff's view) both space and place.[98] That social control, however, had obvious limits.

In this letter about the garbage box, we see revolutionary liberalism's limited reach into the practices of citizens. Like the previous example of garbage burning at the corner of calles 29 and 30, the persons using the box for garbage remain unidentified, as do the cost savings or convenience the box provided for users. Just as little is known about the reported "drunk" (*borracho*) who used the box as a place to sleep. What past do we imagine for him based on this source, and what opportunity did this meager shelter provide? Was the person using the space even a "drunk" as described by the letter's author, or was it simply a member of the poorest sphere of urban homeless set adrift in Guadalajara after coming to the city from the countryside? No matter his individual identity, romantic notions about the smell of damp earth and roses in the song "Guadalajara" had little to do with his urban experience.

At the intersection of health and smell, standing water and flooding drew concerns from residents in the city in various locations. In the case of residents near the maize products plant mentioned above (a petition that has no documented response), the stench from the plant came not only from the air but also from the standing water in the street and from areas near the plant.[99] In another case, state water inspectors responded to leaking hydrants near mercado Alcalde after vendors complained that the stench from the "*charco*" (large puddle) so offended market visitors that business decreased.[100] For Clotilde Saldaña Ruiz, an "immense lake" at the intersection of avenidas Constitución and Juan Álvarez posed multiple problems. The pool of standing water not only threatened to ruin the foundations of a series of homes that Saldaña, who was a property developer and employee of the Comisión Nacional de Irrigación (National Irrigation Commission), had just constructed, but the number of mosquitoes breeding in the water and the "enormous smell" in warm weather made this "impassable" water hole a serious health threat to the neighborhood.[101] In the case of standing water, not only did smell intersect with health and safety for these particular petitioners, but it also posed particular threats to livelihood by means of property destruction.

The issue of standing water in Guadalajara plagued the city because it lacked adequate drainage, particularly during the rainy season, from June to September. This meant that the city at times had an abundance of flooding and standing water. In the past, this water would have filled streams, wells, and cisterns or been absorbed into the water table and been used from September into the dry spring months. Paving and sprawl, however, caused rainy season flooding, and in combination with an insufficient municipal sewage network, the results could be pungent.

Understanding the complications that came with modern hygiene and the sensory problems that accompanied it even prompted one neighborhood to decline water and sewer service. Residents of calle Tabasco in the neighborhood of Mezquitán (near the municipal cemetery) petitioned the city to stop the public works department from introducing water and sewer service. In addition to being too poor to pay their cooperative portion of installation and future upkeep, the residents had had bad experiences with

FIG. 4. Workers hauling pipe for water service in the Los Colomos area on the northern edge of Guadalajara in 1940. The working-class members of the (then) northern neighborhood of Mezquitan at first rejected sewer service because they had seen firsthand (both as city residents and as workers installing sewer lines) the contamination of drinking water that came from improperly installed and maintained sewer lines. Caja 1, Sobre 14, Fecha 1940, Folio 34, Titulo "Obras de drenaje en los Colomos." Courtesy of the Archivo Histórico Municipal de Guadalajara.

city services, which had left a negative impression. Previously, the neighbors had collectively purchased access to a water hydrant on the neighborhood's edge, but water never arrived. Finally, as a neighborhood where every home had an outhouse, they reasoned that any water that came their way would soon be contaminated and not worth the risk.[102] They well understood that almost as soon as the city introduced pipes they began to crack and leak, introducing contamination. In the Mezquitán case, the smell of outhouses for every home in the neighborhood did not outweigh the reality of what modern sewer lines meant for water quality. In this case, the residents used a firm understanding of water levels, the issue of broken water pipes, and the reality of water contamination to make their decision to reject the modernization improvements that, in their experience, had failed from the start.

Perhaps more mercenary but similarly canny, farmers near the city understood the issues with drainage and sewage and their city neighbors and forsook modern notions of odor in their work and living conditions. Faced with immense amounts of runoff from the city in the form of both gray water and *"aguas negras"* (human sewage), farmers on the edge of town took advantage of the cheap irrigation and fertilizer source. Farmers commonly used sewage from the city for irrigation and fertilizer. A 1940 study by the city concluded that only installing hydrants in markets and requiring all vendors to wash vegetables before sale could avoid the typhoid and dysentery caused by wastewater irrigation.[103] In an associated practice supported by the Confederación Nacional Campesina (CNC, National Confederation of Campesinos) in Mexico City, farmers from Tlaquepaque used garbage from the city in compost for their crops.[104] For rural members of the municipal entity of Guadalajara, casting aside the constraints of scent resulted in profits and survival in a world increasingly difficult for agriculturalists threatened by city expansion.

The perception of smells of Guadalajara reflected a range of experiences and contexts for residents. The groups that sent petitions to the city saw themselves as carriers of community through their advocacy for particular olfactory interpretations of Guadalajara, as did those who boldly and openly lived lives that earned them rebuke from petitioners. In some cases—like the people of Mezquitán—petitioners on both sides saw themselves as advocates for health, safety, and civilization. In other cases—as with the farmers backed by agricultural unions versus city residents who complained of the smell—the value of your contribution to society depended on which authority backed you. In large part, this truism marks much of the flexible genius of this era in revolutionary Mexico. With the ruling party not yet fully entrenched in residents' lives, uncertainty meant possibility and opportunities for pragmatic responses. Criminals against clean scents existed as urban residents alongside the authors of petitions, and at times women and men openly rejected the pathways laid out for them by municipal sensory discipline.

Navigating Guadalajara: The Sense of Touch in La Perla

The physical experience of navigating the city overwhelmingly centers the sense of touch, though historians rarely think or at least rarely write explicitly about that sensory experience. As Mirko Zardini has pointed out, how individuals experience the city depends on choosing modes of transportation (cars or bicycles?) and clothing as intermediaries (boots? bare feet?) and, consequently, the class considerations reflected in those choices. Does a person walking along the cobbled sidewalks in high heels and a restrictive pencil skirt feel (and feel about) the city differently than a person in sandals and a flowing dress? What about individuals navigating asphalt streets whose tar stains and wounds bare feet? Additionally, what about the physical ways that we interact with the building materials found in the architecture around us? Plastered walls or hewn stone? Cool tiles or rich, polished wood? Slabs of concrete or walls of shining glass? Touch is also a gateway into the broader world of the previously discussed senses. Eating and processing food requires touch, as does prostitution, most labor, medical care, some forms of worship, and physical violence.[105] Particularly important for city residents, navigation and spatial cognition link to a sense of touch that allows residents to gauge how they move through a city.[106]

As Alexander Cowan and Jill Steward have pointed out, most urban hygiene law intentionally reduced the interaction of human touch and proximity to other humans.[107] Even residents' use of letters and petitions cited in this work indicates a decrease in human connections or situations in which people might meet each other and exchange greetings before discussing issues related to city living with people beyond their neighborhood. This attempted reduction of human touch just as the city filled with more people is no accident. Foundational liberal concepts such as privacy and individualism dominated the modern European city, and Mexican reformers sought to emulate these practices. As Constance Classen has demonstrated, hygiene laws drew people indoors and away from their neighbors for activities such as bathing, washing, eating, or urinating that had previously been done in open or communal settings. For some migrants to the city, this anonymity and escape from the stifling rural village life served as liberation, while for others, the sensory deprivation of less human touch could be disorienting.[108]

Additionally, the pace of life in modern Guadalajara increased intentionally. As public transportation expanded, engineers widened streets for cars, and as police removed barriers to both pedestrian and automobile thoroughfares, the speed of life in the city grew. Slow jostling and physical interaction defined human interaction in eighteenth-century cities, but nineteenth- and twentieth-century city leaders, following the dictates of capitalism, sped up the urban experience to maximize profits. With increased speed, one has to reduce interactions that occur in slow, human ways. As one scholar notes, "An obsession with motion, financial, fictive and corporeal, is arguably one of the major effects of a move into modern capitalism."[109] In short, the sense of touch in the city is about how we physically navigate space and perceive it through time. It is little wonder then that *tapatíos* saw automobiles as a sensory concern, and it is there that we will start with an exploration of touch.

In 1939 mule carts and horse carriages still traversed the urban zones of Guadalajara, though efforts to remove them increasingly found success. Well into the 1930s, "people kept cows and chickens in their domestic space and at night they abandoned dead animals in the street where they rotted in front of passersby and filled the atmosphere with disagreeable smells."[110] As a strategy to reduce the presence of animals on city roads, a new fee on mule carts entering the city while carrying fodder for animals made it more difficult for people to keep animals in the city.[111] The new fee came about after nearly two decades of street-widening projects and paving had created more car-friendly spaces and reduced (but did not eliminate) the number of horses and mules on the streets. In 1923 Guadalajara ranked second behind Mexico City with over 1,300 cars and 100 motorcycles on its city streets.[112] By 1940 Mexico had 7.6 vehicles per 1,000 persons, though the unequal concentration of vehicles in cities like Guadalajara made the number far higher in those areas (closer to 11 cars per 1,000 residents).[113] Thus, street-widening projects in the 1920s and associated paving work brought hundreds of autos to the city center. In 1930 a bus system began running, with its 64 buses increasing the rumbling feel of automotive power on streets and sidewalks. The removal in 1944 of the city's trolleys and their rhythmic passage along predictable rails in favor of more buses (the 60-bus Guadalajara-Tlaquepaque-Zapopan service came on line in 1945), and the proliferation of small industries using trucks to transport materials brought still more vehicular traffic into the city.[114]

Some residents, such as Ernesto Printzen, eagerly welcomed cars and the improved navigation. When a road-straightening project brought an

FIG. 5. City public works crews transforming a dirt road into a paved city street in southeastern Guadalajara. Note the horse and cart still using the path during construction and the small herd of cattle grazing in the background. Caja 1, Sobre 7, Fecha 1949, Folio 6, Titulo "Construcción de la calle Medrano." Courtesy of the Archivo Histórico Municipal de Guadalajara.

automobile route near his home on calle Veracruz, Printzen petitioned the city for aid. Blocked from the street by a neighbor's property line, the German Mexican requested the survey's exact details so he could use them to convince his neighbor to grant access to the road.[115] Others requested paving so that they could improve car access to their properties and neighborhoods, reduce dust, and decrease navigational issues like puddles.[116] For these residents, as well as thousands of others who built garages for their newly constructed homes, drove trucks and buses for work, or who simply toured the city, automotive vehicles provided profit, comfort, speed, ease of travel, and pleasure.

For many others whose letters and petitions appear in the archive, the violence and difficulty of travel caused by vehicles countered any sense of convenience. Transit authorities in 1940 began asking hospitals to contact them when pedestrians struck by cars showed up for treatment because police could not keep track of the growing number of wounded people.[117] The same officials charged with policing cars also referred to cars, buses, and trucks operated by drunk drivers as "instruments of death."[118] Pedestrians weren't the only recipients of vehicular violence: light poles, vendor stalls, construction equipment, and monuments from the colonial period and nineteenth century all faced destruction by cars, trucks, and buses.[119] Cars and fire trucks driven by city firefighters brought their own danger and mayhem to the streets, with the trucks sometimes crashing into vendor stalls or other cars on the road.[120] Still, some youth found a way to shift the violence from cars back toward the vehicles and their owners: youths and young children made a habit of vandalizing cars, then later offered to protect vehicles from future vandalism.[121]

The presence of cars in the city center forced change on residents and pushed them to think of Guadalajara in new ways. In 1941 city officials undertook a widespread effort to expand sidewalks so as to protect pedestrians from cars, and they also made a special plea to drivers of cars and motorcycles to stay off the sidewalks. Additionally, they had to remind residents that the streets no longer belonged to pedestrians and that they should remain on the sidewalks.[122] Even the need for car repair in the city center changed the feel of street navigation, bringing automotive fluids, broken-down cars, and groups of mechanics with their tools, all spilling out of their shops onto the sidewalks and streets, to the chagrin of some residents.[123]

Additionally, the city required property owners undertaking home repairs on corner lots with busy streets to create an "*ochavo*" or a "*chaflán*" (chamfer) corner on the building, flattening the corner and making the street safer for vehicles by improving visibility. For property owners like Dolores Vallarta Rivera, the arbitrary nature of asking some property owners but not others to undertake this kind of transformation seemed fundamentally unfair.[124] Some residents took this order in stride. At a chamfer already created at the corner of calles 13 and 26, one resident saw it as an opportunity to improve the neighborhood. Property owner Fidela Sánchez de Montaño requested that she be allowed to plant a garden (*jardincito*) in the chamfer as well as another garden in a depression in the street and sidewalk where a cable car used to stop and where pedestrians could no longer walk. The city replied, however, that buses required the extra space and that officials had ordered repair work on the corner to improve traffic flow, not to ease pedestrian navigation or add greenery.[125]

The traditional physical feel of Guadalajara for many *tapatíos* meant resisting the invasion of automobiles and the reworking of physical space they brought. For others, however, the vision of the modern city with the uninterrupted flow of cars accompanied by the rapid movement of disciplined pedestrians met their desires. For these city residents, the previously mentioned vendor stalls, not automobiles, served as sensory villains. In one case, María Aguinaga Vda. de González said that she would pay for the pavement along the entire section of road fronted by her property, saving the city their balance of the cost, on one condition: the authorities would order the removal of the stalls located along the street in front of her property, because the stalls impeded foot and auto traffic.[126] The city declined her offer because the stalls were legally constructed, up to date on their inspections and licenses, and properly maintained. City officials could not legally evict them.

Tightly regulated for size, distance between stalls, ornamentation, sound, and location, stalls and the vendors who worked in them formed an enduring presence in the city. Both detested and desired by city leaders and average residents alike, permanent wooden stalls and their presence in the urban spaces in all of Mexico reach well back into the colonial era and forward into the present. Motor vehicles could be particularly hard on stalls located on sidewalks or the street, with the drivers of buses, fire trucks, and personal vehicles all demanding that stalls be removed due to the number of crashes and lives lost.[127] Some stalls grew to such a size that they could occupy half the street or even block all traffic, as in the case with a 1947 drink stand and a neighboring stand selling sugarcane in calle Pedro Loza.[128] Others caused trouble for pedestrians by being too small: Everardo Arrellano complained that a stall built too low had a plank protruding into the sidewalk that caught him on the head, injuring him severely.[129]

The greatest enemy of these *puestos*, however, were not cars but business owners in fixed retail and market locations. *Puestos* appeared in arches (*portales*) and along sidewalks and streets, giving them optimal visual profiles but also allowing for immediate navigation by pedestrians without having to enter a shop door. *Puestos* affected most of the senses, as their vendors called to passersby, used brightly colored signs or banners, and emitted scents that enticed hungry pedestrians. For established businesses in buildings, the physical impeding of pedestrians before they had a chance to enter a storefront served as the great crime of sidewalk and street stalls. Capitalism requires unimpeded urban speed and movement toward consumption—a point of view held by the Porfirian-era Cámara de Comercio (Chamber of Commerce) and other independent and associated groups of businesses established inside buildings.[130] "They are eyesore vendors that obstruct pedestrian traffic and vehicle movement alike" is how one group of business owners described stall vendors. In interceding for business owner Elvira Quezada Vda. de González, they described the *puestos* in front of her store by saying, "Not only do they obstruct passage, but they completely cover her business to the grave detriment of her interests."[131] For these Porfirian-style business associations in a revolutionary era, the physical presence of wooden stands with usually lower-class vendors channeled movement away from profit and required state intervention.[132]

Once more, however, a counternarrative exists between the lines of these petitions. One set of residents linked to profit, speed, and navigation confronted the need for slower, less easily navigable spaces that favored stalls. When faced with eviction from street and sidewalk stands, vendors responded to the city by referencing the work they did to comply with city rules, and they often avoided complete eviction from the city by prevailing on authorities to move them to other areas.[133] Though this shuffling of vendors and stalls might result in complaints from business owners, city officials felt that having evicted the vendors once and seeing them installed and properly regulated, they could not be evicted a second time.[134] For some vendors, slowing down traffic and pedestrians to create customers represented one reason they fought to keep their stalls in place. Additionally, some impoverished vendors used their permanent wooden or metal stalls (covered at night) as residences, creating for them a different sense of tactile contact with the city: a place to rest their heads.[135] For those who came to the city seeking work and shelter, a *puesto* might represent both.

Cities are curious places where people both choose and are forced by a broad array of circumstances to live in relatively close quarters. As Guadalajara's population exploded, longtime residents and newcomers alike had to find ways to reconcile their own senses and sensory preferences with a new urban context that they either arrived in or that grew around them. No matter their gender, sex, age, class, race, ethnicity, physical abilities, or other factors, all of them had to confront this urban world with their bodies and engage in strategies to orient themselves to the world and people around them. As Finnish architect Juhani Pallasmaa has written,

> I confront the city with my body; my legs measure the length of the arcade and the width of the square; my gaze unconsciously projects my body onto the facade of the cathedral, where it roams over the mouldings and contours, sensing the size of recesses and projections; my body weight meets the mass of the cathedral door, and my hand grasps the door pull as I enter the dark void behind. I experience myself in the city, and the city exists through my embodied experience. The city and my body supplement and define each other. I dwell in the city and the city dwells in me.[136]

Tapatíos found a range of experiences stimulating their senses day by day and minute by minute. Whether people were sitting alone in their homes and hearing music from nearby record stores, experiencing the physical agony of a car crash, reading bright and freshly painted signs, or smelling raw sewage pooling around dog carcasses in an empty lot, residents' bodies engaged with the city. It is with their bodies that they interpreted their experiences. For many, the petition process allowed them to see themselves as working for and with officials to create a more ordered, hygienic, aesthetically liberal and modern city. Their sense of place included a city of respectable families engaged in responsible and disciplined actions, both sensorially and morally pleasing. By following these rules, they hoped to avoid what city officials referred to as "sliding fatally toward the abyss of social decomposition!"[137]

Others, however, responded to the growth in ways that made them the subjects of petitions. One response came through sociability.[138] Drinking, soccer, dancing, street food, musical performances, and browsing vendor stalls all represented gathering at sites of shared pleasure for residents. Others found in the city an anonymity that freed them to engage in formerly common but now rejected bodily acts. Public (and at times group) urination, defecation, garbage disposal, and carcass burning present us with not a city subject to the triumph of liberalism but instead an unruly and unruled population following in the sodden, fetid footsteps of millennia upon millennia of urban dwellers. In a similar and darker vein, still others used crowding or darkness to engage in acts of violence against others. Not every petitionable act fell so far from the profit or respectability motives of petition authors. Stall vendors and their *puestos*, singing groups, restaurant owners, mobile vendors, and shouting Pentecostals all saw their bodily interactions with the world as respectable, profitable, and honorable behaviors made possible by the city (and for some, by the 1910 revolution). In rural villages or small, regional market towns, behavior that departed from traditional norms might have resulted in shunning or even lynching.[139] For the people targeted by petitions or those who petitioned in ways counter to city officials' views, the sensory experiences they created or experienced represented a space and place that defined their own belonging to society, not their alienation. Taken together, all of these conflicts over the sensory interpretation represent not only conflict but also community creation through the shared contest over the meaning of city life.

2   Morality and Merriment

In September 1940 eight women renting rooms in an apartment building (a *casa de departamentos*, as they described it) at no. 34 calle Rayón complained that two renters in the building consistently disrupted the other occupants. Modesta Ríos, Concepción Ruíz, María Castro, Jovita Becerra, Concepción González, María de Jesús Ocampo, Eleuleria López Cuellar, and Felicitas Rivera joined together to issue a petition to the city to "evict from their habitations" Librado Oscar González and Esperanza Chávez. "The two aforementioned people live disordered lives in all senses of the word, obviously and scandalously in the company of friends that engage in literal orgies," the petitioners complained. They went on to say that this scandalous behavior spread beyond their rooms and happened "cheekily in the open: publicly in the patios of the apartment house and even in the very street." Beyond exhibitionism and rowdy friends, González and Chávez each allegedly had a spouse outside their relationship. Additionally, each rented different apartments, though they lived together in one and sublet the other to "women from the bad life [*vida mala*]" (a euphemism for prostitution). According to petitioners, this situation led to "the subsequent attack on decent families . . . and different apartments with many children and single women who are owed respect." Facing such immorality, the petitioners saw eviction as the only way to cleanse their homes, neighborhood, and the city.[1]

In this chapter, I explore the petitions of moralizers who portrayed themselves as part of respectable society (*la sociedad culta*) and their engagement in narratives of belonging through conflict.[2] Petitions like these made residents feel involved in the city's direction, empowered them to regulate neighbors, and conveyed their requests to city leaders. According to the definition of belonging presented in the introduction to this book, moralizers asserted their sense of belonging to themselves and city officials by demonstrating that they possessed discriminating tastes that complemented the systems established by the revolutionary state. Petitioners (male and female, rich and poor) discussed in this chapter used a range of moral issues as the basis for their petitions to get city government to regulate their neighbors. For the modern reader, these petitions reveal the city and urban experience envisioned by some midcentury Mexicans. The petitioners, whether or not their language reflected their beliefs, used petitions as narratives of belonging to reinforce their hopes for community.

However, the expectations of certain petitioners for behavior and urban life did not necessarily reflect the dominant views in 1940s Guadalajara. Petitions complaining about rowdy or untoward behavior are simply the views most directly preserved in the historical record. What about different hopes for the city hidden between the lines in those same petitions? A complaint has to have something or somebody to complain about. This chapter also expands on the idea, previously introduced in chapter 1, of reading against the grain of petitions by considering the desires of those being petitioned against. By thinking about the targets of petitions, we discover a world of entertainment, sociability, merriment, and place making that represents the many ways that *tapatíos* viewed urban life and relished opportunities for pleasure. For the aforementioned objects of opprobrium (i.e., Librado Oscar González and Esperanza Chávez in the opening vignette), sex, profit, and partying likely represented some of the opportunities in urban life they valued, and complaints about that lifestyle allow us to learn about that point of view as well. Locations in which to share the pursuit of pleasure served as "nucleuses that attract playfulness of concentrated fun and conviviality."[3] That cities should provide pleasure is also a goal of city leaders, and the actions of those being petitioned against helped them demonstrate that they had found a sense of belonging in the city in their own way.

As two sides of the same coin (or same city), each group represents the urban tension between the mixophobic and the mixophiliac struggling for use of city spaces and definition of place. The petitioners, in this case, were the mixophobics, who feared those who behaved in distinct ways that departed from the mixophobics' perception of an elusive societal and often religious morality. These residents followed a nineteenth-century pattern from France, the United States, and Mexico, aggressively upholding "thrift, sobriety, hygiene, and punctuality" to create a compliant working class supporting capitalist virtues promoted by the consolidated state.[4] For their part, the targets of petitions were the mixophiliacs, who relished the sociability cultivated in nightlife, passion, and the so-called vices that brought together a range of human experiences.[5] Thinking clinically, one could say that petitioners dealt with social pressures through religion, tradition, family, and uniformity, while those petitioned against used sociability and alternative paths of fulfillment to deal with issues of mental health, subversion, or resistance. Both types of resident reinforced senses of belonging in the city in their own ways: the first by engaging in petition and the second by boldly living their lives in ways that earned them the rebuke of petition writers.

Catholic, Liberal, Revolutionary:
General Context on Morality and Petitioners

Morality in mid-twentieth-century Guadalajara motivated petitioners— either in sincerely held belief or as a rhetorical instrument for material gain—as they jostled with their neighbors to define space and make place. Appeals to morality in Mexico (and the Iberian world generally) as a rhetorical tactic of ethos appear in everything from theological debates to letters and plays stretching back centuries.[6] In considering the morality reflected in petitions, note that almost none of the authors and signers quoted religious texts or philosophical guides as a recourse to authority—though they do reference legal codes and constitutional articles. As Ramón Gutiérrez has written of gender in nineteenth- and twentieth-century Mexico, moral codes remain "paradoxical and often contradictory, defying easy binaries, as women and men pragmatically negotiated conflicting desires, duties, and notions of decency, respect, and social standing."[7] This section explores the idea and language of morality that petitioners used to establish their sense of complementary belonging and against which other citizens marked their own lives.

Considering the possible interpretations, how can we tell what petitioners meant when they called for moral or respectful behavior, and from where did that sense of morality arise? Clues such as addresses, paper quality, or names possibly linked with famous families provide some hint as to race and class, but rarely does a petition definitively provide such information. The eight women mentioned at the beginning of this chapter resided in a working-class area and in what they described as a *casa de departamentos*, making them more likely to be mestizo or Indigenous in heritage.[8] Also, according to census data, the women are statistically likely to have been married, born in Mexico, possess some ability to read and write despite having had little formal education, speak only Spanish, and adhere (at some level) to Catholicism.[9] The same can be said, however, for neighbor Esperanza Chávez, against whom they petitioned. These similarities illustrate the difficulty in making any blanket statement regarding morality and class in Guadalajara at the time. No single definition of morality works for all members of certain classes, races, genders, or sexualities according to the petitions filed (and that is not the goal of this work). The most that we can hope for is to see broad patterns generally reflected in the petitions. Petitioners tended to focus on several key areas: the containing of sex to married heterosexual couples; shielding children from adults engaged in sex; protecting children from sexual or physical violence; maintaining appropriate bodily control; safeguarding the community from illness; maintaining community harmony; and safeguarding community material prosperity. All of these are points of view they saw as complementary to *tapatío* society.

Anthropologist Renée de la Torre has described Guadalajara as a city where a division existed between "those who seek to claim place through a fight to keep alive the traditional values of the city under the mottos of 'our morality' and of 'good traditions'; and on the other hand, those who seek to build new spaces of expression."[10] The line between the *gente decente*, or respectable people in the ranks of the middle class, and the working-class masses hinged on morality and manners in late nineteenth-century Mexico. Many in the working class agreed with upper-class reformers on matters of morality, and they also used the language of respectability to differentiate themselves from others in their social class. For example, artisans and public employees wanted to reform laborers (such as mineworkers) and the places they lived, worked, and recreated.[11] In midcentury Guadalajara, the working-class people in these petitions using the *gente decente*'s language may well have become true believers in the cult of morality, particularly if they had passed through the revolutionary Mexican education system by the 1940s.[12] In Mexico, neighbors of varying classes demonstrated their alliances with city officials by trying to eliminate what they saw as threats to public health in the form of their neighbors' behavior.[13] On the other hand, some working-class people mastered only the bureaucratic language they needed to persuade or manipulate (particularly in forged petitions) city officials to work against their neighbors.

Petitioners expressing these general concepts participated in a long history of using morality as a tool to motivate their leaders or to declare against their neighbors. In New Spain, Imperial subjects of all social classes used petitions to motivate royal officials to create or modify policy. These policy changes at times protected various racial groups or provided goods and services to previously unserved or underserved groups.[14] Some secular officials called for laws to defend women by playing on stereotypes of women as weak and defenseless. In issues of Catholic morality related to gender, the characteristic modest, humble, pure, devout, chaste, sweet, and timid women continued to hold social value in the colonial period and the revolutionary era alike.[15] Men, on the other hand, had moral value through their power, reason, respect, and a sense of shame.[16] Men and women both had bounds of proper behavior, but in the realm of sexuality, social expectations particularly regulated women. Still, despite generalized expectations, both men and women engaged in rhetorical gymnastics to exploit the inconsistent applications and interpretations of morality by clerical or royal officials.[17]

Even when Mexico shifted toward political and economic liberalism in the nineteenth century, it maintained broadly the same sense of community, family, bodily temperance, gender boundaries, and economic morality even while adding new layers. When it came to women, "liberals as much as conservatives considered the home the appropriate space for women and that women [should] aspire to marriage," particularly as anticlericalism had closed paths for wealthy women to enter nunneries.[18] Liberals in Mexico had hoped from their earliest appearance in society that "good citizens could be formed by conquering the human body's susceptibility to passion, vice, and immorality through reason, liberal education, and obedience to the laws."[19] Liberals of Mexico's War of the Reform (1858–60) and resistance to the French-imposed emperor (1862–67) established the liberal Constitution of 1857 as Mexico's legal foundation and carried with them deep sentiments of western European morality. For example, Ignacio Altamirano, an Indigenous jurist and author who espoused liberal positions, saw Christianity and democracy as complementary elements that could guide Mexico after years of upheaval and violence.[20] To offer another example, the radical anticlerical politician Melchor Ocampo penned a letter setting out the moral bounds of marriage. In it, he refers to marriage as the only moral family foundation and as the pathway toward "the perfection of the human race." He goes on to reinforce ideas that men should be valorous, powerful protectors of women and that in turn women should engage in self-denial and compassion and be beautiful and obedient. He finished by elevating academic study and kindness in making children good citizens.[21]

In 1876 radical liberalism gave way to a loosely symbiotic relationship between the Catholic Church and the liberal state. Political leaders in Porfirian-era Mexico (1876–1911) explicitly linked morality and state building to the chastity and purity of women, who created a stable, prosperous domestic family that then would be reflected in the national family.[22] This brand of "developmental liberalism" laid aside the desires of individuals, and "the state became a social engineer," pushing Mexicans to be "patriotic[,] . . . productive, hardworking, sober, and conscientious."[23] Additionally, traditional ideas of sin, family, and proper corporate behavior came cloaked in a new guise of "notions of citizenship and social responsibility."[24] The liberals' focus on morality and behavior also intersected with the obsession over economic output, which required productive citizens and workers. For example, while many still saw women as "*hadas del hogar*," or house fairies, who created the moral center of Mexico as mothers, businesses increasingly demanded them for industrial production.[25] Such clashes brought women into multilayered morality. Women workers faced accusations of suspect sexual activity and diminished respectability by being outside of their homes near unrelated men and away from the supervision of husbands and children. Simultaneously, the state saw women as valiant workers toiling for the prosperity of Mexico.[26]

Similarly, when it came to bodily temperance and national productivity, government officials worried that public drinking establishments for the working class promoted "undesirable urban subcultures" and rendered their productive working capacity moot.[27] The Porfirian circle of intellectual advisors known as *científicos* also thought that economic growth should have a goal of improving the "moral and social state" of Mexicans.[28] In Guadalajara these state efforts between 1902 and 1910 combined with those of Archbishop José de Jesús Ortiz and Catholic labor organizations that sought to eliminate vice to improve family and work life.[29] For clerics and politicians, morality and productivity intersected in an urgent mission to shape Mexicans.

The 1910 Mexican Revolution encompassed a myriad of movements against Porfirio Díaz and challenged many nineteenth-century economic norms. It did not, however, mark a sweeping departure from the general sense of morality regarding families, children, women, community, and productivity. Revolution did not usher in a radical, free love, anarchist, bohemian, atheist society nor even produce these kinds of leaders beyond limited examples. Mexico remained a fundamentally Catholic nation whose laity used their political power and ingenuity to hamper the secular plans of government at all levels, or who at least "deepened its presence in civil society" enough to push the state into constant negotiation.[30] For example, religious women in Guadalajara seamlessly merged their Catholic virtues of prudence, justice, fortitude, and temperance with revolutionary state public education by couching Catholic belief in secular revolutionary terms.[31] Protestants and other non-Catholic church-goers in Mexico who saw themselves aligned with the revolutionary government put confidence in government institutions as instruments to promote their own religious views of morality and decent behavior.[32] Indeed, when it came to the topics of family, temperance, sex, children, and community, much of nineteenth-century morality continued to be a focus of Mexico's revolutionary leadership after 1920. Revolutionary leaders saw morality linked to nation building, modernity, and progress.[33] Even some feminists arguing for a revolutionary "new" Mexican woman found congruence with previous generations and imagined revolutionary women as moderate, tidy, and moral.[34] Government at the national and local levels policed actions they saw as counter to revolutionary progress. Drunken behavior, promiscuity, and wages wasted on entertainment merged the worlds of public health and morality to "challenge 'unhealthy' private behaviors" and create an efficient, profitable, successful Mexico.[35]

Morality as portrayed by church, government, and the press centered on traditional families, obedient children, virtuous women, honorable men, unified community, and productivity that together served as both a form of social ordering and an effective state tool. This approach drew heavily on conservative Catholic norms, but it also transferred (or at least added) individual dedication to the nation. Catholics and the various levels of government might battle for the dedication of Mexicans (discussed in more detail in chapter 3), but little space existed between them on morality. Historian Gemma Kloppe-Santamaría refers to the "ideological proximity between the Catholic Church and post-revolutionary politicians, grounded in nationalism, morality, and the importance of the family."[36] Philosophical, political, and violent expressions from a broad variety of Mexican Catholicisms manifest themselves in opposition to secularizing society. However, more often than not, pragmatic decisions on the part of secular political leaders and the Catholic hierarchy created a blended peace that served a goal of both factions: maintaining social order among the masses.

Varios Vecinos: The Desires of Petitioners

While variations exist in approaches to writing petitions, the phrase *varios vecinos*, or "various neighbors," is a ubiquitous heading found in petitions directed to city leaders. Using the term *vecino* in documents helped some residents position themselves in relation to city leaders and established themselves as having rights and responsibilities in civic life.[37] In a city drawing people together from all over Mexico, the concept of *vecino* bound people in a sense of belonging not only to the city but also to the immediate section of neighborhood, as well as the neighbors who joined in signing petitions. The same can be said for the term *comerciantes*, or commercial operators (owners, managers, or employees of those operations), who addressed their letters to community leaders in the same way. *Comerciantes*, much like *vecinos*, established their community-organizing principle around the shared space of commerce, both in physical proximity and in pursuit of a livelihood. In drafting petitions with those identifying labels, residents

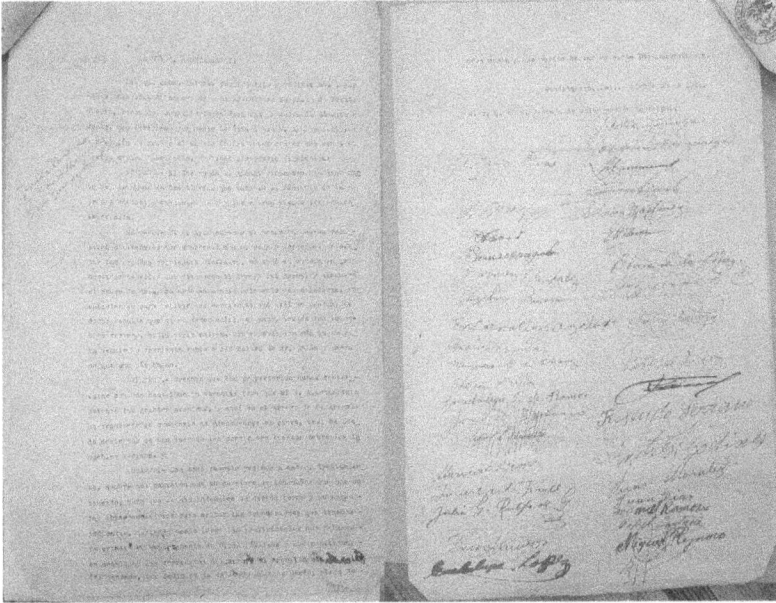

FIG. 6. An example of a typed and signed petition sent by a group of neighbors to city officials as a means of demanding goods and services. Correspondencia, 1946, 1-4-34, AHMG. Courtesy of the Archivo Histórico Municipal de Guadalajara.

could use the effort as a "coping strategy" to help provide a sense of belonging in a changing and growing city.[38]

The sense of belonging came in both the physical act of petitioning and also its imagined reception, as *vecinos* and *comerciantes* anticipated how city officials might interpret their documents. Petitioners in some cases crafted documents with morality rhetoric containing phrases associated with government morality and improvement campaigns (at the city, state, or national level). They sometimes associated their complaint with a city initiative, linked their concerns to a constitutional article, or referenced city, state, or national proclamations and laws. More often than not, the petitions discussed issues of sex, dignity, and correct behavior, as well as moral values presumed to be common to both petitioners and officials. For example, rarely did petitioners pause to explain their moral code's roots or from where their expectations sprang. Morality is simply understood, with no consideration that officials might carry different views. Morality may even function as a mask to obscure alternate motives, with petitioners using words or phrases they hoped would persuade bureaucrats to work on their behalf.

Take the case of Inés R. de Prado, a crockery vendor in a local Guadalajara market. In May 1943 a long-running dispute between her and the nearby Altamirano fruit vendor family resulted in the crockery vendor's arrest. Police took Prado into custody for harassment and spreading disunity in the market and for attacking the Altamirano family with what the police report referred to as gossip and rude comments. Police released her the following day to her husband on condition that she not return to the market. In the face of this injustice, her friends and associates in the market rallied to her cause, and as a group of *comerciantes en pequeño* (small market vendors) they launched a petition to allow Inés R. de Prado to return to the market. In addition to describing the virtues of Prado as "cordial, friendly, appropriate and respectful," they also attacked the expulsion's merit by painting the Altamiranos as bullies: a disfiguring skin condition made Prado the Altamirano family's target for harassment. Petitioners demanded that Prado be allowed back in the market as an "honorable and hard worker who earns her daily bread through work."[39]

The petition also creates the picture of a contrast and lays out how the humble Prado's opponents in the matter are a family backed by a federal legislator (*diputado*), Juan I. Godínez (1940–43). Godínez, they go on to say, used his authority to persuade the police to detain Prado, intimidate her, and threaten her with future arrest. The petitioners hoped that the municipal president could "neutralize" the abusive power that Godínez allegedly marshaled against the humble Prado. To further assault the Altamirano family character, they said that Virginia Altamirano could not be trusted because she had once been arrested (it is not specific on what charge). The petitioners also alleged that she frequented various *casas de asignación*, or houses of prostitution, in the city as a client. The petitioners claimed they could back up those allegations with affidavits from owners of several establishments. "With these antecedents in mind," the petitioners wrote, "it would be painful that a woman of this ilk [Virginia Altamirano] should enjoy prerogatives and preeminence over honorable and hard-working people [Prado]."[40]

At first glance, this petition might seem an argument about community activism performed by vendors and the rhetorical strategies that they used to get the government to respond. Ultimately, however, the petition failed, as Inés R. de Prado remained excluded from the market while the passage of time allowed tensions with the Altamirano family to ease. On stationery carrying the ruling party's letterhead, later letters from labor unions that lobbied for Prado did not overturn the official police decision to bar her from the market (and the original petitioners did not mention union affiliation). We even lack confirmation of Virginia Altamirano's alleged lesbian sexual orientation or even if those who signed the petition actually signed it. At times inspectors reported that petitioners forged signatures or that those being petitioned against did not even live in the place indicated in the correspondence.[41]

In all respects, the petition appears a failure from the perspective of state and resident relations and the view of petitioners as community activists. On the other hand, we do learn about how various *tapatíos* felt life in the city should be lived, and while the petitioners' intent and their considerations of morality are well covered already, we should consider the Altamirano sisters and their position. As fruit vendors in the market, the Altamirano sisters had a stall somewhat close to that of Inés R. de Prado or at least close enough that Prado and Sofía Altamirano came in contact with one another. Altamirano charged that Prado treated her with disrespect (*por haber faltado de palabra*), an act that witnesses claimed came after a long string of slights and comments by Inés R. de Prado, who put on airs because of her membership in a union. In addition, the Altamiranos alleged that Prado also engaged in a "wave of quarrels and difficulties as well as gossip that provoked dissonance among many members of the market." For Sofía Altamirano and others, the lack of humility on the part of Prado inspired ire, and her possible gossip and backbiting created division within the community. Union activity could certainly have fallen outside the scope of good community for some such as the Altamiranos.[42]

Considering the allegations, neighborhood gossip about the sexual orientation of Virginia Altamirano could have sparked the conflict, with the Altamiranos' associates seeing such comments as more damaging to community than the possible use of sex workers by Virginia. Working-class communities might demonstrate greater understanding of lesbian sexuality than middle-class and reformer groups.[43] This relationship of support appears to be particularly true of Sofía, who initiated the fight with Inés R. de Prado, and of Virginia, who supported her sister's account of events. But perhaps visible between the lines lies a different vision of city life if we read against the grain of the petition that condemned Virginia Altamirano. For a woman who sought out sex with a variety of other women, Guadalajara presented a perfect opportunity, as it was an urban environment filled with sex workers. While there is little discussion in historical literature of female sex workers taking women as clients, it is well within the realm of possibility. Fernanda Núñez Becerra, Katherine Elaine Bliss, and Robert M. Buffington have all demonstrated that lesbian relationships developed between women in houses of prostitution or sex workers serving time in jail.[44] If indeed Virginia Altamirano solicited sex, it is possible that she found willing sex workers. While our petitioners argued for their own version of *tapatío* honor and decorum, their petition reveals another world of honor, community, commerce, and sexual pleasure extant in the city. In sum, we have two groups of residents expressing their belonging with two different concepts of community. I argue that this essential conflict doesn't signify two cities for this period (à la Daniel Vázquez) but rather a single community with varied experiences and one where both groups felt open enough to engage in conflict over the meaning of urban society. Petitions represent people of all classes actively engaged in living a variety of urban experiences in the same space. And though politicians relegated sex work to certain neighborhoods, residents of all classes had awareness of its widespread practice beyond approved zones in Guadalajara.

As one might expect, sex work (legal and regulated in Mexico at the time) drew particular ire from *vecinos* and *comerciantes*. Complaints often focused not only on the work itself but the entire complex of adult nightlife at the intersection of gambling, alcohol, food, dancing, music, and sex. Material complaints spanned a range of issues; music, dancing, laughter, honking horns, crowding, government corruption, and blocked sidewalks all perturbed petitioners. These concerns emanated from a range of bars, saloons, restaurants, cabarets, and houses of prostitution, the last often referred to as *casas de cita, casas de mala nota*, or *casas de asignación*. While in chapter 1 I discuss the sensory concerns related to these complaints, it is the petitioners' reference to the morality of sex work and nightlife and the ripples such activity sent through society that are the focus here.

Varios vecinos of calle 45 in Sector Juárez indicated their displeasure with a house of prostitution located at no. 384 and with its owner, María de Jesús Castillo, whom they said "observes very poor conduct." They described the business as a place that employed sex workers but that also admitted couples who turned it into a "den of vice that is an affront to morality." The petition did not indicate if the couples visited for clandestine heterosexual couplings or for frequenting sex workers in a search for polyamorous pleasures. The petitioners continue by saying that a working-class *vecindad* (tenement) filled mostly with families and children stood across the street from the sex workers. They complained that the "immoral behavior" of sex work found its way into the lives of the tenement dwellers and that neighbors discovered a child with a used condom in his mouth, "playing with it like a toy." Finally, the petitioners objected to the sex workers standing in the street, working to draw in clients from among passersby, pulling at men and "using a filthy and profane vocabulary without taking into account that they and their clients are in proximity to people that deserve respect." They requested that city officials "in the name of the aforementioned morality" close the brothel and force the owner into another neighborhood. They finish by indicating that they were sure of the municipal president's help in guaranteeing that "our children are not corrupted at such young ages."[45] This faith in the municipal president seems somewhat naïve when "prostitution abounded in all areas of the city, and regulations to limit where and how they were established were worthless."[46]

An example of so many other similar letters, this one indicates both the pressures of urban growth and the efforts of people living in these spaces to create safe, family-friendly environments for children, even in situations of poverty. While residents knew they had to live in the physical circumstances of working-class penury, they did not believe they had to be subject to moral impoverishment. *Vecindades* became fixtures in Guadalajara during the late nineteenth century, for the first time gathering many more families into small rooms with shared cooking facilities, a single water source, and communal toilets (trenches, pits, outhouses, and then flush toilets). Such cramped locations created a sense of community but also presented challenges for residents in terms of crime levels and public health. The tenements' location in marginal areas also placed occupants in proximity to places like the house of prostitution run by a one Mrs. Raquel. Her home at no. 124 calle Munguía drew condemnation from area residents for serving as a house of prostitution only steps away from "one of the best schools in our city" (as asserted by the petitioners). In this situation, students on their way to classes experienced "extremely sultry demonstrations," with the noise and scandal worsening once alcohol entered the picture. Like the previous letter from calle 45, this petition closed by expressing confidence that the municipal president was entirely in agreement that "the improvement of our people and their culture" required the closure of those houses that cause "constant anxiety for innumerable families living around the aforementioned domicile." The petition closes with a tag line in all caps: "MORALIDAD JUSTICIA Y PROTECCIÓN" (morality, justice, and protection).[47] The final part reads something like a play on the revolutionary phrase *tierra, justicia y libertad* (land, justice, and liberty) most frequently referenced in the revolution of Emiliano Zapata in Morelos. However, much like Mexico's rulers, this letter writer adapted the 1910 revolution slogan for personal purposes.

The two aforementioned examples of petitions complaining about houses of prostitution assume the city's leaders agreed with the petitioners' morality. Such petitions could engage a range of strategies to motivate the city leadership, but these focus on two in particular. First, the latter petition's closing phrase assumes moral rectitude from political leaders and a shared family-centered morality. Politicians on the political spectrum from left to right championed the family, children, and female chastity as the foundation and future of Mexican success.[48] Sex workers themselves recognized this rhetoric and marshaled such language to protect their own honor as mothers of children.[49] Alternatively (or even concurrently), the petition's closing language engaged a rhetorical strategy meant to combine both ethos and pathos and essentially guilt leaders into taking action for the petitioners. From the first example, calle 45, the city inspectors ordered the licensed brothel closed for operating outside the boundaries of decency by spilling out into the street. For the second example, on calle Munguía, the outcome took a different turn: upon investigation, the inspector reported that the house appeared to not be a brothel and that none of the signatures on the petition could be verified beyond the first.[50]

Let us consider for a moment the possibly forged petition about the alleged sex work on calle Munguía. It is possible that J. J. Figueroa, having inscribed the only verifiable signature on the petition, according to the inspector, used a charge of prostitution to attack a neighbor for an undisclosed reason. Residents in the city used legal codes to sabotage their neighbors based on fabricated charges (an issue explored further in chapter 3). According to the inspector, in canvassing the neighborhood he found no neighbor willing to corroborate Figueroa's complaint. He also noted that the homeowner, a Mrs. Raquel (the inspector provided no full name), said that she had many friends "but not like those that are being denounced" and that an inspection showed no signs of prostitution.[51] However, another imagining of the past could take this story in still another direction.

The corruption in Mexico during the 1940s is legendary, not only in terms of real criminal behavior at multiple government levels but also in the imagination of Mexicans and foreigners alike. The system of local laws, licenses, fines, and city inspectors working for paltry wages created an environment ripe for corruption. When it came to the vice trades, however, corruption and profit reached their natural intersection. As historian Paul Gillingham has described it, "state representatives of all levels engaged in the less formal taxation of demanding money to allow businesses across the spectrum of legitimacy to function," working in combination with civic morality and rendering "gambling, prostitution, gun ownership, and even new bars firmly outside the law."[52] In essence, while we see in this petition a resident potentially looking to shape a neighborhood to match their view of community life, it is also possible that what we see is an unregistered site of sex work operating through the corrupt cooperation of civil authorities. Cities provided opportunities for predators with badges or carrying the title of inspector to prey on residents in ways not open to street criminals. For sex workers, the corruption heaped on them by police posed an ever-increasing threat to both their livelihoods and their lives.[53]

Other cases of attempting to regulate neighbors' lives for financial reasons hidden behind a façade of morality are somewhat clearer. In February 1940, neighbors in the area of calle 23 in Sector Reforma petitioned the city to have Marcelina Anguiano removed from their neighborhood of "recently constructed homes." Anguiano lived in a home built earlier than the newer homes in the neighborhood, and her neighbors charged her with keeping in her house a young girl who provided sex for visitors. Apparently using a *cochera* (garage) on the house in a *forma inconveniente* (a euphemism for sex or other immoral behavior), the neighbors worried their own daughters would be exposed to "immoral scenes." Upon conducting an inspection, the city issued a much different report: Anguiano rented the house from Salvador Navarro, currently in prison for beating Anguiano, his tenant. Apparently, Navarro worked to eject Anguiano from the household but couldn't because she kept current on her rent and caused no disturbances. And the visitors to the house? The woman made and sold sweets at a small table just inside the house door. As the inspector reported after speaking with a range of residents, friends of property owner Navarro created the complaint as an excuse to force Anguiano from her home.

During this age of revolution and the long history of liberal individualism in Mexico, neighbors engaged in decidedly conservative and traditional practices of attempting to regulate their neighbors' morality. The slew of revolution-era regulations and inspectors made it possible for residents to use state tools of inspection and eviction to dislodge neighbors they disliked for the greater revolutionary good. Average Mexicans thus attempted to regulate and discipline their neighbors or at least use the tools and rhetoric of the revolution to have the government do their bidding.

In 1942 multiple letters arrived from "Varios Vecinos y Padres de Familia" (various neighbors and parents of children) concerned with "sorcerers and spiritists" living and working in the city. While the letters stated that their concerns centered on the mocking of God, the signers urged the city to investigate one José Lara for reasons linked to the cabildo's public goals. First, they argued that the *brujo* (sorcerer) took advantage of people who did not know any better. The petition appeared during a city-wide antifraud campaign against palm readers and spiritists. They also charged that visitors to the *brujo* exposed the neighborhood's good religious girls to abundant immorality. The *brujo* and his guests not only engaged in a crime against morality but also acted against the beautiful city that they all loved. In 1942 the city ran several beautification campaigns in the face of overwhelming urban decay. What crime did the alleged sorcerer engage in that threatened city beauty? He kept, petitioners contended, fetid, blackened human corpses in his house for use in his ceremonies.[54] While various families in this case certainly drew on issues of religious (most likely Catholic) morality, they took pains to paint the offenses as an attack on the city. Others, however, considered Catholics the public nuisance.

In a 1944 case, J. Antonio Sierra on calle Constitución near the Parroquia de San José de Analco in the working-class Analco neighborhood complained that city leaders allowed "priests to annoy all the residents of the city with their fireworks," which disrupted sleep and quiet. The police refused to intervene and told him that he should take his complaints that religions "disrupted the order of society" to the municipal president.[55] The following year a similar complaint arrived from Antonio Gallardo, also from calle Constitución, who said that the celebratory fireworks set off by the Catholic church in his neighborhood disturbed his sleep. He argued that only uncivilized people used fireworks, as fireworks had been abolished "in the rest of the civilized world." For Gallardo, "order, respect, and tranquil rest" should be guaranteed under the law.[56] A similar complaint from one Fernando Valtierra urged the city and the president of Mexico to ban fireworks to "civilize the Republic."[57] Gallardo, Valtierra, and Sierra (and the authors of many other similar letters) envisioned a liberal, quiet, religion-free city that protected all individuals, allowing them to reach their maximum potential through a good night of uninterrupted sleep.

Groups of residents attempted to dislodge other neighbors by using tactics at times subtle, at times brutally direct, and on occasion duplicitous, hoping to engage city authorities on their side in disputes. The petitioners replicated what they saw politicians doing on the national stage against the voices of dissent or even just Mexicans in the wrong place at the wrong time. Nineteenth-century liberal and conservative politicians alike dispossessed their political enemies, while liberals stripped corporate landholders of their titles and redistributed land.[58] The Porfirian regime allowed large landowners to dispossess Mexican smallholders in its bid to modernize the nation and promote economic growth.[59] Additionally, the Mexican Revolution of 1910 enshrined in the Constitution of 1917 the governmental right to expropriate private property, though presidents applied the article inconsistently.[60] The practice of evicting Mexicans from private or collective property had become deeply entrenched in Mexico by 1941, when the neighbors of Constanza Ruvalcaba demanded the city force her to move because of her rough language and rude treatment toward others.[61] Average Mexicans had seen churches, vendors, criminals, or even just property owners displaced to make way for revolutionary infrastructure or commercial projects, so, by their reasoning, why not also displace an annoying neighbor?[62] However, as the Jalisco attorney general's office responded in the Ruvalcaba case without the slightest hint of irony, "under our current constitutional regime, no authority has the power to oblige a person to leave their residence."[63]

Todo tipo de inmoralidad: The Subjects of Petitions

Daily urban life encompasses a wide spectrum of experiences, none of them simple or typical. As sociologist Luis Rodolfo Morán Quiroz has written, members of society are forced to reflect on what life in the city means for them from moment to moment and context to context.[64] Violence, power, kin, class, work, transportation, physical ability, mental health, gender, sexuality, and an infinite number of physical and mental states of being in combination with an equally infinite number of consequences shape the perception of urban environments. Despite the prevalence of literature dealing with the struggles of urban inhabitants, it is entirely possible for people in a city to enjoy living there. Not only could residents find enjoyment in the urban experience, but they could do so in ways that fell outside of liberal, revolutionary, or religiously moralizing boundaries established by city governments.

As tens of thousands of rural Mexicans departed the countryside and moved to Guadalajara, one factor in their migration frequently cited is the material, pragmatic position of Guadalajara as a regional market power. Guadalajara offered opportunity for a war-torn and economically challenged countryside. However, it is also true that many simply came to Guadalajara looking for more interesting lives, seeking to leave behind the community, familial, and structural limitations of rural life. One frequent style of letter found in the correspondence archive came from parents (usually mothers) seeking their children (usually daughters) who had run away from home to

Guadalajara. For example, Salomé Cisneros de Santos wrote to authorities from Autlán, Jalisco, saying that she had permission from her husband to write and inquire after her fifteen-year-old daughter who ran away to Guadalajara, took up work as a servant, and then disappeared.[65] From farther away, in Veracruz, María Carmen Gutiérrez begged help from officials when her daughter used the pretext of visiting her brothers in Guadalajara to find a more exciting life in Mexico's second-largest city.[66] Men in the vice trade lured others away, like Elena Arredondo's daughter, Margarita, last seen in the company of a man alleged by the community to be a pimp.[67]

For others, however, city life offered the hope of excitement and an escape from the ever-present bogeyman of rural life: boredom. According to mental health researchers, "Some of the alleged risk factors of rurality may be linked to the remoteness, isolation, and seclusion that generally are embedded in rural living and attract rural youth to large cities." Rural life may have provided "stability and control" for some, but for others the simple lack of variety, opportunity, self-expression, or recreation might drive them to cities.[68] Upon arrival in the city, however, the necessity of work and the reality of limited opportunities might push some migrants into difficult, dangerous, and dull work.[69] Recreation, nightlife, street life, and mixing with others from around Mexico and the world provided an escape from that boredom. For transient male workers, such as railroad laborers, salespeople, drivers, or even federal government officials, the drudgery of work and travel from city to city could be broken up by nightlife. And even for the established middle class and the wealthy, parties, dances, and other licit and illicit recreation made city life worth the other challenges it provided. Though liberal Mexican authors like José Tomás de Cuéllar might lampoon riotous parties with drinking and dancing as uncivilized debauchery, they were unwilling to consider that Mexicans enjoyed themselves under these circumstances.[70] Legal or not, noisy, sexual, alcohol-fueled, musically driven entertainment became the subjects of complaint petitions to the city. Consequently, if we read against the grain, we find a different enjoyment of city life than the one experienced by the petitioners.

Consider a case from the northern edge of Guadalajara. Late June in Jalisco brings long, warm days cooled by bursts of rain in the afternoon. This pleasant climate earned the city yet another nickname: the City of

Eternal Spring. It is understandable, then, that some *tapatíos* took advantage of the fine weather to exercise in an outdoor swimming pool located in an open patio area managed by a local hospital.[71] Though the June weather might have been inviting, bathers had already been using the patio for exercise, even during the previously sweltering months of April and May. In particular, they enjoyed the pleasure of entering the pool from a spring diving board.

It is possible that doctors prescribed the swimming and exercise regimen, as the Hospital Alcalde managed the pool. A Catholic priest, Father Luis Sánchez Araiza, had founded the hospital in 1931 under the name Hospital Guadalupano.[72] Hospital Alcalde proclaimed a mission to serve the poor of Guadalajara, and Sánchez Araiza (who served parishioners in the city for over fifty years) affiliated with the charitable organization of St. Vincent DePaul.[73] Did those using the facility to exercise come from the working class or urban poor of northern Guadalajara? Perhaps, but the scene offers a possible picture of a modern, Catholic-associated, healthy activity enjoyed on an idyllic summer day by working-class *tapatíos*—in the nude.[74]

According to pool neighbors, for weeks they had witnessed the surprising spectacle of bathers "given the use of a diving board and lifted to a certain altitude without the use of bathing suits." These petitioners found the entire spectacle immoral and called on the hospital administration to donate bathing suits to the pool patrons. We know little else from the petition beyond the swimmers' nudity, that neighbors and passersby could see the nude bodies launched into the air, and that the bathers seemed to have enjoyed nude swimming for quite some time while the hospital continued to resist complaints from the neighborhood. We can also imagine the past based on evidence from the work of historians on bathing and swimming in Mexico. Although the complaints do not explicitly state the sex of the bathers, most likely all of them were male, especially considering the history of pools and bathhouses in Mexico, which mostly catered to men.[75] Given the many months it took to shut down the nude diving, we can also imagine that the patrons either liked to dive in the nude or doctors from Hospital Alcalde prescribed it. For these swimmers, the urban setting meant medical care, healthful exercise, body expression, possible sexual activity, and recreational play. The city, it seems, felt less positive about the skinny-dipping, and officials requested the hospital provide bathing suits or face closure of the pool.

The city as playground offered clothed options as well. Young men leaving school for the day and others finishing work found opportunities for inexpensive sociability and recreation in the city center. The cool evenings in the narrow, cobbled intersection of calles Madero and Molina in front of an apartment building served as a gathering place for youths (the letter of complaint about this location refers only to "boys"), estimated to be between the ages of fifteen and twenty-five, to gather, gossip, joke, and network. Above all, however, they gathered to play street soccer. Shouting and playing well into the night, they ranged up and down the neighborhood in raucous competition.[76]

Twelve blocks to the west and closer to the central downtown area, Parque Revolución occupied a vast square in the city and served as an informal *fútbol* pitch for local children. Formerly an orchard for Carmelite nuns and then the site of the Escobedo prison until its demolition in 1933, Parque Revolución, as one chronicler noted, offered "capricious paths, islands of well-tended grass, plants and flowers of attractive variety and color, hidden corners of romance, and enviable tranquility."[77] For children and young adults growing up in a sea of brick, concrete, cobbles, gravel, and (increasingly) asphalt, the green and shaded spaces of Parque Revolución represented an ideal recreation zone. Again, late afternoons meant a chance to slip away from duties and families and find conviviality among peers, either in groups or as teams or, as indicated in the quote above, in more quiet pairings in the "hidden corners of romance."[78] For some of the children who had no family or for whom the street served as both home and workplace, the opportunity to gather in childhood games and recreation, face to face with other children and youth, likely marked a bright point in the day.[79]

Not surprisingly, we know of these particular youth gatherings and soccer games not from fond memories of youths left in diaries and oral histories but because of complaints from grumbling adults in the areas where youths gathered. For the calles Madero and Molina pick-up game, the petitioners made aggressive requests. "We demand a remedy for the plague that constantly threatens our decency and tranquility," they raged. Concerned with noise, property damage, and robbery, petitioners asked in what seem to be blatantly classist tones, "Is there no way to protect once and for all the security and rest of our homes which lie so close to the governor's palace and to terrify these lowlifes that really ought to be hauled off to an army recruiter's office?"[80] In the swankier Americana neighborhood, "numerous boys" (*un grupo numeroso de chamacos*) broke the streetlight covers with their soccer play, prompting residents there to similarly demand the removal of kids playing soccer.[81]

The city gave more than children and young men the opportunity to socialize and recreate. For adults, city life offered an opportunity for socializing in ways that may have replaced family or community lost after migrating to Guadalajara. For others, the relative anonymity of cities provided an escape from the restrictions of nearby families. Take, for example, the people who gathered in the garden on the north side of the San Agustín church and the adjacent convent. While the church remained in use, the liberal government confiscated the convent in 1860, and it later served as an artisan training school for wayward youth.[82] Additionally, the space is an example of one of a very few patio gardens not removed from the front of churches to allow for widening streets in central Guadalajara. The garden contained a small plaza with a fountain, bushes, and trees that marked a tranquil and green area between the church and the imposing Teatro Degollado on the north. Here, in a quiet island of peacefulness amid the bustle of the city, a small crowd gathered to play dice and cards. Squatting on the ground, they gambled and chided one another while lookouts watched for approaching police.[83] If law enforcement officers found gambling going on, they might break up the games. They might also shake down the gamblers for their winnings or demand protection payments.[84] Some officials might even have seen it as competition for their own illegal gambling operations, such as that of Luis Ramírez, who allegedly paid a cousin of General Marcelino García Barragán 5 pesos a day to protect his gaming house from law enforcement.[85] Either way, this space gave people a chance to relax and recreate. While some might lose their meager wages, others might supplement their small earned income with their winnings. Either way, gambling in the space gave city residents a chance to enjoy a moment of chance, expectation, and sociality.[86]

Other habits that petitioners found abhorrent included the nightlife of drinking establishments, particularly when they intersected with dancing, loud music, and sex work. Those being petitioned against participated in a lively, widespread nightlife throughout the city, including drinking, music, dancing, flirting, and sex (paid or nonremunerated). Despite Porfirian and revolutionary-era moralizing, these recreational activities labeled as vices continued without significant interruption in the city during the 1940s. At times, revolutionary projects and "centers of vice" even coexisted to mutual benefit. When Severo Herrera rented his building to Felisa Aguilar Preciado for a restaurant, she also added a side room for serving beer. Further, she installed a licensed jukebox and stayed busy all week.[87] What drew patrons to the area of no. 100 calle 26 in Sector Libertad? In that location the city operated an *escuela nocturna*, or night school, bringing literacy and vocational training to working adults. These schools were nineteenth-century relics carried on as part of the Mexican Revolution of 1910 to bring literacy and education to the population, and they helped Aguilar Preciado find a livelihood providing food and a cold beer to students and neighborhood residents alike.[88] These types of gathering places for people might at times become sites of violence, but they also "enhance human growth and social well-being by generating a sense of cooperation, commonality, and belonging."[89] For much of Mexican history, public drinking establishments served as "agents of urbanization" where men and women of various classes "drank together, talked, danced, created social networks, and enjoyed themselves as part of their daily social life."[90] While petitions written to complain about drinking reinforced belonging in society through their appeals to city leaders, those they petitioned against found their belonging in society by engaging in much older forms of belonging.

Nightlife in the city provided opportunities for music, dancing, alcohol consumption, sexual encounters, and sociability that went well beyond beers after night class.[91] The absence of traditional "brakes of morality" and associated "customs" that regulated good behavior made city life appealing for others. Seeking out libations, of course, does not necessarily signal antisocial behavior. For many, cantina camaraderie is precisely the appeal.[92] Consider two adjacent cantinas south of downtown near the train station as examples. For travelers and locals alike, the side-by-side cantinas of La Alhambra and La California (the same mentioned in the previous chapter) provided recreation for travelers in the form of alcohol, beer, and jazz (live and recorded).[93] Patrons looking for hard drinking and occasional brawls found opportunities for both at establishments like La Alhambra.[94]

Other locations for libations and music, such as the cantina Triunfo de Jalisco, offered music more closely associated with stereotypes of Mexico, such as ranchero and mariachi groups. Although it played records during the day, at night the bar offered live music, which spilled out into the streets. Like many other drinking establishments, El Triunfo settled into an area where it had a set clientele: the machine shops of Equipos Mecánicos de Guadalajara and Maquinaria de Jalisco, and the lumberyard of Maderería Guadalajara all surrounded the cantina. In addition to music and alcohol, the location also offered female companionship, with sex workers present in the cantina as well as in the street, in various stages of undress.[95] For workers looking to escape the sober, regulated, and dutiful world of revolutionary industrial labor, El Triunfo de Jalisco offered an escape from the beige utopia of reformers and their regulations. Drinking establishments like El Triunfo appealed to Mexicans by lowering the barriers of class, age, race, or gender and uniting the community through sociability.[96]

More predatory individuals could also find opportunity in the so-called centers of vice. For soldiers, such as the commander who ran a bar and gambling parlor with a roulette wheel, the profit could be direct.[97] Others, such as the police in the Colonia Ferrocarril, spent their time at a cantina where they used their authority to assault or shake down residents in the neighborhood, which had been designed as a refuge for rail workers.[98] Though legal, houses of prostitution could spawn crime among the workers, clients, and passersby. For example, when traveling watch salesman Abel Rodríguez of Manzanillo found himself missing several gold watches and cash, he leveled robbery charges against "the prostitute [*meretriz*] Aurora Hernández . . . from a brothel belonging to Mrs. Guadalupe Marín." A local newspaper, *El Informador*, ran an article on the matter, and the unnamed journalist concluded with an admonition: the police should patrol such businesses and watch out for men like Rodríguez who become so drunk that they lose control of themselves.[99] Of course, adding police to houses of prostitution caused its own kind of disorder. Eight days before the theft of Rodríguez's watches and cash, a police officer seeking a suspect found his quarry dancing in a *casa de asignación*, and when the suspect tried to flee, the officer started shooting, wounding a young girl working in the house.[100]

While I have explored a social past in which petitions let us imagine a world where residents or visitors see urban space as recreational, vice historians also remind us that narcotics, stimulants, or other addictive substances are often linked to uses beyond entertainment and sociability. Alcohol in particular serves as a licit (during the period under study here) psychoactive that allows users to alter their consciousness—a property welcomed in the industrial, urban world.[101] Intoxication is the foremost way that most humans have dealt with post-traumatic stress through the ages, and that has remained the case for Mexico in both the twentieth and twenty-first centuries.[102] The Mexican Revolution of 1910 and subsequent religious conflict consumed generations of Mexican lives in traumatizing warfare, illness, famine, and small-scale violence but with no adequate public reckoning beyond an official patriotic narrative.[103] It is little wonder that some found comfort in the conviviality of drinking and self-medication in "the altered state of consciousness known as the *borrachera*."[104] If we consider not only war trauma but also immigration trauma experienced when going to work in the United States (either as one whose family goes or as an individual migrant laborer), domestic abuse, internal migration, abusive corruption (both syndical and government), workplace struggles, and the physical toil of labor, the potential for immense trauma exists. While the revolutionaries of 1910 extolled revolutionary virtues and the economic boom of the 1940s, many of the people who acted as instruments of that revolution drowned their nightmares in alcohol.

Such thinking, then, might lead readers to imagine the past experiences of alcohol imbibers and the camaraderie of liquor and prostitution. The seemingly endless options for gambling, drinking, prostitution, fighting, vandalism, music, and dancing in the face of respectable and traditional society can also be seen as a source of subversion and resistance. Scholars of colonial New Spain and modern rural Mexico have well interrogated the potential for alcohol—particularly to excess—as a form of subversion and resistance. The consumption of psychoactive substances occurs well beyond the passing trends of politics, revolution, and reform. As one scholar has noted, "Once established, a drug will typically persist in some form across generations. Drugs have legs. They have outlasted beaver hats and hoop skirts and other once fashionable items long since relegated to museums."[105] Alcohol and sites of consumption such as parties, festivals, and cantinas have plagued secular and religious reformers in colonial and modern Mexico for five hundred years.[106] This is, he continues, a way for those without power to make chaos of the order imposed on them by those in power, thus escaping the constraints of time regulation, control, and status performance.[107] Though the corrupt hand of government officials dipped into the vice trade's profits, that very trade provided a psychological resistance and escape to the "violence, corruption, and impunity" that denied urban residents dignity, democracy, and justice.[108]

Groups of neighbors in 1940s Mexico engaged in a long tradition of petitioning their city officials to work cooperatively with residents to improve urban life. From those petitions, we can find groups of neighbors who valued moral behavior such as controlled marital sex, appropriately chaste and deferential women, hardworking youth, respectful young men, and environments free of distractions from respectable labor, school, rest, and home life.

In most ways, these values mirrored those of the Catholic Church in Mexico at the time. In a 1935 joint pastoral letter from the Mexican bishops, they sought the preservation of home, family, hygiene, worker protections, honest work, and protection for single women. The missive stated that together with the "just and wise laws" of government, the Church and the "Mexican People" could return to a time before 1910 to better engage in "taking care of the physical needs of the most poor, and mostly contributing in building a beautiful society with lovely churches and religious institutions."[109] It also mirrored efforts by the secular government of that time to create a society of "honor and industriousness" on the part of both the government and Mexicans, who could work together to stamp out "abusive or immoral acts by any party who sees themselves as a repository of authority." Workers, educated children, and wise teachers did the heavy lifting of morality formation and anticorruption. Society members, opined Luis Álvarez Castillo (municipal president, 1939–40), should model themselves after the new governor of

Jalisco, Silvano Barba González (1939–43), who lived as "erect as a straight line." Thus, "a harmonious understanding between authorities and citizens will build the *tapatío* collective."[110] What better way could residents orient themselves to city leadership and other members of society than through letters and petitions helping to police the collective?

Petitioners writing to the municipal president and other city officials between 1939 and 1947 sought to uphold those goals. When neighbors and authorities alike violated the norms of morality, propriety, and social justice, residents of Guadalajara dutifully bound themselves together, as urban residents from all over Mexico had done for generations, to report and regulate community members.[111] They provided details in the names, addresses, acts, locations, dates, and times of what they termed as abuses, immorality, depravity, and any number of behaviors that they felt violated the social norms of society in Guadalajara. In doing so, however, they engaged in not only a discourse of hegemonic state formation but additionally located themselves within their urban space through their attempts to shape their sense of urban place. First, by supporting traditional morality, residents hoped that city officials would do their part in building a city that they as residents imagined by disciplining or relocating unruly neighbors. Secondly, they also participated in community through the very act of writing the petition and conflict.

Community is conflict. Utopia exists in word and in deed in no place, and as study after study of utopian communities in Mexico and around the world indicate, communities without conflict do not exist. In the case of petitions by residents against their neighbors, the very process of complaining, rather than conflict-free coexistence, bound them together in ways that went beyond simple citizenship rights. Conflict over morality allowed *tapatíos* a sense of belonging in the community linked to an unchanging aspect of urban life—the conflict of neighbor against neighbor over differing definitions of the good life.[112] For the petitioners, shaping urban space happened not only when inspectors and police responded to and complied with requests but also in the act of petitioning together as neighbors. Even in the cases of forgery or false reports, authors understood that the collective complaint gave them authority as they imagined themselves part of something larger—even if the problem never existed or if city officials never responded.

However, petitions only tell us how some residents imagined themselves into a sense of community. A sense of belonging and community also grew in those being petitioned against. Making place in Guadalajara for some residents appears in the acts they do that anger their neighbors. Rather than just taking into account the influence of reformers who rejected the so-called vices, we can also imagine that pleasure attracted new residents to Guadalajara. For those who sought to sever the bonds of so-called traditional morality, diversions such as drinking, jazz, dancing, gambling, fighting, larceny, and paying for sex presented themselves as opportunities that defined city life as an indulgent amusement. For others, participation in such actions—particularly drinking—preserved their mental health and created their own escape from the rigors of modern, postrevolutionary Mexican society. Finally, as other historians have discussed at length, the so-called vice trades also offered opportunity for the poor and working class in production and distribution.[113]

Traveling the streets of present-day Guadalajara, one is struck by the near constant presence of graffiti, the smell of urine, the shouts of soccer players, and—as the city grows dark at night—pounding music, the sight and smell of inebriated people stumbling into a ride-share vehicle, and the beckoning gestures and words of sex workers. Indeed (with the exception of sex workers), recent municipal presidents of Guadalajara have leaned into nightlife as part of urban planning, joining cities around the world that recognize evening pleasures as fundamental parts of city life.[114] Though explorations of liberal, Catholic, or revolutionary reforms are more pervasive in historical studies of urban Mexico, the partyers, DJs, street defecators, and bartenders have left their own less explored yet long-lasting imprint on urban life, persisting into the present. The urban experience varies for different members of society. Vice, pleasure, progress, or modernity—all residents lived or sensed these concepts differently, but all saw themselves engaged in them in relation to others in *tapatío* society.

3 Divine Hygiene

The previous two chapters have explored the sensate and moral ways that residents found belonging in the city through correspondence with officials. At this point, the focus shifts to spiritual communities and their attempts to find belonging in the changing city and nation. The 1940s in Mexico marked an era of dynamic transformation for religious Mexicans. The growth of existing Protestant congregations, the appearance of entirely new religious groups, and divisions within both Catholic and Protestant congregations all placed the religious on uncertain footing. Additionally, even as Guadalajara changed, the influx of migrants who modified the religious landscape added more uncertainty and tension. Where did religious Mexicans fit in society, particularly in the 1910 revolution's shadow, with its debates on the role of religion in society?

Because urban growth and hygiene crusades allowed residents to proclaim their support or rejection of the revolution in daily behaviors (including worship), religious individuals and their associated groups seized on debates around public health and hygiene to assert their belonging in the city. As discussed in the introduction, a sense of belonging helps individuals find a feeling of "personal involvement in a system or environment" by either helping people feel needed or accepted or by proclaiming that their way of being "complements the system or environment" they are in.[1] For many Protestant and Catholic Mexicans, petitions to municipal authorities allowed them to demonstrate that their religious beliefs complemented the work to improve the new urban reality. Rather than continuing to be outsiders as Catholics in a secular revolutionary state or Protestants in a Catholic nation, taking a stand on health and hygiene gave all religious *tapatíos* a sense of insider status and belonging. However, their petitions carried other significance as well.

Clean water and functional sewer lines mattered to the people of Guadalajara, but residents also sought clarity in conflicts over infrastructure when they intersected with their religious lives. Consequently, religious *tapatíos* attempted to redirect the power of city, state, and at times federal law from straightforward urban planning and hygiene enforcement toward ordering the sacred spaces of Guadalajara. The liberal state may have been the lexicon of their hygienic language, but it was in religion that some urban residents found its application. The authors of letters and petitions discussed here saw themselves as firmly belonging to a city led by politicians who would help them cleanse and preserve their sacred spaces. In return, residents would help forward the city's public health mission. Guadalajara residents experiencing rapid growth with all its associated challenges faced a constant stream of language on urban planning and hygiene directed at their daily lives. Such planning intended to control a wide array of social issues related to public health, such as labor reforms.[2] That doesn't mean, however, that the correspondents would respond affirmatively to that intent. Instead, they found ways to turn secular municipal programs toward their own sacred ends.

The Secular Revolution and Religious Residents: The Context of Unbelonging

Religious Mexicans found an opportunity in public hygiene discourse to argue that their beliefs complemented the goals of city government and to reassert their belonging, both to themselves and to municipal leaders. These authors and congregations firmly refute older arguments that the religious are disinclined "to seek the solution to their problems in political or other secular forms."[3] But why did they see using the language of public hygiene as necessary? This section examines the context of religious conflict in Guadalajara after 1910. Not designed as an exhaustive recounting of Mexican religious history, this section is intended to help readers understand why both Catholics and Protestants sought a chance to establish themselves as belonging to broader *tapatío* urban society by 1939 due to a sense of dislocation or uncertainty beyond that of domestic migration and changing community.

The 1910 revolution left the city of Guadalajara comparatively untouched by large-scale violence. However, an initial anticlerical wave in 1914 and 1915 unleashed secularizing forces on the city, and these emanated from the ultimately victorious Constitutionalist faction of Venustiano Carranza.[4] The Constitutionalist occupation of Jalisco under Governor Manuel Diéguez (1914–17) relied on humiliation, "rumor and slander," and violence to curb Catholic clerical power.[5] Additionally, networks of young firebrand revolutionaries and supporters in Guadalajara's Masonic lodges undergirded Governor Diéguez's approach to religious conflict.[6] For some revolutionaries who drew on decades of skepticism or disdain about religion, the Catholic Church posed a threat to progress and modernization, despite Catholic support of revolutionary social goals such as labor unions and social safety nets.[7] The threat came particularly in areas of gender equality, education quality, productive property, and national autonomy. On the national level, this period culminated with the 1917 Constitution's anticlerical passages that strengthened the 1857 Constitution's limits on the public and political visibility of churches. Seeing Catholicism as a hindrance to modernity and progress, secularizers viewed the anticlerical laws of 1917 as a welcome return to Mexico's earlier regulation of religion under President Benito Juárez.[8] The Catholic hierarchy responded by trying to convince Carranza (unsuccessfully) that the Constitution's anticlerical provisions contradicted other provisions that protected the professions of all Mexicans or that called for equality under the law.[9] However, as Catholic resistance grew, first President Carranza (1917–20) and then President Álvaro Obregón (1920–24) reduced their own anticlerical rhetoric. To avoid violence, each held back from fully enforcing the constitutional restrictions on religion at the national level and instead focused their limited political capital on more pressing issues, such as education and security (both also hoping to avoid additional civil war as well as invasion by the United States).

Despite this temporary reduction in tension, Catholics in Guadalajara could not rest easy. Secular revolutionaries around the nation still condemned religion and decried the Catholic clergy as suspicious foreigners born outside of Mexico or as agents of a foreign government (the Vatican).

Considered a city of safety by Catholics elsewhere in Mexico, Guadalajara attracted activists seeking shelter. Those who did so instead found in that city struggles similar to those they had faced in other areas of Mexico.[10] Material acts such as appropriating furniture from Catholic churches for government offices and "unscripted anticlericalism" by municipal and state officials and employees became a part of everyday politics between 1920 and 1922.[11] At the state level, governors countered the traditional influence of Catholicism by drawing the populace toward a "secular national culture" of nationalism and state ritual.[12] Regional anticlericalism grew, and by 1923 it had become a formal state strategy to block the possibility of renewed Catholic political power.[13] In 1923 Catholic resistance in Guadalajara grew in the face of hostility from Jalisco governor José Guadalupe Zuno. The governor banned Catholic political organizations and later shuttered Catholic hospitals, schools, and seminaries.[14] By recognizing only secular labor, peasant, and educational organizations, training young teachers to keep education secular, and working with Mexican feminists to attract popular support, Zuno effectively froze Catholics out of mainstream politics in Jalisco.[15] While Catholics might have held political citizenship, their religiously oriented sense of involvement and participation in their social environment faced explicit opposition from government-supported forces.

Starting with his 1924 presidential campaign, Plutarco Elías Calles joined a slate of other politicians attacking Roman Catholic clergy—or at least priests he saw as intervening unduly in political matters.[16] By 1926 regional anticlericalism had grown into a national movement, sparked when the newspaper *El Universal* reprinted a 1917 pastoral letter attacking the Constitution's anticlerical articles. This might have gone unnoticed, except that by 1926 the central government was enforcing these articles and Archbishop José Mora y del Río publicly defended the nearly decade-old letter.[17] The federal response from the Calles government (1924–28, informal rule from 1929 to 1934) was enforcement of constitutional restrictions on religion, which led to violent conflict and the erosion of "local power arrangements and cultural traditions in certain regions."[18] The individual motivations for both regional and national anticlericalism are varied, and not all can be attributed to atheism and a hatred of religion.[19] The rhetoric used to explain enforcement of the Constitution's religious restrictions provided Mexicans with a glimpse of how secular government proposed to rule. That official language of religious regulation tended toward the scientific, with goals of stamping out superstition and using the nation's resources for reform or modernization instead of religion.

Additionally, by choosing to enforce the 1917 Constitution's religious restrictions instead of looking the other way, as his predecessors had done, Calles argued that he could establish the rule of law in Mexico.[20] And finally, the establishment of the Iglesia Católica Apostólica Mexicana (ICAM, Mexican Apostolic Catholic Church) with state and union support signaled the revolutionary state's willingness to undermine the Roman Catholic Church via alternative religious pathways.[21] The tension between Roman Catholics and the federal government worsened with a government clampdown on popular Holy Week celebrations in public, as well as riots over the occupation of Roman Catholic buildings by the aforementioned ICAM.[22]

In Jalisco the clandestine Catholic resistance organization known as the Unión Popular (UP, Popular Union) gained support from the laity and some clergy (though not a majority).[23] By July 1926 and under the attempt to enforce the rule of law, Congress passed laws enforcing constitutional Articles 3 and 130 prohibiting religious education, regulating the number of churches and clergy, and limiting Roman Catholic clergy to Mexican citizens.[24] Anticlerical federal soldiers and agrarians pulled down the statues of saints in Catholic churches or removed children from religious schools and placed them in state schools.[25] In protest, the Mexican episcopate suspended religious services at the end of July 1926. Clandestine Catholic groups, some local priests, and many lay Catholics in Mexico's center-west region rose in armed rebellion to support the clerical strike. Through August and September 1926, successful revolts erupted in rural western Mexico, and sympathizers in Guadalajara supported them.[26] Lay Catholics not closely associated with the rebels assassinated Álvaro Obregón after his reelection in 1928 as part of a wider (but disorganized) resistance to secularism and federal power.[27]

The Catholic rebels enjoyed early success, but by June 1929 the church's hierarchy and the Mexican state had recognized the conflict as a bloody stalemate, and the U.S. embassy aided in negotiating a peace deal between the Mexican government and Catholics—referred to as the *arreglos*—thus ending the revolt. The government agreed to ease enforcement of religious restrictions while the Roman Catholic leadership barred the clergy from politics.[28] With the *arreglos* of 1929 that reduced tensions between the Catholic Church and the Mexican central and state governments, Mexico gradually entered an uneasy détente with religion. Still, secularizers disliked the new arrangement, and Cristero hardliners who had not been party to the arrangement felt betrayed by the Roman Catholic Church. The antagonism did not vanish overnight, and violence between Catholics and secular schoolteachers continued in areas such as rural Jalisco. Calles again stoked tensions in 1934, declaring in a Guadalajara speech that Mexico must begin a "psychological revolution" to take command of Mexican children's minds and lives. "It would be a grave error for the men of the Revolution to not wrench the youth away from the claws of the clergy," he proclaimed.[29] Nevertheless, the Catholic leadership's silence in the face of such speeches, consistent Catholic victories to roll back local secularism, and pragmatic restraint by the Lázaro Cárdenas administration (1934–40) all contributed to an uneasy peace between religion and government by the end of 1938.[30]

This reduction of tensions began a period known as the modus vivendi. Bishops signaled their relaxation of opposition to the 1910 revolution by supporting the nationalization of foreign oil companies in 1938 (a move led by Guadalajara's Archbishop José Garibi Rivera). Furthermore, the bishops limited their role in society to serving as religious teachers and supporters of social and educational reform. In addition, they promised not to stand in the way of Mexico's economic transformation. For its part, the Mexican government left in place constitutional restrictions but simply chose not to enforce them, particularly in matters of public worship and the existence of private Catholic education.[31] They also dropped their goals to replace the "backward ideas" of Catholicism with ideas of development and liberalism.[32] Should the Catholic Church renege on the deal and begin engaging in politics, the 1917 Constitution remained in place as a kind of sword of Damocles. We now enter a gray area where the Roman Catholic Church no longer had to exist under the aggressive hand of state repression, yet it still functioned under a layer of state regulation and later even had to partner with the state apparatus in Cold War anticommunist crusades.[33]

The context of religious conflict and accommodation just reviewed centers the high clergy and political leadership. But how did religious Mexicans on the ground react to the end of militant persecution of Roman Catholicism but with a seemingly cowed Catholic Church? How did the much smaller Mexican Protestant congregations react to a Catholic Church free of official state persecution? What about the possible loss of status for Protestants as supporters of liberal reform in Mexico? A détente between the upper echelons of the Catholic hierarchy and the federal government could not instantly create a sense of community belonging after decades of tension and in the context of growing Protestant congregations in Guadalajara. City by city and neighborhood by neighborhood, religious Mexicans of all affiliations had to wrestle with a state whose secularizing language remained prevalent but whose willingness to treat churches as a threat to Mexico had diminished.

The cessation of direct conflict did not eliminate the daily regulation of churches as federal property. After the government declared the churches to be the property of Mexico, it handed them over to *juntas vecinales*, or *juntas de vecinos* (neighborhood associations), to manage. The central government created these secular neighborhood associations in 1926 to control, care for, and monitor churches now considered the nation's patrimony. The state did not recognize any entity calling itself a church, but it did recognize the right of residents to form neighborhood groups in buildings designated for special purposes such as religious worship. Though the Catholic *juntas vecinales* in Guadalajara appear to follow the pattern seen elsewhere in Mexico, such as Oaxaca or Campeche, where the neighborhood associations became proxies for local priests, congregations still heard the language of government inspection and supervision with regard to church buildings, even if they had no real say in how clerics administered those properties.[34] How did lay members themselves react to these inspections and regulations?[35] For many Protestant churches, the *juntas* represented a shared voice in governance in an otherwise pastor-centered hierarchy, and often congregants took the power bestowed on them by the state as a recognition of that authority.

After 1938 religious *tapatíos* interacted with a city in which congregants worshipped without threat of state violence or continuous activist harassment, but they still faced layers of city, state, and federal inspection. Their response to that regulation subjected them to secular power, but the way they engaged with that regulation also made them partners and innovators—partners in that they legitimized the state's regulation by acquiescence but also innovators in that they took that regulation and turned it to their own ends. If the armed resistance to the state and the failure of that resistance marked the end of formal Catholic political power in shaping the Mexican Revolution, as Robert Curley has argued, individual residents used religious thought, action, and motivations to shape it informally.[36] Political Catholics had "spent their cartridges in the [Cristero] war," and they joined Protestants in seeing themselves as part of a state that they demanded pay attention.[37]

Hygiene and Religious Competition in Guadalajara

Before Protestants had even established formal congregations in Guadalajara, the presence of their literature and Bible versions alarmed the archbishop of Guadalajara and moved him to issue a pastoral letter warning *tapatíos* against reading Protestant material.[38] In 1874 the same office issued a full ban on any interaction with Protestants.[39] Though the growth of Protestantism in Guadalajara has never surpassed the single digits as a percentage of the population (as of this writing), their mere presence caused panic among Catholic leadership from the start. For Catholics, Protestants simply did not belong in Mexican society.

Baptists, Congregationalists, and Methodists created the first Protestant congregations in Guadalajara in the 1870s and 1880s, with Anglicans and Presbyterians joining the scene soon after. These groups all saw themselves as allies of liberal thinkers and anticlerical politicians.[40] This affinity came as an extension of not only progressive theology that sought to educate and missionize Indigenous populations and pull them out of Catholicism but also pragmatic needs to find allies opposed to Catholic power in Mexico.[41] From the start, the Protestant sense of belonging came about by demonstrating how their practices complemented the Mexican state's goals. With less than half a dozen Protestant congregations having been established in the city by 1900, a sense of affinity with the national government undergirded their sense of security. Demonstrating how they complemented the liberal and later revolutionary "environment or system" reinforced their sense of belonging.[42]

Because of this alliance, the overthrow of Porfirio Díaz had nuanced meanings for Protestant *tapatío* leaders. While they saw his ouster as positive, they also hoped that a new regime would not bring disorder or upheaval.[43] They need not have worried, as over time the revolutionary leaders found allies in some Protestant congregations, which helped maintain public enthusiasm for the 1910 revolution and, in its wake, the ruling party.[44] According to some Mexican scholars, a growing number of Protestant congregations and Masonic lodges "were a permanent presence in Mexico's revolutionary process" and attempted to further shared goals of "social engineering" by "'bettering the population' . . . with the purpose of causing the rise of a new physical society that has been morally regenerated."[45] Church educational programs (particularly in literacy, physical fitness, and civics) underscored the Protestant/liberal affinity.[46] And while the late nineteenth century saw only a handful of Protestant congregations (mostly serving foreigners), by the 1930s Guadalajara had acquired dozens of Protestant and other non-Catholic religious groups, many of them populated and directed by Mexicans themselves. While the population of Protestants as a percentage came in at less than 1 percent in 1950, disdain from Catholic leadership for their presence remained firm.[47]

In May 1933 the small Protestant congregation of the Iglesia Episcopal Mexicana in Guadalajara sent a petition to the municipal president of that city requesting to use the Santa María de Gracia church, a former Dominican convent in the city center. They also requested use of the Templo de la Soledad, situated across the street northward from the cathedral in the city center. Had they occupied either location, this would have put Protestants at the very heart of both the municipal and ecclesiastical city space, being only steps from both the Catholic cathedral and state government buildings such as Congress, the Supreme Court, and the Governor's Palace. Although the conflict between the Roman Catholic Church and the state had entered into a period of reduced tension, colonial properties remained part of the national patrimony and therefore under federal regulation. To protect and preserve these properties, the state inspected, inventoried, and required upkeep of the buildings for both aesthetic and hygienic purposes. Against Catholic objections, many of these buildings eventually housed state-sponsored entities such as universities, union halls, or hospitals, and the Secretaría de Gobernación (Policy Secretariat) even turned a few properties over to Protestants. The Iglesia Episcopal Mexicana congregants hoped for such a property, and they felt Mexico's recent federal history of anti-Catholicism supported the Protestant position.

The Iglesia Episcopal Mexicana had its origins in the nineteenth century and a group of excommunicated Roman Catholic priests. Like many other reform-minded Catholics, they supported the liberal Constitution of 1857 that disestablished Catholicism and allowed other religions in Mexico, and this earned them expulsion from the Catholic Church.[48] Their 1933 petition reflects this historic alliance by stating that "liberal public servants" had always been friendly with their congregation. The petition then states that the Iglesia Episcopal had itself been a supporter of Mexico "for the evolution and good of the people." At this point, the letter departs from the expected nineteenth-century language of liberalism and instead turned to using the 1910 revolution's language to define exactly how the group planned to work for local residents without causing conflict with other churches: "In our case—if you will provide us with the church we are requesting—we desire to offer programs independent of our religion such as antialcoholism conferences, other discussions of hygiene and culture, stripped of any religious meaning and that tend toward the education and progress of our people."[49] Antialcohol crusades undergirded state-sponsored hygiene and social improvement projects.[50] The letter's authors hoped to affiliate themselves with campaigns to improve the health and safety of residents, increase work productivity, and better the cleanliness of public spaces by referencing existing government projects. They hoped, in light of their plans, that the city government would offer a favorable opinion to the federal government regarding their petition to occupy a Catholic Church property.[51]

Though the record is sparse, it appears that the federal government rendered an opinion in the *episcopales*' favor, granting them the Templo de la Soledad next to the cathedral. The Episcopalians never took possession, however, stating in correspondence with the municipal president of Guadalajara that they had been unable to occupy the "Romanist temple" for "diverse reasons."[52] Two years later the Episcopalians stated they could not occupy the building but that "only the federal government knows why."[53] No additional clarification for that phrase appears, though references to the building's deteriorated condition might mean a lack of funds to refurbish the large structure. Eventually (in 1936) the Iglesia Episcopal Mexicana purchased land and built their own building, and the State of Jalisco pulled down the Templo de la Soledad to make way for the Rotonda de los Hombres Ilustres, completed in 1952 (now known as the Rotonda de Jaliscienses Ilustres).[54] Episcopalians placed their new property in the heart of Guadalajara's working-class Catholic urban space. At the nexus of the congregations of Mexicaltzingo, Nuestra Señora de Aranzazú, San José de Analco, and San Juan de Dios, the Episcopalian Templo de Cristo on calle Antonio Molina existed at the crossroads of southern Guadalajara's middle- and lower-class Roman Catholic fervor and many of its most established Catholic worship spaces. When the regionally important Virgen de Zapopan's image was taken on a tour to local chapels in Guadalajara, the route during the period under study went from San José de Analco, up calle Prisciliano Sánchez, to San Francisco de Asís.[55] For Catholics, the presence of a Protestant church marred her passage. Moreover, being just two blocks from San Francisco de Asís, the Templo de Cristo stood at the center of what had been the region's missionary heart, with San Francisco de Asís having served as the conversion center for the region's Indigenous population who had settled in the neighborhoods surrounding the proposed Templo de Cristo. The church of San Francisco de Asís also served as the southern starting point for the colonial-era *via sacra*, or urban travel route from the south to the north that identified Catholic colonial power in the city.[56] San Francisco de Asís had been mysteriously burned in 1936, and during this era the Catholic Church was busy renovating the structure—contexts that could also have increased tensions. So, with Catholic antagonism ramped up, the *episcopales* discovered that Catholics could also adapt the state's language to regulate ideological foes.

Outside of Jalisco, Catholics in states such as Hidalgo already checked state power and socialist programs through social networks and popular mobilization, often under the powerful and charismatic guidance of lay and clerical firebrands.[57] Guadalajara's Catholics may not have been led by a

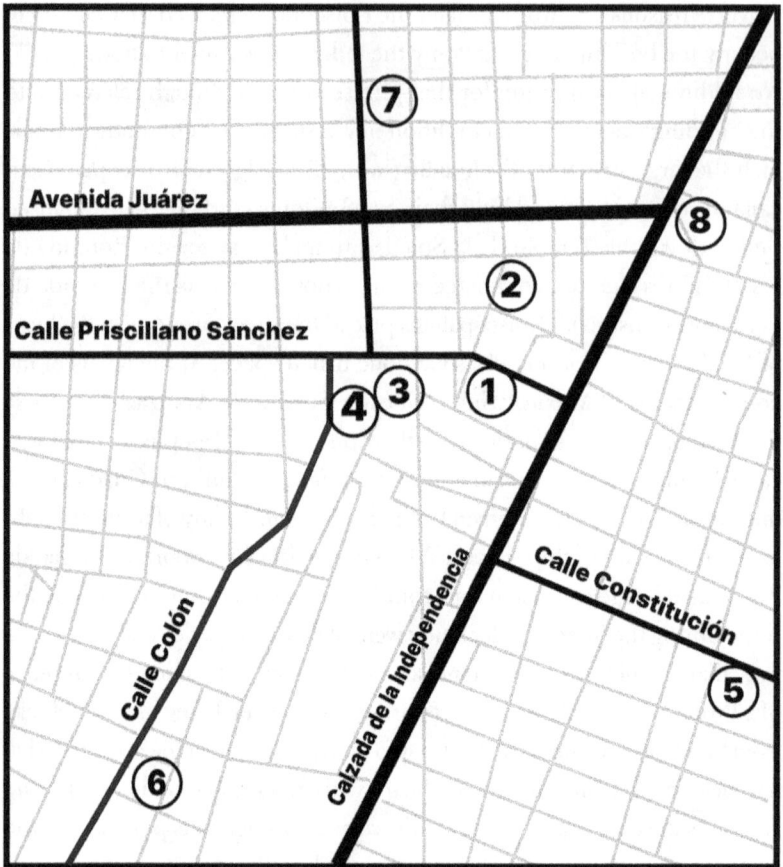

FIG. 7. The location of the Episcopal denomination's Templo de Cristo in relation to the major Catholic congregations in the city and the Masonic lodge: (1) Templo de Cristo (Episcopal); (2) Gran Logia Occidental Mexicana (Masonic); (3) Templo de San Francisco (Catholic); (4) Parroquia de Nuestra Señora de Aranzazú (Catholic); (5) Parroquia de San José de Analco (Catholic); (6) Parroquia de San Juan Bautista de Mexicaltzingo (Catholic); (7) Catedral-Basílica de la Asunción de María Santísima (Catholic); (8) Parroquia de San Juan de Dios (Catholic). Map by the author.

clerical caudillo, their leader being the bookish, music-loving Archbishop José Garibi Rivera, but the Guadalajara native set a tone for his congregants that appears to have helped them navigate a changing city as well as turn the discourse of revolution and hygiene in their favor.[58]

On the national level, joint letters from the Catholic Conference of Mexican Bishops (including Archbishop Garibi Rivera) lamented the poverty and persecution of Roman Catholics, as well as the ineptitude of secular government that was holding back Catholic efforts to improve Mexican society.[59] Locally, however, Garibi Rivera gently reminded his clergy to follow local laws, encouraged patriotism via Acción Católica Mexicana (ACM, Mexican Catholic Action), and tempered the fervor of young Catholics toward using political parties to enact the Church's positions.[60] Nevertheless, "José the Archbishop" (as he signed many of his letters) did not shy away from taking a hard edge with Protestants. When he learned that the Asociación Cristiana Femenil (ACF, or the YWCA in English), which operated social services such as literacy and health education (the letter does not mention family planning) in downtown Guadalajara, had origins in Protestantism, he responded promptly. Garibi Rivera issued a diocesan circular forbidding Catholics from affiliating with the group and warned them that they risked exposing their children to canonical "perversion" if they associated with the ACF.[61] This mirrors a general trend in Catholic leadership arguing that the Mexican sense of community suffered after the 1910 revolution because the Protestant presence in Mexico increased.[62] In April 1938 the archbishop reminded the diocese in less than gentle terms that they lived in times of "great insubordination" and that any person, including civil authorities at any level, who attempted to hinder the work of a priest in any way deserved excommunication.[63] Garibi Rivera may have encouraged patriotism, but he would not back down from his ecclesiastical mission or his view that the Catholic Church "was the true mother . . . and constant developer of true progress" in Mexico.[64]

At a time when President Cárdenas was expanding the populist welfare state through land distribution and social services, the Catholic Church was responding that it, too, desired to improve the temporal lives of Mexicans. After the election of Manuel Ávila Camacho to the presidency in 1940 and his declaration of adherence to Roman Catholicism, conservative politicians in the ruling party used statements on religious tolerance from liberal Benito Juárez to defend the right of Catholics to worship unmolested by the state.[65] Where the liberal Juárez had called on Mexicans to respect the belief of others as a sword against Catholicism's dominance over society, conservatives turned it into a shield of defense. Lay Catholics learned to do the same with the language of municipal laws as they carried on the long tradition of Catholic civic engagement in Mexico.[66]

On the neighborhood level, Catholics utilized these strategies in less formal ways against their religious enemies and reinforced to themselves and city leaders their sense of belonging in the wider society. To start, they adapted tactics they saw applied to their own facilities during the height of revolution-era religious persecution. For example, in 1924 police raided the Catholic seminary in Guadalajara "on the charge that the people studying there were lazy and dirty. The Departamento de Salud Pública declared that the building did not meet standards of public hygiene."[67] Similarly, the Secretaría de Gobernación bombarded Catholics with questionnaires about building conditions, restricted repairs or improvements that might damage colonial-era buildings (possibly to harass congregants), and forced the diocese to justify every action and clergy assignment.[68] With the pragmatic influence of Archbishop Garibi Rivera behind them, as well as the language of religious regulation around them, Catholics faced off against the Iglesia Episcopal Mexicana and their new church in the Templo de Cristo building at no. 274 calle Antonio Molina.

With the new chapel still under construction in December 1938, Pastor José N. Robredo submitted his paperwork to the city, soliciting their favorable opinion about the new Templo de Cristo in his bid to win approval from the state and federal Secretarías de Gobernación to use the space provisionally. He assembled a neighborhood association (*junta vecinal*) of congregants charged with caring for the building and provided an accompanying petition, with four pages of signatures from members of his congregation, seeking a positive ruling. Confident of a favorable outcome, Robredo communicated with the city using Templo de Cristo letterhead already emblazoned with the building's address, though the chapel still didn't physically exist.[69] Although the city demurred from supporting the petition, officials did say that if Robredo would resubmit his request after the building's construction, the city would afford him the same religious liberty as all other Mexicans.[70] Nevertheless, even before Robredo's request to use the Templo de Cristo arrived in the municipal offices, resident complaints began arriving in those same offices.

Two letters from neighbors concerned about Robredo came from near his private residence in calle Pedro Moreno. The authors asserted that the pastor used this home as a clandestine and illegal "house church." These two letters to the municipal president of Guadalajara indicated specific days and times that people visited, allegedly "looking around to make sure no one sees them." The letter writers then stated that they had been following Robredo around the city, including to the village of Zoquipan, where he held meetings. They voiced concern that he had not registered as a religious worker (he had), and they expressed disgust with his "mockery of the law." Finally, they communicated fear at confronting a *"capitalista"* (capitalist), and they asked the municipal president to step in. All signed the second letter as "workers in this city."[71]

When the Templo de Cristo finally moved beyond the planning stage and became a fully furnished and functioning church building, more letters sought to close the building and jail Robredo. In a letter to the state's governor, a group of concerned neighbors wrote to draw attention to the affront Robredo and the *episcopales* represented to their neighborhood. They informed the governor that "the schismatic priest named José Robredo commits infractions of the law every day," and in a shot at city authorities they go on to say that "of course since nothing happens to him he does whatever he wants."[72] What are the crimes of which they accused Robredo? The letters display knowledge of laws governing sacred and public space at the time but also hint at a network of informal surveillance in Zapopan and Guadalajara marshaled to ferret out the crimes committed by what the letter writers call the "schismatics."

Mexican law strictly forbade religious meetings in private homes, and the neighbors looking to stop the Episcopal priest claimed that "all through 1938 he met in private houses." The writers attempted to rally authorities by also claiming that "they are having religious meetings with a political character" and that these meetings of "all their *curitas* going late into the night" could only happen because the *episcopales* sneaked around to avoid detection.[73] According to the authors, not only did the congregants and the *curita* (a diminutive reference to priests that challenges their status and masculinity and draws on the language of anticlericals) allegedly plot against the government, but they did so with full knowledge of their crimes and attempted to hide them. In engaging the same anticlerical language used against Catholic priests' sexuality and gender, the petitioners appear to motivate the city by finding common cause with officials but directing that anticlericalism toward an Episcopal priest. These authors firmly establish their own belonging in the city by asserting their compatibility with the state through signifying language while simultaneously rejecting the legitimacy of Protestants as community members.

Finally, the letter closes by going after the perceived ideology of the group as well as their origin. The letter writers encourage an investigation and prosecution that would result in the building being instead used by the *"verdaderamente extranjera"*—the truly foreign. Both liberal and revolutionary critiques of Catholicism used such language, arguing that Catholics took orders from the Vatican, owed allegiance to a foreign head of state (the pope), and used a network of transnational employees (the clergy), thus making Catholic leaders "truly foreign." The letters turned that language on its head and used it to attack a tradition—Protestantism—associated in the minds of Catholic Mexicans with northern Europe and the United States. They then questioned the group's political leanings (despite the group's leaders being excommunicated Mexican Catholic priests loyal to the 1857 Constitution), encouraging the governor to "investigate this José Robredo that is in charge of the schismatic sect that, so they say, is bathed in liberalism," before referring to the tragedy of having a building in the city led by this "bourgeois *curita*, Robredo, mocker of our Government."[74]

Failing to get a response, the neighbors sent a letter to President Lázaro Cárdenas the following week. His office promptly forwarded it to state officials, who in turn sent it back to the city for investigation. The letter contains similar complaints about the priest, stressing his clandestine visits to private homes as well as his "mockery" of the "magna carta" of Mexican law. The letter also demonstrates the extent of surveillance that the neighborhood had over Robredo, claiming that their efforts at vigilance had broken up church meetings in a home when Robredo noticed his observers. There is one variation in this letter, however, that does make it stand out. In the letter to Cárdenas, not only do the signatories call for having Robredo and his associates investigated and tried, but they also advocated seizing the premises and turning it over to unspecified revolutionary programs "for the good of the nation instead of foreign sects."[75] Once more, the neighbors took the state's anticlerical language, inverted it, and used it against their ideological foe in an ever-important debate over physical space. In this regard, their letter functioned as a narrative of belonging that demonstrated to city leaders that they not only sympathized with the state project of religious regulation but they had mastered the language of anticlericalism to regulate the community.

A third letter in the historical record came from Zapopan, located on the western limits of Guadalajara, on April 3, 1939. Even though the *episcopales* had maintained for several years a small worship space in Zoquipan, located between the city of Zapopan and the western edge of Guadalajara, it wasn't until they built their church in the heart of Guadalajara that complaints from Zoquipan appeared. This letter addressed the municipal president of Guadalajara and not Zapopan, under whose jurisdiction the Zoquipan chapel fell. The authors also inverted the political language once used to paint Catholic priests as tyrannical, self-serving rulers lording over barely converted dupes and applied it to their Protestant foes. The authors claimed Robredo had few congregants truly versed in the religion of Protestantism, and those who attended services did so only because they, as employees at the priest's *rancho*, feared for their jobs. For this reason, the chapel did not even have a registered *junta vecinal*, they claimed, because no villager truly belonged to Robredo's congregation.[76] Beyond being targeted by the traditional language of anticlericalism, the Episcopalians found themselves facing charges regarding another practice—bad hygiene.

According to this letter, Robredo kept the building in poor physical condition, unfit for worship. Such inadequate upkeep in everything from sweeping to roof maintenance, they argued, resulted from the Episcopal priest's refusal to care for the building. The authors use the edifice's allegedly filthy state to claim that the Episcopalians used the space for dubious reasons and that the pastor forced congregants into the chapel. The petitioners also protested that the building went to waste in the possession of "schismatics" who kept it full of "garbage and bats." By complaining to the municipal president of Guadalajara, the neighbors tried to persuade the government to close down the facility on the grounds of hygiene. If Robredo kept the building in its current state, the authors feared that "instead of progressing, our village will be left in an even more destroyed state than it is already."[77] Having found no relief from the state or federal authorities, complaining neighbors turned their attention back to the local level—where all their correspondence had been returned—and took a new tack. This time they hinted that the worship space in Guadalajara would follow the Zoquipan building's pattern and end up a hygienic menace to the community. Additionally, the letter writers urged the city to confiscate the building and dedicate it to any use that municipal government determined appropriate. Using the Cárdenas-era language of light Marxism with a heavy dose of liberal hygienic and social reform, each letter engaged the state as a mediator or even ally in their own religious cause. Additionally, this language of conflict also reinforced for the authors and for the recipients that their own traits made them complementary participants in society.

Might there be other reasons for the dislike of Robredo and his congregation? In the Templo de Cristo's case, a hint exists (without firm evidence) that Pastor José N. Robredo may have been a member of the Masonic Gran Logia Occidental Mexicana. The only reference to Robredo in Guadalajara newspapers lists him in attendance at a 1940 dinner at no. 112 calle Manuel López Cotilla. The dinner happened a mere block and a half from his chapel on calle Antonio Molino, across from the Masonic lodge headquarters. The dinner appears under the single-word title "Agape" (used in Masonic ritual), and a reporter describes the gathering as an "interesting" moment of "scientific study" hosted by sculptor and well-known Master Mason Victores Prieto.[78] Robredo is listed only as attending the January 6 dinner (also the feast of Epiphany), and no noticeable Masonic marks, symbols, or indications of membership are used in his letters and petitions. The possibility exists that Robredo held membership in a wider upper- and middle-class network of professionals linked to freemasonry. However, his possible social status did not appear to result in city officials obviously bending rules in his favor nor did it earn him much recognition by a city government unsure of the group's existence in subsequent years. If he did hold membership, it might have offered useful connections for his print-ing business. No other known Templo de Cristo congregant appears in the list of dinner attendees.[79] While Catholics saw Masons in Jalisco as a threat, it is telling that in the reports made by those surveilling Robredo, involvement in Masonry or visiting the Masonic lodge so near his new chapel never received a mention.[80] Did he never visit the lodge, or did his observers simply not see him there? It is also possible that if Robredo was a Mason and his critics knew it, perhaps they understood that appeals to the perceived threat of Masons would have little sway with city officials in a time when Catholics perceived Cárdenas-era politicians as mired in Ma-sonic networks.[81] Instead, Robredo's observers opted for a focus on legal foundations based in hygiene and clerical regulation laws.

Why hygiene? The go-to answer on why Catholics turned to the language of hygiene might be the presence in Guadalajara of Acción Católica Mex-icana, an activist organization designed to promote the tenets of Catholic social doctrine and reduce the influence of more militant Catholic organiza-tions.[82] The *Boletín de Acción Católica* proclaimed that "the Catholic social doctrine teaches that Catholics—as citizens—are obligated to exercise their rights and to comply with the corresponding responsibility, just as they should defend the Faith and moral health, the freedom of conscience, etc., which is to say that they must participate in civic life as well as political life."[83]

It is possible that ACM may have served as the prime mover for engaging with government on religious matters using the state's language. On the other hand, that might be expecting too much of the organization in the Guadalajara of 1939 and 1940. None of those writing the letters appears on the rolls of ACM or its affiliate organizations for the Catholic churches near the Templo de Cristo, and neither do they appear as members on extant *junta vecinal* lists that would have marked them as trusted leaders in their respective parishes.[84] Even had they appeared on the membership lists, the various organizations of ACM in Jalisco functioned minimally or at unor-ganized levels. In activity reports submitted to the archdiocese, meetings might be irregular or the attendance low. Regarding cleanliness (of people or property), no parish in the entire state was shown in extant reports in the archive to have discussion circles related to issues of public health or hygiene.[85] As active participants in the ACM, women tended toward issues such as "religious instruction, support for priests and seminaries, mothers, and enthronements [a type of devotional ritual] . . . Catholic schools, charitable works . . . and personal piety."[86] While tempting to paint the ACM as the only driving force moving Catholics to use hygiene as their weapon of choice against Protestants, it is more likely that other factors are also at play, namely a longtime local tradition of political leaders and elites emphasizing health and hygiene and linking it to life in the city.

During the colonial era, Guadalajara faced public health challenges, though it actively tackled them in direct and public ways that caused the residents to laud the quality of public services.[87] As the Bourbon Reforms and their focus on health and hygiene swept through the Americas, Eusebio Sánchez Pareja, as the governor of Nueva Galicia (1771–76, 1777–86), ordered a series of hygiene guidelines and rules to remove garbage, animal slaughter waste, vegetation, and other trash from cities and to set time aside for street sweeping.[88] When famine and then disease struck the city in 1785 and 1786 along with an influx of unemployed rural migrants, city elites proposed a range of solutions, from the absurd that never came to pass (city walls to keep out the poor and sick) to the useful (expanded health care and charitable institutions).[89] Subsequent construction of medical hospitals, modern markets, guides for the disposal of animal corpses, fines for promoting contagion through unhygienic behaviors, and the expansion and improvement of water delivery services further improved urban health in the city at the nineteenth century's start.[90] The Belén Hospital (1794) became a point of pride in the city and a beacon of providing health and education to the urban working class of Guadalajara.[91]

As their counterparts in the twentieth century would do (and as discussed later in this chapter), working-class residents often used water and health infrastructure for their own ends. For example, the city nearly closed a well near the Santa Teresa convent because water carriers and others used the area for socializing, often in ways that offended the discalced Carmelite nuns inside the walls. Unknown persons marked buildings with graffiti, waterways became toilets, and quiet corners became places for socializing and sex. Both Crown and clergy expressed their displeasure, and municipal officials responded with increased vigilance and ordinances for street cleaning and bodily restraint.[92]

While the independence era brought a continued interest in the protection of health and hygiene in Guadalajara (and Mexico generally), limited funds often made grand projects for water and sanitation related to public health improvement difficult. In the late 1800s, Porfirio Díaz elevated thinkers obsessed with liberal and scientific thought and also invited foreign investment, bringing a renewed vigor to sanitation and hygiene in urban Mexico and an increasing number of public health codes.[93] Governor Luis C. Curiel (twenty-three different terms as substitute governor or governor between 1893 and 1903) brought water from the Los Colomos forest area to the northwest, thus providing a year-round supply of water for the first time in the city's history. However, the expansion of sewerage and potable water systems paid for by bonds issued through U.S. companies and the introduction of flush toilets and other indoor water systems dramatically increased water use.[94] Concurrent with these developments, city leaders and police officers worked to encourage Mexicans to "improve their daily habits, especially when it came to bodies, hygiene, and public health."[95] Porfirian-era officials also joined North Atlantic nations in equating health with prosperity and "bright" national futures.[96] And while it is certainly easy to dismiss public health concerns as simply another area where elites sought to control working-class lives in the name of productive capitalism, hygiene and public health had real consequences for urban residents. Between 1887 and 1896, just over 50 percent of children in Guadalajara died before the age of seven, frequently due to environmental factors like polluted water, inadequate nutrition (during pregnancy and after birth), and issues related to hygiene.[97]

Leaders of the 1910 revolution intended to extend the benefits of Porfirian society to the masses, and this included improvements in health and hygiene.[98] In addition to the more famous issues of land, rural water, nationalism, and race, many engaged in rejecting Porfirio Díaz and his administration over issues such as urban water supply, fire control, paved roads, law enforcement, public sanitation, and a host of other services previously limited to elite neighborhoods.[99] Mexicans who saw themselves as respectable members of society called for expanded modernization plans that the Díaz administration bragged about but could not evenly deliver.[100] For Mexicans who engaged in the liberal dream of "hard work, hygiene, sobriety, and progress" for the entire nation, the Díaz dictatorship failed miserably to create a civilized society.[101] For these revolutionaries, issues like public health marked Mexico as a progressive, civilized society. Such devotion to the ideas of development and modernization through public infrastructure led to the "political culture of developmentalism" in Guadalajara. This culture of promises (though not always one of completion), constantly appeared before the general population in official slogans painted on the walls of public buildings and banners or tacked onto every official communication or publication.[102]

In the late 1930s and early 1940s, few *tapatíos* would have missed the language of hygiene in daily life. Effective revolutionary state intervention in hygiene started in the Calles era, but the language also drew from an earlier Porfirian impulse associated with controlling and regulating Mexican lives.[103] As Claudia Agostini has argued, "Public health became, during the course of the late nineteenth and early twentieth centuries, an important instrument for expanding the authority of the state . . . and for enlarging a technically proficient state apparatus."[104] In hygiene and health laws, we see states displaying their power through what they could do not only *for* bodies but also *to* them. By 1938 the Cardenista-era leaders of Guadalajara seemed more concerned with campaigns against gambling, alcohol, dirty streets, and unsafe food than the threat of religion.[105] For example, in Guadalajara there are more citations issued against barbershops open on Sunday than illegal church and church school closures. Municipal records contain hundreds of documents related to closing down vendors of tortillas, milk, bread, and charcoal for public health violations, while extant municipal records show the city closing only two clandestine religious schools in 1938 and none of the many unregistered Catholic and Protestant churches.[106] Though on a daily basis residents of Guadalajara might have gratefully witnessed authorities checking on vendors' cleanliness and removing from the streets anyone selling adulterated or dangerous products, the physical assault on the churches of Guadalajara for ideology no longer occurred as frequently as it had in the 1920s or early 1930s. For the working class of Guadalajara, appeals to hygiene could be seen as a way to move the government to action in ways that religion once had.[107]

The state also reinforced this view by constantly reporting its work on hygiene, infrastructure, and public health. The *Gaceta Municipal* of Guadalajara contained year-end reports and speeches (required by law) from municipal presidents and state governors that touted spending on public works, water, sanitation, and fees collected for code violations. City and state officials narrated these reports as accounts of actions fulfilling the revolution's promises. Officials also invited members of society to participate in the city's improvement by communicating their desires to city leaders. When municipal president Luis Álvarez del Castillo (1939–40) took office, he issued a proclamation to the public stating that diligence and honesty (*labrosidad y honradez*) should be the "norm of the Tapatío Commune [Comuna Tapatía]." To accomplish this work, he promised that his office and the city council would be at the disposal of city residents to "receive with interest and a spirit of cordiality all your suggestions or queries tending to improve public services." He went on to say that all "social elements" functioned as deputies to report corruption, suggest improvements, and help build the *tapatío* collective.[108] While the Cárdenas presidency's (1934–40) light socialism is clear in the communication, so is an encouragement to all residents to participate in improving the city.

By the early 1940s, the city of Guadalajara had become more aggressive about the shared duty of public health and hygiene. In January 1940 city leaders proclaimed that "a happy absolute and perfect reality" in a city should be the ability to live in a tidy environment that was free of rubbish. However, "the population itself" stood between that beautiful dream and reality. To help the residents, the city threw its ideological and financial support behind the Sindicato Único de Trabajadores en la Limpia y Aseo de la Ciudad (Workers' Union of City Cleaners) branch of the Confederación de Trabajadores de México (CTM, Confederation of Mexican Workers). The city hoped that these "distinguished" workers and residents could cooperate to make Guadalajara "an example of its progress in modern ideas and social policy."[109] City leaders said they did their part to promote cleanliness and public hygienic safety, but they asked the citizens to contribute as well.

To encourage this participation, city leaders went beyond school lessons and hortatory newspaper notices, organizing full-scale parades to celebrate "Security and Hygiene at Work Week" the first nine days of May, followed

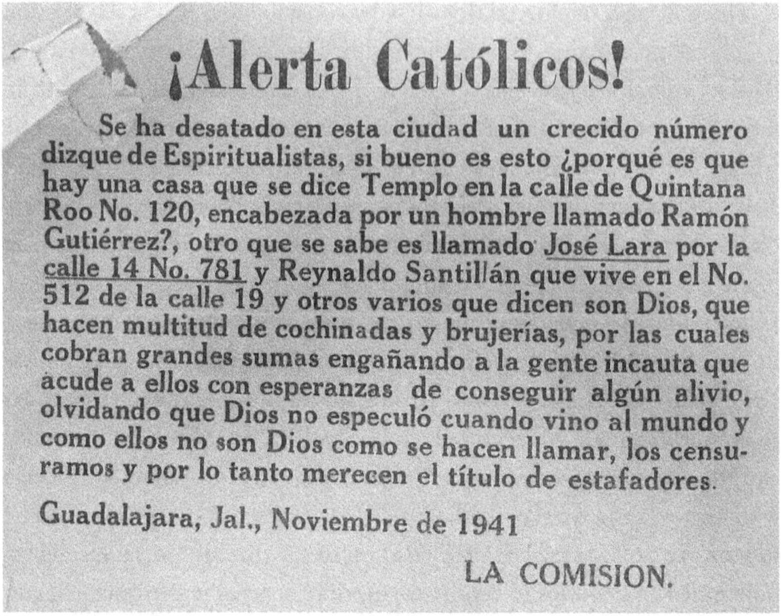

¡Alerta Católicos!

Se ha desatado en esta ciudad un crecido número dizque de Espiritualistas, si bueno es esto ¿porqué es que hay una casa que se dice Templo en la calle de Quintana Roo No. 120, encabezada por un hombre llamado Ramón Gutiérrez?, otro que se sabe es llamado José Lara por la calle 14 No. 781 y Reynaldo Santillán que vive en el No. 512 de la calle 19 y otros varios que dicen son Dios, que hacen multitud de cochinadas y brujerías, por las cuales cobran grandes sumas engañando a la gente incauta que acude a ellos con esperanzas de conseguir algún alivio, olvidando que Dios no especuló cuando vino al mundo y como ellos no son Dios como se hacen llamar, los censuramos y por lo tanto merecen el título de estafadores.

Guadalajara, Jal., Noviembre de 1941

LA COMISION.

FIG. 8. This flyer was sent to municipal authorities as part of a handwritten petition from two individuals claiming to represent a commission of neighbors concerned that spiritists and sorcerers threatened the spiritual and physical safety of young Catholic women in the neighborhood. Correspondencia, 1942, 1-1-08, AHMG. Courtesy of the Archivo Histórico Municipal de Guadalajara.

by "Rural Hygiene Week."[110] Aside from the parade, events included visits by health officials to *vecindades* to inspect living conditions, teach cleanliness, and offer free in-home medical consultations for women expecting children.[111] Individuals had the duty to help the wider community maintain health and safety not only in practice but also by reporting public health issues to officials.[112] Government at all levels provided religious *tapatíos* with the language that they hoped could unlock the state on their behalf.

Protestant versus Protestant disputes about hygiene also underscore the idea that the language of government armed working-class *tapatíos* against their religious opponents, though not necessarily as a means to achieve the state's liberal ends. In autumn 1942 the famed Guadalajara-based church known throughout Latin America as Luz del Mundo (the official name is La Iglesia del Dios Vivo, Columna y Apoyo de la Verdad, La Luz del Mundo) faced the tumult of an internal schism over pastoral authority and abuse.[113] Founded in Guadalajara in 1926, it had recently lost hundreds of members in Mexico City, with the conflict rippling back to the church's headquarters in Guadalajara. The division grew from disaffection with the group's founder, Eusebio Joaquín González (known to his followers as the Apostle Aaron), and his elevation beyond pastor into a prophet. The conflict may also have sprung from charges of sexual assault brought by a woman in the congregation against the group's leader.[114]

Disaffected members of Luz del Mundo challenged the legitimacy of the group's sacred space. In October 1942 twenty-seven members of the congregation wrote to city officials of Guadalajara denouncing alleged "anomalies, injustices and abuses" by the church and its leadership. They also attempted to sway authorities by saying that a chapel in the working-class eastern half of Guadalajara still failed to meet "the requisites of security and hygiene" in maintaining the building and keeping it clean.[115] Why did congregants think this might be an effective way to close the chapel? City health inspectors had closed the building in January 1942 (prior to the schism) for failure to meet construction standards relative to hygiene and zoning for buildings with large crowds. The inspection process kept the congregation out of the space for nearly four months and had city health officers inspecting the building regularly until August 1942.[116] In addition, the former municipal president of Tala, Jalisco, J. Jesús Nuñez (1934), signed the petition requesting the group's ouster from the chapel at no. 1680 calle Gigantes. An early convert to the group, by 1942 Nuñez had become a vocal opponent of the church as Apostle Aaron drew more power to himself. As a former municipal president, Nuñez had a working knowledge of municipal public works and health inspection services. Responding to the petition, the public works department dispatched inspectors to the building, but it remained under Apostle Aaron's control without closing.[117] The proposed line of attack had failed, but the attempt to close the building tempers the idea that only the civic encouragements of Catholic clergy or their associated groups such as ACM pushed congregants to work against religious opponents.

Other Protestant congregations, such as the Iglesia Apostólica de Fe en Cristo (one of the largest denominations in Mexico as of this writing), experienced similar disputes in which congregants attempted to use their position in the *junta vecinal* to activate city government on their side and seize the chapel from their church leadership to make it their own.[118] This complaint followed a decades-long dispute between congregants in Guadalajara and the church's leadership in northern Mexico as well as two prominent preachers, Monclovio Gaxiola and Melesio Gaxiola, two brothers who were working to expand the church.[119] In 1947 roughly 115 adults in the congregation complained that the Gaxiola brothers attempted to evict them from the no. 716 calle Zarco chapel built by congregants themselves on land donated by María de Jesús Mejorada. They noted how they had watched as the Gaxiola brothers had misappropriated construction materials and funds over the years to enrich themselves and how they expelled from the congregation any member who complained. Now they complained that another Gaxiola (Heriberto) was trying to impose an unqualified pastor on the congregation, and, as the government had the power to approve preachers, they begged that the city not agree to his appointment.[120] The dispute endured into the 1950s, with various courts and government officials siding with one faction or the other through the years.[121] These cases also cast aside the notion that only Catholics experienced laws regulating worship space and clerical registration.

Not only did non-Catholics have to follow laws regarding the use of religious space, but they also had to observe laws that prohibited foreign clergy. With the absence of foreign clergy and supervising missionaries, Protestant churches saw a growing divide between their congregations and their European or U.S. benefactors, who could no longer police the religious practice of their adherents in Mexico.[122] Mexican Protestants also had to master the same bureaucratic language as Catholics, because many non-Catholic groups failed to properly register with the state simply because they referred to themselves as a "church" (the state recognized no such entity) instead of a "neighborhood association." Even if the Secretaría de Gobernación granted exceptions, non-Catholics had to understand the rules from which they wanted relief or exemption, and they needed to ascertain the best way to navigate the language necessary to extract an exception. For example, in 1928 a different Anglican organization (the Iglesia Anglicana), requested permission for a foreigner to hold clerical services in Guadalajara.[123] The request specifically indicated that the foreign priest—Frank Creighton—would not be providing clerical guidance to Mexicans but only to English-speaking congregants (and thus only to foreigners).[124] Creighton requested a limited period of service (six years), during which Mexican Anglicans could train his Mexican replacements.[125] Though this request is the only one of its kind I encountered in the Guadalajara municipal archives, it demonstrates that even at the height of conflict between Catholics and the Mexican state, Protestants still needed to engage in rhetorical strategies to navigate or circumvent state regulation.

In the years of reconstruction and economic growth, religious Mexicans in Guadalajara harnessed the language of anticlericalism in areas such as productivity and hygiene. This practice expanded beyond the hierarchies of churches and became standard at the local level, whether employed by congregants in small Protestant movements or by Catholics annoyed with their Protestant neighbors. In the attempt of secularists to get religion out of government (by using the Constitution of 1917) and to disempower the religious, they unwittingly provided the average members of congregations with a new way to use the language of the government reformers to involve government in the affairs of religious disputes even more often, not less. President Calles and local politicians like Zuno might have "made clear that the new order would repress the only serious competitor" to state power, but it could not stop residents from seeking ways to bend that power to suit their own ends.[126] Every petition that reconciled the state's goals with the theological ends of various churches reinforced to its authors and congregants that they belonged to *tapatío* society.

In revolutionary Mexico, all levels of government from the Obregón administration (1920–24) forward emphasized hygiene, and Guadalajara's churches of all denominations adapted the language of hygiene to question the right of opposing churches to exist, thereby emphasizing the perceived power of language to shape space.[127] The strategy of using the language of science, hygiene, and rationalism has never been entirely absent from religious conflict in modern Mexico. Hygiene served as a tool in the conflict between baroque and Spanish Enlightenment Catholics during the Bourbon Reforms, and the Catholic hierarchy also attempted to quash popular religious expression using science during the independence era.[128] By the postrevolutionary period in Mexico, health and hygiene were already serving as "a new realm of authority: sensate experience carefully moderated by scientific reason."[129] However, health and hygiene also served as a "sensate authority" in a Kierkegaardian sense, in that it represented a temporal power and authority in the political world where religious Mexicans lived and participated.[130] For that reason, religious Mexicans excelled at assimilating the language and popular vocabulary of secular government to further their own goals or to ma ke conversations happening in religious contexts understood in secular contexts. Unlike the residents of Mexico City who resisted or ignored city policy regarding funerals and corpses, the religious residents of Guadalajara doubled down on rules and regulations to serve their own ends.[131]

Mexicans of faith recognized that the state actively used health to "control the country's regions as well as its residents' private habits and beliefs."[132] As such, the state ordered the physical and political world, but it also aided religious groups' attempts to order the spiritual world. Historiography on hygiene has followed engineer and writer Alberto J. Pani's lead in centering the state as the prime mover of health initiatives in the revolutionary era.[133] However, correspondence in the Guadalajara archives demonstrates how some Mexicans then appropriated that hygiene language to communicate the rewards they expected from the 1910 revolution and became "savvy negotiators and correspondents with the municipal authority."[134] In doing so, they oriented themselves in the community, finding a sense of belonging through religious conflict because conflict marked participation in the broader social conversation of the age and served as a narrative that reinforced a sense of belonging among the authors of petitions and letters.

But historian Christina Jiménez places brackets around the conceptualization of space and identity and the use of that negotiation power, focusing on what she sees as "the key relationship" in the city "between urban residents and the local government."[135] Her focus is on secular concepts of citizenship, citizen identity, public space, and public good, for which religion is a tradition from "the colonial past."[136] Jiménez argues that "*vecino* identity" empowered Mexicans to evoke "citizenship, public rights, and notions of accountability of belonging."[137] For many residents of Guadalajara, the key relationship for them existed between themselves, their community, and

God. A liberal state and secular revolution served as a means to improve that relationship.

If revolution meant the betterment of everyday life, why could it not provide a shelter for religious lives? While the state had created a dominant new secular discourse of health and hygiene, religious residents of Guadalajara learned to harness that language to their own holy ends and to carry on that conversation not just between themselves and the state but also between multiple social entities such as neighbors and churches. Historian Eric Van Young has argued that the Mexican Revolution of 1910 to 1920 largely lacked the messianic and local religious fervor present during the colonial-era movement for independence. While messianism may have largely been missing from the leadership of the 1910 revolution, "that most of the Mexican population, still so Catholic even today, should somehow have lost its religion in the century between 1810 and 1910 seems implausible, even if a degree of secularization did accompany the accelerating modernization process."[138] It seems just as implausible that all urban Mexicans would have abandoned their religious identity in total submission to liberal goals of hygienic civic identity alone. Rather, religious Mexicans adopted liberal hygienic language in defense of their enduring religious beliefs and sacred space, not in spite of them. What the religious use of hygienic language does, then, is to conceptualize the articulation between popular interpretations and applications of law "on one hand, and social, political, and cultural constraints on the other."[139]

The letters and petitions of both Catholics and Protestants use terms such as "honor" or "justice" and frequently refer to the patriotism of their various groups (and lack thereof in their opponents) for upholding the law. The reality in reading the city's limited responses to these groups can be almost heartbreaking to see in the face of such earnest enthusiasm from the petitioners. As the reader may have noted, few religious petitioners mentioned here seem to have accomplished their goals, at least completely. In Templo de Cristo's case, additional correspondence reveals a disinterest on the part of municipal officials regarding the Protestant church and the disturbance over its existence.

A January 1940 city inventory of churches lists the Templo de Cristo as still under construction, with some concern that the church might not be registered.[140] By February, a query from the federal Secretaría de Gobernación had arrived in Guadalajara asking if city officials had any concerns with registering the Templo de Cristo as a worship space. The city responded in April that it had no concerns.[141] Just two months later, in June 1940, the State of Jalisco queried the city statistics department as to the number of Episcopalian churches in the city. The city responded just twenty days later with the answer: none. Later that summer the State of Jalisco fine-tuned their request, asking the statistics division specifically if the Templo de Cristo on calle Molina offered services. The city responded in November 1940, stating that the church had opened to congregants in 1939 and that both the priest and the church had legal registration.[142] A final letter to the city once more related that the state government thought the *episcopales* on calle Molina had never registered: this letter came twenty-three years later (1963) and after Templo de Cristo had appeared consistently on inventories of Guadalajara churches for two decades.[143]

In fact, inventories of Protestant churches in Guadalajara and the clergy that staffed them could be inaccurate, and small Protestant house churches continued to skirt the law.[144] Even as the populace had an expectation that the intrusive state could be engaged on the level of hygiene, public health, patriotism, or justice regarding religious issues in the détente era of church/state relations, it was the gradual drift toward nonenforcement and general bureaucratic inefficiency that shielded all churches, not rigorous law enforcement or a change in written law. Alternatively, beyond simple inefficiency, perhaps what we see is a city apparatus that mobilized only when a group reached a critical population mass that warranted its inclusion in the network of informal corporate bodies that bound the party and the populace, such as happened with the aforementioned Luz del Mundo. When that group's membership grew to the point that they could populate their own neighborhood in the mid-1950s, the municipal government granted the church exemptions from planning regulations.[145] Connections, contexts, situations, and relationships defined a pragmatic governing style in 1940s Guadalajara and during the presidency of Ávila Camacho. Protestants and Catholics similarly found pragmatic paths forward. Both religious groups heard the Mexican state's goals and responded with their own efforts to make the state work for them on their own religious terms. This improvisation allowed them to create their own narratives of belonging to community in Guadalajara.

To read documents from the municipal archive of Guadalajara while centering the state reveals a limited story. Resolving issues of a religious nature did not rate as particularly important for city leaders facing a doubling population outstripping its supportive infrastructure. However, the value in the municipal correspondence archive is reading the intentions of religious *tapatíos* who took their own stand for local concerns and actively involved themselves in the city's physical space on multiple levels. By centering the petition authors, we see their aspirations during changing times and can thereby refocus on the strategies they employed in hopes of realizing their desires; they could harness the power of secular city government for what petitioners saw as both patriotic and holy ends. Just as important, that they wrote petitions and engaged in neighborhood conflict demonstrates that they felt a sense of belonging and the desire to fight for their place in the city. In this process of petitioning, they engaged in both the ritual and the creation of a narrative that defined their relationship to the city and its residents.

4   Concrete Requests

The processes of petitioning and conflict served as ritual acts of establishing belonging in the city, and the artifacts of petitioning functioned as narratives that reinforced to petitioners their place in society. What role did women play in these petitioning processes? As we have seen to this point, women led or participated in petitioning campaigns on a range of topics regarding the changing city. Particularly as seen in chapters 1 and 2, *tapatías* engaged in correspondence and conflict with city leaders, inspectors, and especially their neighbors in an effort to build urban space and a sense of place that aligned with their own. No gender norms excluded women from defending their use of private property, shaping the city's public spaces, or at times using both public and private spaces for purposes not always intended by city officials.

Women served as organizers and participants in a range of local movements to improve life in Guadalajara, and this has been well covered by various scholars.[1] However, an aspect of women's lives little examined or explicitly considered for the revolutionary era is that they shaped public space and the public sphere through their roles as property and business owners. Although Mexican law and social tradition saw property ownership as an acceptable role for women, many conceived of it as occurring in an imagined bifurcated world with a domestic sphere for women and a public sphere for men. Social custom in postindependence Mexico placed property ownership in women's domestic sphere. In this chapter I explore how *tapatía* women owned property and actively managed it to enrich or support themselves and their families and thereby physically shaped the urban space of Guadalajara. While their property development or business strategies often mirrored those of *tapatío* men, women also strategically used perceptions of gender to elicit desired responses from civic leaders or neighbors. In the process, the petitioning and conflict they engaged in to defend their businesses and properties served to instill in them a sense of belonging and give them an avenue for exhibiting their contributions to city life.

Building Women: *Tapatías* as Property Owners and Developers

Women as property owners in urban Mexico is a common occurrence, though few scholars have thoroughly examined women's work in actively shaping urban space through their property ownership. That women who owned property or contributed to the physical shaping of Guadalajara are almost invisible beyond a few key individuals in city chronicles is no surprise. Idealization of male engineers and architects runs deep within modern Mexican thought. Liberal thinker and historian Daniel Cosío Villegas, for example, dedicates much of his three volumes on "economic life" in his *Historia moderna de México* to the minutiae of engineering reports.[2] In Mexico after the 1910 revolution, educated men becoming engineers and architects represented an economic path forward into modernization that meshed well with the technocratic "politics of centrism" and focus on development and industry during the presidency of Manuel Ávila Camacho (1940–46).[3] Engineers built "a more permanent revolution within the material structures of Mexico—the city streets, highways, railroads, ports, irrigation, housing, factories and stadiums"—in an effort to leave "lasting peace and prosperity" as the revolution's legacy.[4]

A high-profile example of blindness toward women's role as property owners or of dismissiveness toward their importance involves a legendary moment in the construction of modern Guadalajara. When city leaders decided to widen avenida Juárez, they expropriated every building along the north side of the street—every building, that is, except the telephone exchange building, which the authorities considered too important to demolish. Instead, between October 24 and October 28, 1950, engineer Jorge Matute Remus and his workers picked up the 1,700-ton building and scooted it back to make way for the newly widened avenida Juárez. Even more notable, they moved the exchange while operators worked inside and kept connecting calls for western Mexico. This monumental project required hundreds of hours of legal maneuvering, planning, and labor, and for his efforts Matute Remus earned engineering awards in both Mexico and France.[5] Not often discussed in the reports on the project or among the accolades for Matute Remus is that women owned an existing building that had to be demolished so the telephone exchange could be slid into its new spot. In a 1996 interview, Matute Remus stated that moving the building and working with the telephone company had not been difficult; however, "convincing the women [*las señoras*] who owned the land where the building is now to sell their property—now that was hard."[6]

With a single quip, Matute Remus dismissed women as an active force, erased their names by simply calling them "*las señoras*," and labeled them as obstacles to his version of progress rather than as agents whose property allowed for growth and whose savvy negotiating power brought them security.[7] Rather than being the obstacle suggested by Matute Remus's remarks, women actively managed and developed property in the city. *Tapatía* property owners shaped the public spaces of Guadalajara and engaged with (or against) men in politics and the bureaucracy to make the city livable, aesthetically pleasing, a place of safety, and a space for economic opportunity. In very literal terms, women shaped the public urban space, built a sense of place, enriched themselves materially, and declared their position of belonging in Guadalajara. Let's look at an example and then review larger trends.

The *plaza de gallos* (cockfighting pit) at no. 339 calle 2 in Sector Reforma (today calle Insurgentes in the Analco neighborhood) is not a striking building. The 1939 remodeling plans show little remarkable about the building. In fact, as of this writing, the building still stands, and not much about it draws the attention of passersby. In addition to cockfights, the circular space also hosted *lucha libre* (wrestling) and boxing matches.[8] The building owner also rented it out for events and parties.[9] And unlike the anonymous but able "*señoras*" from behind the telephone exchange referenced above, we do know the owner of this building: Marina Ayala González. Thirty-two and single, she owned at least one other piece of property with her older sister, Otilia, in the nearby town of Tonalá. Ayala remodeled a small,

FIG. 9. This statue of Jorge Matute Remus celebrates the engineer for successfully moving the entire regional telephone building away from a street-widening project without disrupting phone service. The statue shows Matute Remus pushing the building, creating the image that the engineer worked as the primary force behind the street-widening project. Statues like this leave an impression of the men who built modern Guadalajara but say little about the women property owners who were instrumental in making the projects possible. Photo by the author.

two-bedroom apartment at the building's front. She had the roof repaired, added an indoor bathroom, and separated the dining area from the kitchen. Considering that her family owned properties in Chapala and Tonalá, it is unlikely that Ayala lived in the space in this working-class neighborhood, and she most likely rented it out (or it served as caretaker rooms), just as she did with the *plaza de gallos*.[10]

Marina Ayala's property repair represents just one of hundreds of licenses for reconstructions and new construction issued to women in Guadalajara between 1939 and 1947. City officials issued 7,301 licenses during those years, and 2,407 went to clearly identifiable women property owners. That number represents 32.9 percent, or one-third of all construction and remodeling licenses issued.[11] Some scholars hold that the revolutionary era signals a decline in respect that women received as property owners and marks a decrease in women's ability to manage property that they did not regain until the late twentieth century.[12] This view emerged from research on rural areas where the central government and its various state-level revolutionary experiments undertook distribution of agricultural land and intentionally blocked or limited most women from holding title to distributions. They did so by arguing that adding women as title holders would place undue pressure on communities by fragmenting parcels into smaller lots incapable of sustainable agricultural production. Other rural investigations of women property holders focused on the vast agricultural holdings of hacienda owners in the colonial era and nineteenth century or in Indigenous communities during the early years after the European invasion.[13] John Tutino, for instance, has charted how powerful oligarchic women challenged patriarchy as silver capitalism declined and Mexico transitioned to independence, as well as how women used their power in property to fight for Mexican independence.[14] Finally, a third area of scholarly study addresses the relationship between urban property and divorce (generally excluding a discussion of single women) or property patterns in the colonial and nineteenth-century eras, primarily in central Mexico.[15] Still others made strides in examining either early or late twentieth-century women as business owners, particularly in alcohol or market vending.[16] For the mid-twentieth century, however, we know very little about women as business and urban property owners.

While we can see that some women—such as the *solteras* Marina and Otilia, who had no brothers or brothers-in-law at the time of their property development—managed individual properties, other women tackled far larger projects. Carlota Cano de Carballo subdivided several hectares into thirty-eight lots in the quickly growing area along southern avenida Colón.[17] The daughter of one of the principal families of the city, she called the much older businessman Domingo Carballo Espada of Spain her husband, and together they had five children.[18] She also developed two more properties along the Calzada de Independencia. The Calzada represented an expanding commercial zone running south out of central Guadalajara. One property had two stories, with the first floor occupied by a large commercial space while the second story contained a five-bedroom apartment. The second building differs from the properties previously mentioned, as both wife and husband owned it, and both signed the development request for the lots. This building had a series of four connected single-story storefronts. It would be tempting to see this as a case of husbands controlling jointly held property, and that still might be the case. However, that Carlota developed the other two properties without her husband's signature (meaning she had sole ownership) indicates the possibility of other independent projects. At the very least, it is possible that she actively engaged in developing both the marital community property with her husband as well as the individual holdings she brought with her into the marriage or accumulated for herself later.[19]

We might conclude that the 1910 revolution and the first Cristero War took their toll on the number of men in the city and increased the percentage of women owning and developing property in Guadalajara. Several factors resist this narrative, however, and differentiate Guadalajara from Mexico City and the capital's growing population of women due to the 1910 revolution.[20] The population of Guadalajara already numbered at least 5 percent more women than men before the 1910 revolution and the 1926 Cristero War.[21] The applications for construction licenses offer several ways to indicate the marital status of applicants, and that status is apparent for 61.5 percent of applicants. The most common is that the letter of application from the property owner indicated marital status via the labels *señorita*, *señora*, *viuda de*, or *célibe* (young, unmarried, married, widow, or never

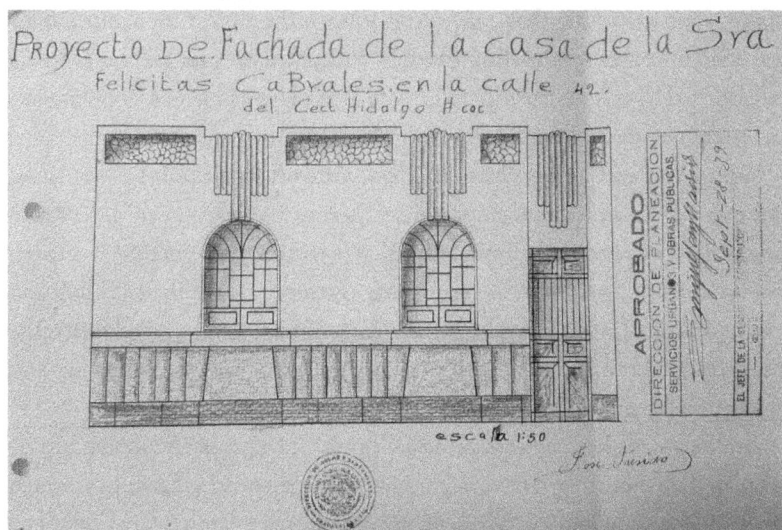

FIG. 10. Blueprint for a project to remodel the façade of the home of Felicitas Cabrales. This is an example of both remodeling work and women's ownership of a smaller property. Licencias para Construcción, 1939, plano 266, AHMG. Courtesy of the Archivo Histórico Municipal de Guadalajara.

married). Blueprints submitted with the letter of application also signaled the property owner's marital status by using *señorita*, *señora*, or *viuda de*. Finally, the return letter from city officials also responded to a *señorita* or a *señora* and on occasion *viuda de*, if the clerk wrote out the applicant's full name. In analyzing the records, widows account for the smallest number of property owners, at approximately 11 percent of total applications of both women and men.

We might then think that single women would be the largest group; having inherited property from their families, they would have greater freedom to choose or reject marriage and manage their own property affairs. Nevertheless, single women take second place at approximately 21 percent of total applications. Married women made up the largest number of property owners, at 28.5 percent of total applications. More simply, in applications where marital status of women appears, married women represent 46.5 percent, single women 35 percent, and widows 18.5 percent.[22] Just under 40 percent of applications from women carried no indication of marital status, demonstrating that a significant proportion of women applied for construction and remodeling permits without their marital status being considered by city authorities. The role men played in managing women's property clearly had limitations.[23]

Education and employment are also difficult to pinpoint using these records. In the rare cases among these permits when women indicated a status that references employment, it states either "*sin profesión*" (without profession) or "*propietaria*" (property owner). Unlike the middle-class and working-class women of Mexico City linked to a labor identity, the *tapatías* in these records used property to establish their standing and sense of belonging in society.[24]

Still, it might be easy to read more power into property ownership by women than there might have been. As scholar Shauna Huffaker has argued in reference to women as property owners in the Islamic world, scholars should be cautious at being overly optimistic about women's agency when fathers, husbands, brothers, or actors in the state might limit women's use of property.[25] Certainly in the case of Guadalajara construction permits in the correspondence collection, limitations on women are visible. There are cases when the property of a woman is dealt with as a family property, where a husband is writing for his wife, or where a father is developing his underage daughter's property under *patria potestas* (*patria potestad* in U.S. legal parlance means parental authority). Of the 2,407 licenses, those incidences of clear intervention by men account for 11 cases (0.4 percent). Still, permits cannot report on conditions in the home and the level of discussion among family members on the use of property. Neither can those records account for any cases where a man might hide property under the name of a wife, sister, or other relative.

It was also difficult to consistently see the income and class level of each woman based on construction-related correspondence and permits after I cross-referenced them with genealogical records and other municipal documents (by creating a database of all women's names in the records I consulted). It was difficult even to ascertain if the buildings these women built are still standing today or to pinpoint their exact location. Even if one is able to navigate the changing street names (the city changed its entire street-naming system from names to numbers and then partially back again), house numbers often followed families when they moved and adhered to no strict ascending or descending order in this era.

However, we get a simple view of class privilege when we consider the sector where the building activity occurred. City planners divided Guadalajara into four administrative sectors. Sectors Juárez and Hidalgo generally contained more upper-class residences (though not exclusively), while Sectors Libertad and Reforma generally contained the lower middle and working classes. Though street addresses are difficult to pinpoint with certainty, the sector indicated on the applications is easy to track. Officials issued 33 percent of permits to Hidalgo residents and 28 percent to people in Sector Juárez. Those two areas are the wealthiest sectors. Libertad accounted for 21 percent of construction permits, with the solidly working-class Reforma sector in the southeast coming in at 18 percent. While this does reflect the number of applications per sector, it does not account for the size of construction projects, the number of people in each building, type of construction, and so on. Such a breakdown requires additional quantification and analysis.

The prominence of some families, however, makes their larger stories somewhat more accessible. Some women building homes came from connected political families in the ruling party's Jalisco wing. For example, Virginia Iñíguez de Parra purchased and repaired at least two buildings during the time under study. One was a single-story construction with a house on one side and space for a business on the corner, and another was a two-story building with two apartments on the second story and two businesses on the first floor.[26] Less is known about Iñíguez de Parra than her husband, Alfonso Parra Zepeda. The two had shared seventy-one years of marriage at the time of her death in 1996. It is difficult to imagine that her property holdings remained independent of his political position.[27] Parra Zepeda served as a delegate in the city's Secretaría de Hacienda, working in license enforcement, then as municipal treasurer of Guadalajara, and eventually as the State of Jalisco's pension fund director.[28] While Iñíguez de Parra exercised no formal political power, her property deals in the 1940s may have paved the way for her husband's political ascension in the PRI apparatus in later years. It could even be that the property originated with Parra Zepeda, but the couple decided to shelter the property under Iñíguez de Parra's name for political or financial reasons. Alternatively, it could be that her property holdings increased each time Parra Zepeda ascended a rung of the party's ladder of power.[29]

New constructions and renovations are not the deepest or only footprints made by women in the urban landscape of Guadalajara. The Archivo de Instrumentos Públicos del Estado de Jalisco (AIPEJ) contains the notarial records of property transactions for the State of Jalisco, including the *municipio* of Guadalajara. Of 1,840 property transactions sampled in the notary records between 1939 and 1947, 1,412 involved women as either buyers or sellers, or about 76.7 percent of property transactions. To break that down, sales by women to other women account for 23.75 percent, sales of men to women reached 21.68 percent, and sales from women to men account for 31 percent.[30] In short, women bought, sold, and developed property at a significant level in Guadalajara in the 1940s. This percentage is a marked increase from urban property ownership in the colonial era of roughly 16 percent.[31]

The importance of women in property sales and development increases after considering how growth in Guadalajara took place: between 1940 and 1950, 69 percent of expansion occurred on private land.[32] Because the cost of public housing appeared prohibitive to political leaders, the private sector met housing needs for the working class in Guadalajara on readily available private land. Consequently, building housing for average residents (not just luxury developments) netted profits for developers.[33] While scholars such as John Walton have pointed out that private Mexican developers and businesses invested heavily in real estate, while foreign investors focused on industry, he and others have not recognized that women participated in property development.[34] In form and function, both the construction permit and the notary records present us with archives of possession, documenting the property ownership and power of women in 1940s Guadalajara.[35]

The network of single sisters, nieces, and female cousins from the Asencio family serves as an example of women with extensive property networks in Guadalajara.[36] Juliana Orozco and her husband, Manuel Asencio, had at least ten children, six of them daughters who never married. Originally hailing from Arandas, Jalisco, the family had relocated to Guadalajara permanently by 1900. By 1930 Manuel and Juliana had both died, and their sons and daughters then lived in two homes in an upper-middle-class neighborhood on calle Hidalgo, snug against San Miguel del Espíritu Santo (a church finished in 1904 and elevated to parish status in 1917).[37] Amalia Orozco de Asencio and her husband, Emilio Asencio Orozco, as well as their ten children (seven daughters and three sons) made their home at no. 1187 calle Hidalgo. Next door, at no. 1193 Hidalgo, we find Emilio's older brother Francisco, younger brother Ignacio, and five sisters: María Guadalupe, María de Jesús, María Inés, Juliana, and María Encarnación. While none of the sisters had married, Emilio had already married and been widowed twice, leaving him with four children.[38] By 1936 both Emilio and Francisco had died, leaving a bevy of aunts with significant property investments in Jalisco and Colima to guide their brothers' children.

Juliana, born in 1886, left a paper trail of the most actively managed property. Between 1939 and her passing in 1946, Juliana engaged in fourteen confirmed property transactions, all purchases. The transactions ranged from small houses on lots valued at 100 pesos to a housing development in Colonia Villaseñor for 1,200 pesos.[39] What did she do with her properties? A cross-referencing of her property purchases with construction licenses suggests that Juliana developed property lots into multiple housing units and then rented them out.[40] This also appears to be the case with her sister-in-law Amalia; sisters María Guadalupe, María Inés, María de Jesús, and María Encarnación; and nieces María Mercedes, María del Carmen, Adelaida, and Esperanza, who also purchased and developed houses around the city's south, as well as farmland near Tlaquepaque.

When an Asencio woman died, who received their holdings? A June 1940 will and testament left by María de Jesús Asencio gives us a clue as to how some women divided their property. After making her declaration of faith, María de Jesús requested that all her property be divided between her sisters María Inés and Juliana.[41] Leaving property to sisters and other women in the family is a pattern. A survey of other testaments left by single Asencio women indicates that they unanimously privileged their own sisters, nieces, and single female cousins when bequeathing their property. The Asencio family cultivated a wide family network originating in Arandas, Jalisco, and it included distant cousins Jacoba Asencio and María Agustina Asencio Padilla. These women also appeared as *soltera, propietarias,* or *célibe* (single, property holders, or never married) on notary records, and they also left all of their property to their sisters.[42] Finally, despite all of their work as developers and rental proprietors, they frequently listed themselves as *"sin profesión por su sexo"* (no employment for reason of gender), indicating their status in society as women wealthy enough to not need employment outside the home.[43]

Women could also be involved in more detailed property exchanges with family members. In 1944 Magdalena Calleros Iñíguez purchased the house where she lived with her father on calle Liceo, close to the cathedral in the heart of the city. Magdalena bought the home from the company Magdalena Calleros y Hermanos; records list her father, Ramón Calleros Moreno (age seventy-four), as the company manager.[44] Ramón came to Guadalajara from rural Jalisco (Zacoalco de Torres) at the turn of the twentieth century, marrying there in 1905 and eventually becoming the owner of at least three small industrial businesses: a lumberyard, a tannery, and a braided cordage (or possibly braided fishing line) factory. He lived until 1953. It is possible that Ramón intended the transaction for the home of 508 square meters (just over 5,400 square feet) to provide security for the unmarried Magdalena as he aged.[45] The full nature of the business owned by Magdalena and her brothers is not discussed in the records, but Magdalena is listed as a *"contador titulado"* (certified accountant). In another example from 1939 of a woman managing a business with family, Mariana Alvarado registered her new small-goods store (*tienda de abarrotes*). A single woman who never married, Mariana entered the business with her brother as equal partners. Her profession, however, appears in the records as teacher in a public school (*profesora normalista*).[46]

The civil registry privileges information on reproduction, the married, and the dead, but the notarial records and construction licenses open up an entire world of women's lives for those of various statuses. As Huffaker has argued, it is not enough to see that women owned property; we must also consider the nature of that ownership and how it is used.[47] We see women engaged in building a network of businesses across a growing city, investing their funds in strategic areas of Guadalajara that are exploding with both the inflow of migrant workers from the countryside and a growing Mexican middle class. Property records also let us imagine family networks of sisters,

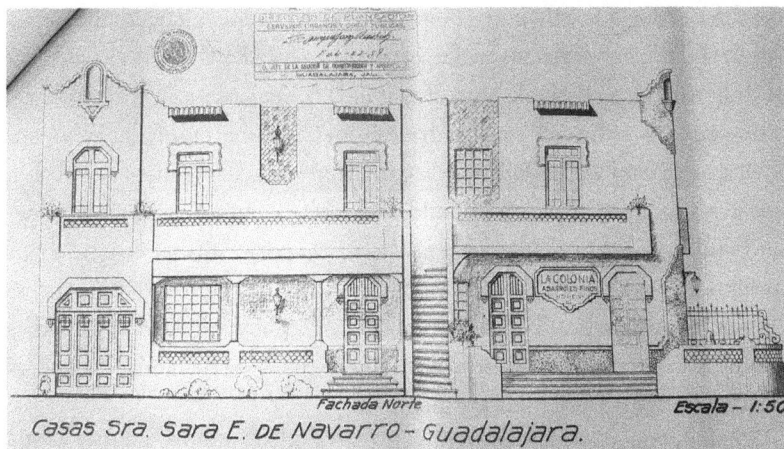

Casas Sra. Sara E. DE Navarro - Guadalajara.

Fachada Norte   Escala - 1:50

FIG. 11. Blueprint for new construction for Sara E. de Navarro. This building still sits at the same location as of this writing. It is an example of a multifamily residence in combination with a business. Licencias para Construcción, 1939, plano 72, AHMG. Courtesy of the Archivo Histórico Municipal de Guadalajara.

nieces, and female cousins who cared for each other and used their material resources to make a final declaration of love or support at their death. The construction registration and notary records give us a picture of women and their use of property, particularly in relation to its use in families, but the materials in the correspondence archive give us another perspective. Letters from women to the city help us envision a past where women actively managed the property. While we may have seen women in business and property ownership in the notary records, in the correspondence archive we see their level of involvement in managing property.

For example, Micaéla Larios de Arocha joined her fellow property owners in first challenging the expansion of avenida Niños Héroes. Once a small street on the city's southern edge, by the mid-1940s Niños Héroes was a significant thoroughfare whose widening required extensive property con-demnations.[48] In 1947 Larios not only signed petitions to city officials for better reimbursement but also had permission from her brother Isidro to advocate for him because he lived in Santa Maria, California, in the United States. It is telling that Isidro authorized his sister to advocate for him and not his brother Marcial, who also petitioned for reimbursement. Eventually the three siblings and their neighbors won the fight.[49] Incidentally, the Larios family did not have extreme wealth, with Isidro listed on his U.S. World War II draft card as a vegetable worker and in U.S. censuses as a farmworker.[50] Authors such as Daniel Vázquez have argued that the "good families" and the "known families" of Jalisco relied on property accumulation for wealth, social status, and the power to build Guadalajara, but a myriad of working- and middle-class property owners also participated in shaping the space around them and manifesting their belonging to the city.[51] Both the process of buying property and engaging in its development or defense served as tools for women to orient themselves in the changing urban landscape, as well as to have a hand in its shaping.

Women engaged with government frequently on issues related to the care of their homes, rental properties, and businesses in Guadalajara. In doing so, they demonstrated their active knowledge of city laws and urban planning and worked to make the city a livable space and protect the wealth they had invested in property. This is a textbook example of engaging in a narrative of belonging as women expressed their value to the community around them. Additionally, like the often women-led petitioners discussed in previous chapters, the individual petitioners to the city hoped to pressure bureaucrats to be more responsive. Candelaria Espinoza drafted a letter to the city in March 1943, complaining that another woman with a portable wooden stand had set up on the sidewalk in front of her own store. Since Espinoza ran a general goods convenience store, she said the stand "is a threat to my interests as it is an open air store selling groceries, aspirin and other medicines." To get the stand moved, Espinoza took several approach- es so that the municipal authorities saw her not only as aligned with their interests but also as deserving of their response.[52]

Espinoza began her letter by pointing out her nationality as well as her address in the respectable Sector Reforma. She then indicated that she ran a small store and stayed current on her taxes and licenses, "as I like to have all my business well ordered according to the law," she adds. This contrasted, according to Espinoza, to the nuisance wooden stall blocking the movement of people and traffic (she did not mention its license status). Speaking the state's language, Espinoza informed the city that she participated in their plans for development and prosperity in Guadalajara by running a business, but it rested entirely in their hands if she would be remaining that way. The wooden stand, she argued, cut into the sales she needed to cover the costs of her store. Those sales kept her an honest Mexican and helped, she said, "cover my taxes to the state."[53] After an inspection by city officials, it appears that Espinoza had both exaggerated the stand's size and lied about its inventory, with inspectors reporting that the stall owner sold nothing in competition with the complaint's author. Still, her attempt to mobilize the city on her behalf had been somewhat successful, getting a city inspector on the spot within five days of receiving her letter.

Women also used their knowledge of city services and law to either gain access to resources or change their economic relationship with the city of Guadalajara. Carmen Somellera Martínez Gallardo contacted the municipal offices to request records regarding her property. Unmarried and the heir of nineteenth-century Spanish immigrants from Santander with commercial investments around western Mexico, she developed property in various areas of what became the city's working-class southeast.[54] Her actions with regard to undeveloped and rural lands aligned with those taken by a landed family stretching back to the colonial period.[55] Later, Somellera Martínez donated land for the creation of the Ciudad Universitaria neighborhood and the accompanying Centro Universitario de Ciencias Exactas e Ingenierías of the Universidad de Guadalajara.[56] However, in this particular correspondence, she dealt with issues of expansion. As construction of new streets connecting Guadalajara with the nearby towns of Tlaquepaque and Tonalá progressed, the value of her rural properties declined. Somellera Martínez adjusted their value down with the State of Jalisco land office to reduce her tax burden.

Women who inherited wealth from their family agricultural estates managed large property concerns, but women of more modest means also dealt with the day-to-day issues affecting them, their businesses, renters, and families. In this way they not only managed their properties but also reinforced in writing their position in society as *propietarias* to whom the city belonged and where they belonged. For example, the widowed Cecilia Camarena de Leal faced property damage due to water runoff exacerbated by poor paving installed by the city near her home. Camarena herself negotiated a reduction of costs for development in the area, and that offset her losses on the property damage.[57] Mundane but far more common, women's negotiation with city officials regarding water billing disputes demonstrated their active management of property. With limitations on the availability of potable water, the city utility office billed by the number of *tomas* or *mercedes* (shares of water used) allotted based on the home's size, number of people, and types of water use. Frequently the city overcharged its water customers, and women requested an inspection to lower their water bills. The city itself recognized that it frequently undercharged owners of the largest properties and overcharged smaller property owners, and it cited that practice as one reason that people in the city suffered from a lack of water in "an almost distressing way in recent times."[58]

For example, when María Trinidad Verduzco asked for an evaluation of her home after being charged for multiple water uses, the inspector found "one sitting room, one bedroom, and a plumbed kitchen" and reduced her costs to a single *merced*.[59] In another case, in April 1947, Dr. María González Rodríguez (a single woman living across from Morelos Park) noted to officials that of all her neighbors, only she lacked water service. Recounting to the municipal president that she had written, telephoned, and visited the relevant municipal office in person without a satisfactory outcome, she demanded that the municipal president intervene. His office forwarded her demand to the public works office, and by June 1947 repairs on the water line got underway.[60] Whether in the mundane affairs of water and sewer bills or the negotiation of property values and property use, women directly engaged with municipal authorities over the management of their property.

Because women owned and developed multiple properties, some naturally served as *terratenientes*, or landladies. While this situation came with profits that could help sustain them or a family, renter relationships required property-owning women to be actively engaged in management. For María Nieves Patiño, the lack of renters who followed city regulations proved frustrating. In January 1946 the city fined Nieves Patiño because her renter ran an unregistered bakery on the property (all bakeries had to be licensed and approved by city health and safety inspectors). The woman made an *amparo* (judicial appeal) to authorities requesting that the fine be revoked because her tenant had assured her that he had been inspected. When authorities confirmed that the illegal baker had failed to produce paperwork for Nieves Patiño, they let the fine stand, saying she should have been more vigilant about her renters.[61] In another case, Victoria Madrigal tried to balance her cantina business with renter safety. After a flood undermined the foundations of her establishment at no. 501 avenida Colón in the Nueve Esquinas neighborhood, the bar and rental units became unusable.[62] Unfortunately, Madrigal could not convince her second-floor tenants that their safety required their eviction, and she asked police to remove the squatters before the building collapsed. Property ownership required that women take on the risk of loss, particularly to tenants. They hoped to mitigate that risk by turning to city officials for help in protecting their property and renters.

Women also used their property to contribute to the revolution's goals, though much like the era's bureaucrats, whether they did so from belief or for profit (or both) is mostly unknowable. For example, education was a primary goal of national leaders, and women served as key owners of rental properties used for public schools in Guadalajara. Despite rhetoric at the national level supporting the funding of public education, as the city grew in the 1940s few new public schools were constructed. Instead, the city negotiated with private property owners to rent properties for use as public schools. Parents begged the city for more schools, as they did in an example from the El Retiro neighborhood. That area boasted a university medical school and new government buildings but no public school for children. The people of El Retiro complained that children walked fifteen blocks to get to school even though the government had already built other administrative buildings in their area.[63] Why couldn't one of those buildings be a school?

Guadalajara had such a pronounced shortage of schools that in 1946, when Concepción Ocampo Vda. de Rosas attempted to end her contract with the city, officials denied her request and forced her to keep renting to them due to the "very few locations" for schools. Why did Ocampo try to get out of her contract? Because of "age and failing health," the woman needed to sell her own home as well as a portion of her property, leaving her a small portion to live on. The widowed Ocampo was just one of a wide range of women renting to the public school system.

In 1941 city officials issued fourteen contracts for public school rental properties: nine contracts went to women and five to men. For the women's contracts, three went to single women, three to married women, and three to widows. No couples or families received contracts. In 1942 Francisca Herrera Vda. de Velázquez and her daughter María Refugio Velázquez Vda. de Tsubuku signed at least two contracts for school properties and received advance payments on the rents for both.[64] Refugio in particular needed the payments: she cared for her aged mother, Francisca; her husband, Dr. Guillermo K. Tsubuku, had died; and she had at least one teenager at home (her daughter Lilian).[65] The school contracts helped a widowed mother caring for both a child and an aging parent to survive in the city and fill the community's need for educational resources.

Other women, such as Maclovia Jiménez, provided the city's public works department with access to springs on her land so that working-class people would have their desperate need for water fulfilled.[66] María Guadalupe Jiménez developed a formidable nineteenth-century property that belonged to her family, turning it into a much-needed public hospital.[67] Mexicans also remember Carmen Arce de Zuno in the public sphere as wife to José Guadalupe Zuno, the socialist mayor of Guadalajara and later governor of Jalisco. She also bore twelve children, one of whom went on to be the First Lady of Mexico (María Esther Zuno Arce de Echeverría, 1970–76). Left out of her biography, however, is her construction of working-class housing developments in the 1940s, when Guadalajara lacked affordable housing of any kind.[68]

One type of land deal that women frequently engaged in was the purchase of a cemetery plot for themselves or family members. With private burial plots regulated by hygiene laws to near nonexistence and a limit on the size of private graves and crypts, the business of securing a plot in a city-owned cemetery could be difficult, and hanging on to that plot after the burial might be even more so. Buyers had to pay off the plot in a lump sum or in monthly payments, as well as pay a small yearly fee to keep their relatives in the burial space. Such payment schedules led to disinterment and disposal procedures that drew complaints from residents.[69]

Many women took on the task of keeping possession of their ancestors' plots, as well as guaranteeing a plot for themselves so that those they left behind would not have to deal with the matter. Securing a plot at a reduced price or for free required some understanding of what would generate a sympathetic response from city leaders. For example, Marina Quijas asked for and received a free plot because her father served in the 1910 revolution and for years as a police officer in Guadalajara.[70] Around the same time as Quijas's appeal, Catalina Trujillo also requested a free plot for her father but without any reference to the revolution or having any city connections. The financially struggling woman had less luck than Quijas. City officials responded that they, too, struggled financially and denied the request. However, they did offer her a 50 percent discount on the plot and a payment plan of 10 pesos a month.[71] Access to a plot could also be determined by the supplicant's willingness to accept a smaller plot. Plots came in various sizes, from first-class plots of three square meters that accommodated larger tombs, down to fourth-class plots of much humbler aspect. Some women attempted to haggle plot sizes and prices with the city in a sort of marketplace of death. For example, María Refugio Velázquez in 1945 attempted (unsuccessfully) to trade up from her second-class plot of two and a half square meters to a larger first-class plot of three square meters so she could improve the space with a small *capilla* (chapel or crypt).[72]

Connections, however, sometimes ameliorated the financial burden of burial costs. For example, Carmen Gil appealed to the city for a third-class plot for her mother, Sofía Herrera. Herrera, she argued, had "given service to the state in various roles for various officials" over the years. No specific mention of those roles appears in the short letter, but not only did officials grant Gil's request, but the city also upgraded her burial space to a first-class plot.[73] The city death registry confirmed the move with a note stating that "she is to be buried in a first-class plot by order of the Municipal President."[74] Whatever her role in state government, her connections and network in Jalisco proved influential enough to ease the financial burden on her daughter after her passing.[75]

From the banal management of water bills, to the dramatic development of entire neighborhoods and the care of ancestral remains, women managed property directly. This stands in contrast to women of earlier eras forced by social expectations to be more circumspect and employ men as managers of property and businesses.[76] These *tapatías* may have been connected to larger family networks or simply managed property as best they could as single women with few connections, attempting to engage authorities in an effort to better the city they loved. Every registration of a building, every water record complaint, every piece of property passed to a niece or sister also emphasized the material and communal ways that women belonged in the city, as well as the way the city belonged to them. Far from being some imagined world of a private domestic sphere, property ownership and active management placed women squarely in the active, public sphere shared by all genders.

Managing Women:
Women as Small Business Owners and Entrepreneurs

For many women, the management of property also included the management of businesses. While scholarly research on working women in Guadalajara tends to examine them as laborers and not owners, women directly operated their own businesses.[77] Considering the limitations of public city records, what good is the registration of an act or the archiving of a piece of paper if it does not contain the historical subject's voice? In the correspondence archive's case, we are looking at more than form letters, a smattering of biographical information, and some names jotted down in registry books. From the letters and petitions submitted by women, we are able to see how they wanted the city government to see them, how they thought their city should be run, the development of their own expertise in urban planning, and how they wanted city officials to see the way they interacted with their neighbors, customers, and business associates.

María Hirata Aoki serves as a good starting introduction to the small-business women of Guadalajara. Hirata Aoki operated a small café and ice cream parlor on the southern part of calle Independencia at its junction with avenida Juárez in a retail expansion area. She does not indicate in her letter to the city whether she is Mexican by birth or naturalization in the way that many Mexicans did when writing to the authorities. Other Hirata family members in Guadalajara became naturalized citizens before World War II. The family was later moved to Guadalajara by the Mexican government in 1943 as a larger relocation of Japanese Mexicans and Japanese nationals away from the coasts.[78] María Hirata Aoki may even have lived nearby in the working-class neighborhood of San José de Analco, an area that had been the center of life for many Japanese Mexicans and where the Aoki family appears in the local Catholic parish records.[79] She did not indicate her national origins or citizenship status, but she clearly declared herself a *propietaria* (property owner).

The subject of Hirata Aoki's letter also demonstrates her knowledge and ability to protect her property. She understood city ordinances and knew that inspectors could not charge an annual registration fee for her business. She stated directly in her letter that after reading the official periodical of the State of Jalisco from December 26, 1946, she knew that the state legislature exempted cafés and ice cream parlors from licensing fees. Nevertheless, inspectors had repeatedly levied fines against her business for lack of licenses. Hirata Aoki refused to pay, and she instead demanded that city officials step in and deal with the corrupt inspectors. Their imposition of informal fees formed a fundamental part of the "black economy" and constituted one of several kinds of bribes and shakedowns referred to popularly as a *mordida* (literally meaning a bite).[80] The letter from Hirata Aoki produced a single response from the city: she was correct, no annual payment was required, she owed no fines, and all she had to do was pay her regular taxes. María Hirata Aoki not only owned her own business but understood the rules governing it and willingly challenged inspectors to protect her business. No matter her national origin or gender, her correspondence declared her membership in the wider community and underscored her position as a business owner aware of state and city laws and her ability to defend herself.

Women owned and operated a wide variety of businesses across the city, and these business operators' communications with the city lay bare women's participation in the commercial world and how it drove the economy of Guadalajara. The widow Esperanza M. Vda. de Maupomé, for example, ran a business in the Mexicaltzingo neighborhood in which she loaded and sold shotgun shells, while Concepción M. Vda. de Ramírez (also a widow) sold Remington hunting rifles.[81] Enedina Michel took her business to another level by making, transporting, and using industrial explosives for construction.[82] Others, like tailors Hilda Lange and Virginia Vargas, found themselves thrust into the spotlight through the suspicions of their neighbors. When the neighbors of calle 5 in Sector Hidalgo became suspicious of the single, widowed, German national (Lange) and her Mexican employee

(Vargas) for conduct unbecoming of women, they reported them to police as sex workers. For many of Mexico's polite society, "the prostitute was a woman alone" whose autonomy alarmed *gente decente*. In Lange we see a woman both alone (a widow) and autonomous (a business owner).[83] Mexicans in the mid-twentieth century routinely leveled charges of prostitution against working women in commercial enterprises with male customers.[84]

Outraged, Lange responded to the chief of police with a scathing letter, laying out that as tailors, she and Vargas were poor women but still deserved the respect that every woman should receive. Lange flipped the script on gender and used it as a strategy to garner respect for her business dealings. She said she could put the city in contact with all the respectable people with whom she did business and others who knew her. However, she would much rather have a list from the city: Lange demanded an accounting of all the neighbors who complained about her so that she could charge them with the crimes of "calumny and defamation of honor."[85] Women in Guadalajara faced the challenges of corrupt city officials, daily business management, and nosy neighbors in their quest to care for themselves and their property. Like other women whose documents remain in the correspondence archive, Hilda Lange matched threats to property and reputation with equal ferocity. Her declarations made it clear she saw herself not as a subject for wagging tongues but as a person with honorable connections across society and someone who contributed to and belonged in Guadalajara. For Lange, her profession, nationality, and marital status had nothing to do with her sense of belonging in *tapatío* urban society, and her counterattack reinforced to her and city officials her right to claim membership in the community.

Frequently, of course, women's managing of property and engaging with the city aligned with strategies to benefit their own businesses and use city rules to undercut competition. For example, María Refugio Higareda had five files in the correspondence archive, all routine requests for a license to open either a tortilla stand, a corn-grinding stand, or a combination of both. The records stretch from 1941 to 1947 and, taken individually, are unremarkable. Taken together, however, we see not a simple tortilla vendor, whom the historiography often refers to as hired labor, but instead a canny entrepreneur.[86]

In 1941 the city granted Higareda permission to install a nixtamal grinder, a machine that turns maize kernels into dough for tortillas. Electric grinder use had grown since the 1920s, though some women still applied for permits to use gas or diesel grinders in the 1940s.[87] There is no indication if the city government gave her the grinder as part their crusade to unchain women from the manual labor of grinding kernels into nixtamal dough by hand.[88] Indeed, because of her use of electricity, she had to delay installing her nixtamal stand until she had a reliable electric outlet, causing a man with his own stand to charge that she had failed to provide the neighborhood with fresh tortillas and therefore lost the right to own and run the nixtamal stand. Higareda not only defeated her challenger and installed her electric grinder; that year she also took over two stands of another male nixtamal grinder.

Higareda grabbed up another stand in 1944; in 1945 she took over nine more stands, and by 1947 she had acquired at least one more before disappearing from the public record. Although Higareda enlisted the nixtamal grinder union's help to defeat the man who attempted to take her location in 1942, she did not rely on the union in subsequent years to seize the other stands (or at least she did not involve city officials in those efforts). She ran a business with locations throughout the city and developed (according to the records) only women as business partners and employees who helped her create a small tortilla empire based on buying out other vendors, all of them men. During the same time that Higareda expanded her tortilla business, not all women experienced success, particularly as laborers in tortilla and nixtamal production. Men dominated the Guadalajara unions that represented the larger nixtamal and tortilla facilities and ruled via sympathetic women, who purged radical women agitating for better pay and conditions from the business.[89] Similarly, in Mexico City, the mechanization of tortilla production and grinding shifted production to men and pushed down women's wages.[90] On the street, María Higareda carved out her own space and removed men from local neighborhood production. This is just one of many examples of small business owners who built their networks around the city but also deftly used laws to sabotage their competitors, often successfully engaging inspectors and even the courts to defeat their rivals.

Revolutionary Urban Belonging and Public Space

Jocelyn Olcott has brilliantly explored the "contingent, inhabited, and gendered" aspects of citizenship in her path-making *Revolutionary Women in Postrevolutionary Mexico*. Denied access to the vote and elected office by the ruling party, women in Mexico demonstrated their citizenship (the term used by Olcott) in the revolution by engaging in levels of social activism appropriate for their local and regional context, national and transnational trends, and gender norms.[91] Unlike political and social activism, however, the ownership and management of property fell within acceptable gender norms and did not risk relegating the owner to the status of *marimacha* (tomboy).[92] For women property owners, this inclusion in the Mexican revolutionary experiment took on more than just figurative meaning.

Olcott states that the "language of citizenship dominated postrevolutionary political discourse, where the title *ciudadano* (citizen) designated one as a legitimate revolutionary."[93] In that regard, correspondence demonstrates the limitations placed on women in their communication with the city. Whether they are writing about a water billing error, purchasing a cemetery plot, or complaining about police corruption, responses to women nearly always refer to them as "Mrs." or "Miss" (*señora* or *señorita*). There is one exception: on correspondence regarding licenses for new constructions or property renovations, women receive the honorific of "C.," for *ciudadana* (citizen).

For example, when single sisters Natalia and María Refugio Barrera submitted plans in 1939 for the construction of seven contiguous houses at the corner of calles 46B and 39A in Sector Juárez, the response from the city did not go to their engineer, who had submitted the plans, but instead addressed the women directly. Additionally, the Dirección de Planeación, Servicios Urbanos y Obras Públicas (Office of Planning, Urban Services, and Public Works) addressed each with the title of "Citizen," abbreviating the honorific with a "CC" (for *ciudadanas*, or citizens) before their names in the letter's salutation. For individuals, the title appeared as the letter *C*. A leading textbook on Mexico states that outside of education and moral reform, men in the revolutionary state did not receive women's participation with respect. By contrast, in construction correspondence we see women extended an honorific rarely if ever offered in any other interaction with authorities.[94] It seems that property ownership garnered women respect from civil authorities in a way similar to what women in education received.

This pattern repeatedly holds for individual women as well as groups of women, married or single. This is no clerical error either, since letters to the city as well as the blueprints all indicate the gender and marital status for the majority of women applying for a construction permit, demonstrating that the clerk drafting the letters knew their gender. Though the city started using preprinted form letters in 1944 with the "Citizen" honorific on a template, that a secondary form letter excluding women was not generated indicates that officials saw no problem in referring to women with the honorific of "Citizen." While the 1917 Constitution failed to establish women as citizens (and constitutional convention delegates even laughed at the thought), when it came to property ownership, male leaders took women more seriously.[95] Writing petitions regarding property issues acted as rituals of belonging, establishing the relationship women had with wider society through owning, developing, buying, selling, and managing property in accordance with the goals of city, state, and national leaders.

The inclusion of women in revolutionary society extended beyond honorifics on letters. As discussed earlier, the process of improving cities through public health codes and projects expanded with eighteenth- and nineteenth-century liberalism. In the case of propertied women at any class level, their participation in the liberal state and its focus on the power of private property also had much earlier roots. Continuing the shift from communal and corporate property to individual property elevated during the Bourbon period, the liberals of Mexico's nineteenth and early twentieth centuries defended the rights and development of private property for capitalist production through both legislation and violence.[96] For women in particular, the great liberalism-caused shifts in the conception of "citizenship, secularization, changes in laws of marriage, urbanization, and the expansion of . . . employment" proved crucial to redefining the legal and formal power of women in Mexican society.[97] At the intersection of all these areas resided property ownership and the ability to manage that property with minimal interference.

As Mexico entered the revolutionary era, the Constitution of 1917 addressed the issues of private landownership on the one hand and related concerns about the public aspect of private property on the other. The constitutional convention's Jacobin wing understood the tension between private property and its public value and sought to limit property use and subordinate it to the "social interests."[98] Their full vision only partially came to fruition under the Constitution's Article 27. That section allowed for both urban and rural expropriation of property for the public good, but subsequent legislation focused mostly on rural land issues. The convention's radical members (such as Francisco J. Múgica) or others who experienced land reform during the 1910 revolution advocated for a more expansive land program, but they focused exclusively on the rural experience.[99] Others saw land reform as a tool of pacification for rural revolutionaries.

When gathering input on the creation of Article 27, the committee reviewing the article took comments from convention members like Luis T. Navarro, a veteran of Zapatismo's agrarian struggle against the counterrevolutionary president Victoriano Huerta (1913–14). However, Navarro later switched his allegiance to the less radical Constitutionalists. Navarro argued that redistribution of land as laid out in Article 27 would keep people from joining Zapatismo and also get them to lay down their arms.[100] Clearly he did not have a radical view of social property, and his thinking indicated that property (particularly urban property) was generally of little concern to the delegates on a deep level. Additionally, delegates came to Article 27 as a compromise—one not deeply discussed, debated, or even fully understood by the delegation as a whole.[101] In short, while the 1910 revolution radicalized some aspects of private property, no hard break between the importance of private property ownership and national success emerged.

As had been the case in the colonial era and through the nineteenth century, women of the revolutionary era demonstrated their participation in the nation and national agenda through property. In fact, Mexico after the 1917 Constitution deepened its commitment to women's ability to control property even while redefining property rights as no longer "absolute or inalienable."[102] Single women had already gained greater control of their property before the 1910 revolution, but the 1917 Law of Domestic Relations and Property gave full legal capacity to married women to function in their own legal affairs, administer property, draw up contracts, and take part in lawsuits, all without a husband's permission. Additionally, it removed the legal duty of husbands to protect wives and for wives to obey their husbands.[103] By 1928 the Código Civil para el Distrito y Territorios Federales (Civil Code of the Federal District and Federal Territory) had begun to consider women in those jurisdictions to be political citizens in their own right. The code argued that "judicial standing is equal for men and women; consequently, women are not subject, by reason of their sex, to any restriction in the acquiring or exercise of their civil rights."[104] Such changes had a broad range of influences on various members of society depending on class and context. Sex workers, for example, increasingly used laws against pimps couched in the language of both revolutionary law and traditional gendered honor to control their own labor, property, and income.[105]

Despite the law, nineteenth-century men exercised de facto power over property, particularly the property that entered marriages as communal. Such circumstances drove activists to fight for the improvement of women's control of communal property or even for the abolition of private property altogether as a way to reduce men's ability dominate women's lives.[106] Revolutionary Mexico did not do away with private property, but the Código Civil of 1928 extended explicit, full legal equality in household representation and management. For single women, the code forbade any distinction based on gender. It still had its shortcomings, though, since it focused on women as domestic laborers within the home and encouraged them to direct household affairs even if they worked outside the home.[107] Despite the remaining issues, the clear trajectory of including Mexican women in the economic development that increasingly defined the 1910 revolution, as well as its liberal heritage, is clear. The Mexican Revolution helped broaden certain aspects of women's participation in society. However, this chapter in no way argues that most revolutionary men saw women as equals or that women attained full gender equality.[108]

Women's eventual political citizenship and voting rights came about (in part) because men stressed the difference between women and men, linking women's political rights to motherhood and housework.[109] Certainly economic power is an easier level of influence to attain in society compared to other social powers like political-hierarchical position, physical force, and ideology.[110] However, the existence of women's economic power does argue for the possibility that they maintained some ability to shape the world around them despite the ongoing discrimination against them in Mexico. Though Mexico after the revolution followed the liberal tradition of separate spheres for men and women, by relegating women to the domestic sphere (including property management) while at the same time opening opportunities for property ownership, the revolution brought women further into the public space of urban life.

The participation of women in the developmentalism of Mexico's economic growth is no small matter, particularly in the period under consideration. While Lázaro Cárdenas is known for his expropriation of oil companies (1938) and the redistribution of rural property to men in the countryside (1934–40), he also claimed other accomplishments. Cárdenas highlighted his investment in the infrastructure that fed urban development and private business expansion; markets, drainage work, paved roads, increasing automobile use, and the growth of businesses all served as bridges from the Porfirian capitalist prosperity ethic.[111] Nevertheless, as the redistributive revolution and accompanying social reforms withered under presidents Manuel Ávila Camacho (1940–46) and then practically disappeared with Miguel Alemán (1946–52), they each worked to replace those losses. Investments in infrastructure and development projects turbocharged both import substitution industrialization (ISI) and private capital. As Paul Gillingham notes, "This radical shift in state priorities was predicated on rapid and stable economic growth."[112] Guadalajara functioned as a particularly key area for such evolution, with the city serving as a testing ground for the larger national push toward ISI to fuel the growth of domestic wealth.[113] Partly due to inertia and partially planned, the official policy of Mexico moved the nation toward a hybrid of state control and a "revived capitalism, a renewal of the Porfirian model" that set aside more radical revolution "in return for social stability and economic development."[114] Cities provided a particular showcase for Mexico to demonstrate its success and draw in foreign visitors and investors. The improved infrastructure also helped the head of the Secretaría de Gobernación, Miguel Alemán (1940–45), to "refashion the image of Mexico" as "metropolitan, up to date, and businesslike."[115]

Every building updated, every street rendered free of sewage, every empty lot filled with housing demonstrated that the revolution marched on. At the state level in the same era, Jalisco's governors presided over an expansion of infrastructure and development projects in the state.[116] Guadalajara itself became a linchpin in the machinery of development and urban prosperity, serving as the location for the founding of the Confederación Nacional de Organizaciones Populares (CNOP, National Confederation of Popular Organizations). CNOP functioned as the party wing representing the general population and civilian organizations "pledged to defend private property, foster small industries and landholdings, and combat fanaticism."[117] For women, involvement in developing the city gave them an alternative path of revolutionary belonging. Every woman in the correspondence record who performed an alignment with that agenda demonstrated participation in the revolutionary process as well as the local shaping of public space and a sense of place.

Historians Stephanie Mitchell and Patience Schell have both argued that women made the 1910 revolution's gains work for them and, by extension, the rest of Mexico. Mitchell notes that rural women played key roles in agricultural landholdings and that in urban areas they drove labor activism that improved the lives of workers, industrialization, and consumer growth. In addition, women had significant power in the household; from that position, they directed the revolution, because women decided "how much [of] that agenda was implemented and how much of it remained in the ephemeral realm of revolutionary slogans."[118] In a related vein, Catholic women "fostered their own version of revolutionary Mexico," one based instead on Catholic social doctrine and maternal morality.[119] In essence, women exercised their revolutionary participation both directly and indirectly and with their own interpretation of the household's private sphere. By extension, both single and married women who controlled property engaged in a similar process, deciding how the 1910 revolution's developmentalism in cities would both look and provide for urban Mexicans.

Private and Public in Making Place in Urban Space

Private property is not strictly private in the urban setting. It establishes the public aesthetic, its liabilities of waste or decay affect public hygiene and area property values, and it fills the space and decorates the stage where residents improvise urban life. It does not matter who holds the title or who sets the social rules; any property in a shared physical and visual space helps define place. In this regard, women developing property shaped public space in two direct senses: they created an aesthetic "character of the city, that allows people to recognize it [the city] and live there," and they developed space that "enriched urban practices and increased public participation" in the city.[120] Indirectly, the process of developing the property worked through layers of public institutions for initial approval, licensing, development coordination, and connection to and management of public services, particularly in the case of larger housing developments.[121] Because Mexican women owned and actively developed property, they directly defined the cities that male revolutionary leaders held up as signifiers of their success. As the 1917 Constitution's Article 115 indicated, the "free municipality" established the basis of "popular, representative, republican form of government." Cities functioned as the beating heart of Mexico's public space and public sphere.

Feminist theorist Carol Pateman argues that women in societies guided by principles of liberalism are associated with nature and private space while men get linked to public urban space. The result is a false, gendered dichotomy between public and private. Additionally, liberal feminism tends to draw an imaginary hard line between the public and the private.[122] Similar to the Euro-U.S. social norms studied by Pateman, the hard line between the feminine private and masculine public is overemphasized. Contrary to popular perceptions, the hard division between women in the private sphere and men in the public sphere is not some long-standing Hispanic trait. For example, women in the colonial households of New Spain had significant economic responsibility.[123]

Historian Silvia Arrom argues that a variant of Victorian moralism borrowed from external neocolonial Euro-Anglo influences had come to reign supreme among elites in Mexico by the nineteenth century's end. This imposed thinking put an emphasis on women as the moral guide of families in the home and therefore as guardians of Mexico's future.[124] Over time, that thinking affected perceptions in daily life, where even popular music limited women to the roles of mother, wife, girlfriend, or targets of love and lust.[125] At loftier state levels (whether during times of independence, colonization, or neocolonial domination), limiting women to a private sphere allowed for legislated control of women's bodies. For political leaders, controlling women and reproduction meant improved commercial productivity, increased and better-behaved labor, and, consequently, profits.[126] This imagined domestic sphere for women indicated their key role as inculcators of patriotic and nationalist behaviors that undergird "civic pride," which created the thrifty, efficient, dedicated employees, managers, and entrepreneurs that ultimately powered the capitalist engines of a modernizing Mexico.[127]

This Victorian focus on motherhood and morality in private versus public spheres distracts from an important aspect of domestic life: property ownership and management. If conceived of in a strict binary, the public sphere of urban space is left primarily (though not exclusively) to the domination of men. As scholar Agueda Jiménez Pelayo has argued, "For many years the role of women in Hispanic America focused on their isolation in the home caring for the family. Little participation in economic or political activity was conceded to women."[128] Because of this male-centered narrative (that also excludes the long history of working-class women in the public sphere), many popular histories are rightly dedicated to a counternarrative revealing the power women demonstrated in public spheres of labor (both as organizers and workers), the arts, teaching, medicine, and political activism. For example, Susie S. Porter's exploration of working Mexican women has successfully demonstrated their participation in the public sphere through their role as workers and their creation of public discussion about that role.[129] Additionally, she locates them in public space through their physical presence in work and other public venues.[130] Ageeth Sluis argues that the Mexican Revolution opened up space for women in the "public sphere as workers, teachers, consumers, and activists," as well as the entertainment industry.[131] When indicating the importance of women in Jalisco during and after the Mexican Revolution, scholar Aurea Zafra Oropeza lists educators, poets, historians, journalists, musicians, authors, artists, politics, and student activism in her history of women in Jalisco but lists no women engaged in business and property ownership.[132]

Similarly, María Teresa Fernández Aceves's path-making *Mujeres en el cambio social en el siglo XX mexicano* examines women in religious activism, social justice, education, and labor as "militant feminist women in the public sphere."[133] As noted in a collection of pieces about twentieth-century women's lives, "in the area of education, politics, and the creative arts, Latin American women's achievements are worthy of global recognition."[134] This kind of writing tends to examine roles for women in society in areas outside of property ownership because that is perceived as being in the private sphere. However, if Mexican liberalism drove a capitalist ethic and system both before and after the Mexican Revolution, what could be more capitalist than accumulation, development, management, and speculation of and in private property?[135]

In an example of failing to account for property management as being in the public sphere, consider Margarita Maza de Juárez, the wife of Mexico's famed liberal president, Benito Juárez (1857–72). Of Maza de Juárez, one author notes in passing that, while her husband ruled Mexico, she "directed the family's affairs" from their home outside Mexico City without mention of what that work entailed. Instead, the author focuses on her political acumen in the public sphere.[136] For writing on women who excelled in business ownership and property development, the emphasis falls on late twentieth-century women, such as industrialist María Antonieta Pacheco Gaytán, whom scholars considered a rare "incursion" into the world of men in the 1990s.[137] However, Pacheco Gaytán got her start in the same kind of street vending and small business ownership as many of the women discussed in this chapter. Though "only 6% of the large businesses are directed by women in Mexico" like Pacheco Gaytán, at the local level the proportion of women who own and manage the affairs of their property and direct the interests of their businesses is much greater.[138] In this regard, women engaged in business and property ownership or development pushed back against "gender binarism, heteronormative sphere separatism, patriarchal kinship, and the instrumentalities and inequalities they secure."[139] Though they may not be engaged in the powerful feminist separatism of refusal that would provide them greater control over their own lives, purses, and bodies, they are seizing the opportunities afforded them in the era's context, particularly as they worked together in networks of women.[140] They find, as Sarah Ahmed puts it, "ways to exist in a world that makes it difficult to exist."[141] Rather than being objects moved about by the circumstances of revolution or urbanization, the women who bought, sold, improved, and managed property built the physical and aesthetic world around them. Much like the women of Mexico City who took active roles in shaping modernization and urban imagery in the 1920s and 1930s, property-owning *tapatías* used their agency to shape urban society.[142]

The historiography on women varies in theme and methodology, with many (though not all) works on women in Guadalajara taking a biographical approach, one example being the scholarship of María Teresa Fernández Aceves on the political work of women.[143] Biography is a tool frequently used by other leaders in the field of Mexican gender and women's history, as Ana Lau Jaiven and Elsie McPhail Fanger have done.[144] This strategy allows for a picture of life outside the full control of men and their bureaucratic machine. Historian Anayanci Fregoso Centeno has argued in support of biography over using traditional but problematic government archives because "the respected tradition in the West of registering on paper all public events—to legitimate them as true events—denied for a long time the subjective nature of these documents, and as a consequence, the lessons drawn from these documents [were] incomplete; they limited the idea that other documents could also be used as sources of information, denying the power to see in those sources what they said but also who created them, how they spoke, and other implied meanings such as visual language, for example."[145]

Certainly this is the case for most civil registry records where women submitted notice of births and marriages (and little else), thus providing a limited view of their role in society. But the municipal correspondence archives show us a side of women not generally discussed in the literature: property owners and entrepreneurs. Thus, the correspondence archive allows us to get a sense of women's lives; such records are themselves personal declarations of how they wanted others to see them in relation to the public sphere of urban life. As Ana Lau Jaiven has written, "Everything is related to personal history."[146] In this way, the narratives of belonging declared in the ritual of petitioning and correspondence allow us to hear the voices of women that otherwise might be lost in avenues of preservation.

Indeed, the very foundation of Guadalajara rests on the efforts of Beatríz Hernández, an upper-class Spaniard, conquistador, and the partner of Juan Sánchez de Olea. When Indigenous resistance to Spanish imperialism drove colonists away from Guadalajara's earlier location, Hernández placed herself on the city council and pushed the governing body to take refuge southward in the Atemajac Valley (the city's current location). "The king is my leader [*mi gallo*]," Hernández declared, before announcing, "I think it best we move ourselves to the Valley of Atemajac, and if we make any other move, it would be a disservice to God and the King and a demonstration of cowardice."[147] The colonists departed in the fall of 1541 for the Atemajac Valley, and the Spanish Crown chartered Guadalajara in its current location on February 14, 1542. In a way, Hernández sealed the fate of the city's later development with her actions and declaration. Her "daring and aggressiveness" (as the commemorative plaque about her in the city center states) saved the city of Guadalajara's existence and set a pattern for generations of women who helped build, guide, and define the city into the twentieth century.

Contrary to the opinion of Jorge Matute Remus, the engineer who named women as an obstacle that he needed to eliminate in order to promote property development, construction licenses and notary records show women actively engaged in the urban landscape of Guadalajara. The celebration of male engineers and architects paired well with the conceptual relegation of women to a narrow set of private, domestic roles in the context of a patriarchal midcentury Mexico, particularly when dealing with the growing city's challenges. From conservative presidents to leftist radicals, a cult of masculinity dominated political leaders' attitudes regarding women's participation.[148] However, Mexico has a long tradition of women as property owners or in positions of influence and power, from the colonial era forward. Women's presence in these roles increased into the early twentieth century, as laws considered women fully mentally capable to "buy, sell, rent, inherit, or bequeath property of all kinds."[149] Arrom notes that while men in the colonial era thought women too weak to have free control of their property (though it did not stop women from owning property), after independence, the rise of liberalism gradually provided women more latitude in the home, and expectations about women's roles changed.

This latitude under liberalism, however, came generally as a result of a growing division among elites about the private sphere of women and the public sphere of men. Some argued that women acted as rulers in the "empire" of the home. That positioning banished women from the public spheres of political office and suffrage.[150] Nevertheless, as in the colonial era, "the impropriety of women's 'mingling publicly with men'" went by the wayside when it came to managing property, including dealing with the legal aspects of property ownership.[151] After the 1910 revolution and the increasing number of city, state, and federal offices related to property ownership, management, improvement, construction, demolition, and confiscation, the participation in property ownership by women is nothing less than a distinct form of Olcott's "revolutionary citizenship."[152] I argue that property ownership and small-business entrepreneurial behavior did not set off the same widespread moral panic that occurred when women took positions as office workers.[153] As scholar Elizabeth Quay Hutchison declared of women in the workforce in Chile, "Despite the abundant evidence of female participation," the actions of women as property owners is not well studied.[154] Julia Tuñon has argued that middle-class and upper-class women had failed to "come down into the streets to make concrete requests" in the public sphere of politics.[155] In their work as property and business owners, women's participation in the public sphere and public space demonstrates them making figurative and literal concrete requests and not simply being isolated in a cocoon of autonomous individuality and domesticity.[156] The agency of women in Guadalajara to manage their property and businesses is noteworthy, but in the context of the era under examination here, their actions for the public good become even more notable. While I am examining this topic in the limited scope of Guadalajara, scholars interested in this topic may find other regional cities that offer fertile ground for this area of research.[157]

After 1920, the city of Guadalajara changed dramatically, in both demographic and economic terms. Between 1920 and 1940, the population increased by roughly 100,000, to between 240,000 and 250,000.[158] Having avoided the Mexican Revolution's worst destruction and subsequent religious violence, the city expanded its role as the economic engine for western Mexico. However, as economic historian John Coatsworth has argued, growth does not always equal development.[159] The failure of revolutionary leaders in Mexico City to use its resources to develop a broad base of social

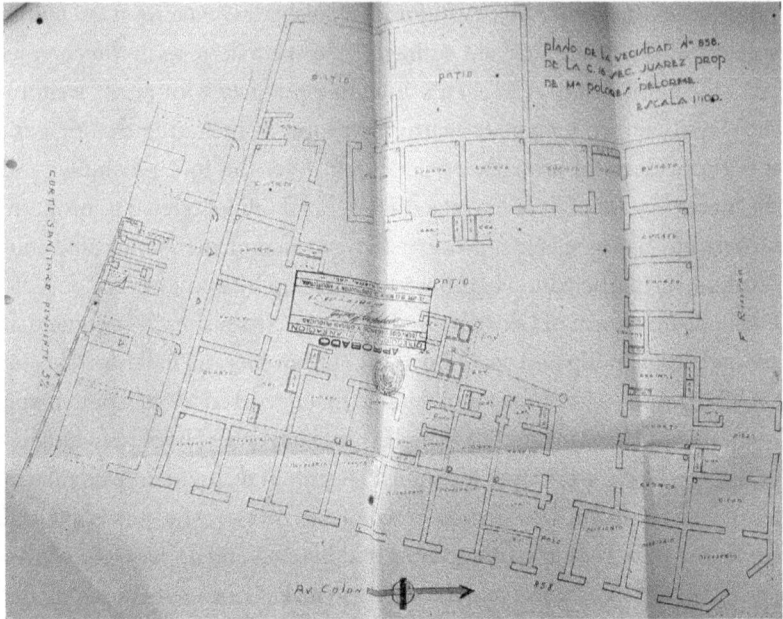

FIG. 12. Large, multifamily apartment buildings, or *vecindades*, began to appear in Guadalajara during the late nineteenth century. This plan for a new *vecindad*, to be built for María Dolores DeLorme, is just one example of larger-scale projects built by property-owning women. Licencias para Construcción, 1939, plano 44, AHMG. Courtesy of the Archivo Histórico Municipal de Guadalajara.

justice reforms that would materially support the population made urban life increasingly difficult.[160]

What kept Guadalajara from collapsing during the period under study? Over nearly a decade in which the city gained little help from federal funding, how did municipal officials and private companies shelter, provision, and supply water for its inhabitants? One possibility is that the capital and land provided by women and their businesses in key areas of provisioning, such as tortillas and dairy products, helped the city survive. As engineers struggled to provide water or housing, women built on their land not only various apartment buildings and housing developments for the working classes and professionals but also homes for middle- and upper-class residents. When the city struggled with a shortage of market buildings, women developed home businesses that supplied food to the public from structures they built or rented. Although the nation touted its education system while failing to adequately fund it, women provided the space necessary for urban education. Men visibly dominated construction, industry, and business ownership in the city, but the rate of population growth and infrastructure pressure would have outstripped their ability to provide jobs, food, and shelter. The contribution of women to activate their property and power for the population's benefit not only helped the city survive but demonstrated their belonging as *tapatías*, illustrating their work to build space and make place in Guadalajara.

Conclusion

Dozens of photos of Guadalajara from before 1939 exist, and thousands exist for the years after 1947, but few photographs in the city archive document city life between those years. Those the archive does have are primarily of political rallies and public works. The Archivo Histórico Municipal de Guadalajara does have one candid photo of 1940s street life. For a moment, I want to use that photo to think of the history of everyday life in Guadalajara (using the social history approach taught by John Mraz).[1]

Taken in 1942 by an anonymous photographer, the picture captures a portion of the city torn down after 1947. The area is now a large, open plaza (Plaza Guadalajara) located across the street and to the west of the cathedral. The businesses, residences, and sidewalks that once filled the space are now gone, and the city and state erected a fountain there. The photograph shows the northeast corner of the lot, looking south, and takes in a miniature sweep of street life. On the ground level, we find a street vendor like those mentioned in chapters 2 and 3, dispensing what appear to be drinks from his stall on the edge of the sidewalk in front of a clothing store. His client leans to the side awaiting his purchase, and to the right we find middle-aged men at rest. One leans on a power pole, a cigarette dangling from his hand as he observes others on the sidewalk, while the other leans back against the clothing store, apparently smoking too. Both seem to be taking advantage of the shade on the east side of the building in the early afternoon. Moving to the right, a slightly built man bends forward, struggling with the cumbersome shape or weight of a box as he readjusts his grip. In front and facing him, a youth stands still. Is the young man turning to help the older man, or is he about to receive the box from him? Behind them, a man in a dark suit and white hat appears stationary, turning to face

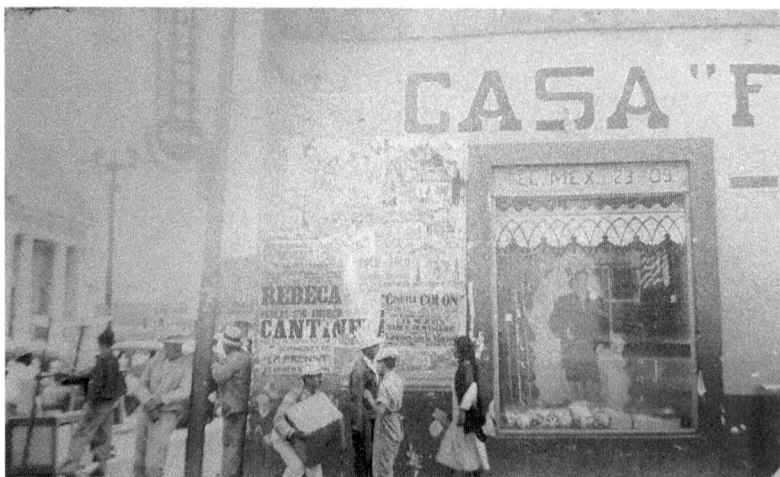

FIG. 13. This is one of the Guadalajara municipal archive's very few candid shots of downtown Guadalajara from between 1939 and 1947. These buildings were later bulldozed to make way for a large plaza that helped form a giant cross in the center of the city. Caja 1, Sobre 1, Fecha 1942, Folio 1, Titulo "Esquina Noreste de la Manzana 9 derribada por la Plaza de los Laureles hoy Plaza Ayuntamiento." Courtesy of the Archivo Histórico Municipal de Guadalajara.

an oncoming woman. Is she on her way to the cathedral, whose southern edge is visible on the far left of the picture? Or is she simply approaching the man against the wall facing her, his dark suit in contrast to the white hat illuminated by the sun?

Behind it all, the decorative wrought-iron lampposts of dragons (still found around Guadalajara to this day) stand guard against the promise of nightfall. The sign for the Casa Franco clothing store looms above the people in the photo, and the store itself provides the backdrop and shade from the sun for the picture's human subjects. Casa Franco's display window at the far right exhibits a mannequin with the dress of an upper-class woman, surrounded by Anglo-style Christmas ball ornaments scattered along the floor of the display.[2] Plastered on the wall are text-only posters for movies, such as Alfred Hitchcock's *Rebeca* (1940) and *Amores son Perlas* (the Spanish-language release of *Back Door to Heaven*, 1939), as well as a broadside advertising a Cantinflas film, whose title is too faded to decipher.

Advertisements for movie houses and beer, as well as layers of previous posters long pasted over, peek from around the edges. Behind it all, the paint on the wall peels away, and decorations from past celebrations hang near the top of the wall. Finally, we see how automobiles and parking had permeated the center of the city by 1942.

This space indicates multiple levels of use and meaning. The sidewalks are acting as a place of both movement and rest. Consumerism and advertising reach out from the posters and the clothing store, but so do the people who make consumerism possible. What we also see is a decidedly working-class picture of street life. There are the obvious moments: the street vendor and his stall or the man lifting the box are clearly people engaged in labor. However, the picture portrays class status in other ways as well. Are the two men on the corner pausing from work for a smoke break? What about clothing? In the case of all the men in the photo, their clothes hang in ways that portray their untailored fit, some with visible signs of dirtiness. Baggy pants appear on the men and not the tailored, pleated, and pressed trousers of the age that would rest lightly on the tops of shoes for the middle and upper classes. Nevertheless, the clothing reflects an urban Mexico of the 1940s and the aspirations of the working class to dress in the style of the period. Perhaps less tied into the modern clothing styles are our two remaining subjects. The young man in the picture (or is he an older child?) has his pants cinched up tightly, the seat broad enough for an older, heavier man and thus bagging in the back as his too-large shirt is tucked in and the sleeves are rolled up to keep his arms free. And finally, the lone women in the picture with her simple dress (most likely cotton), dark shawl, and long hair trailing down her back indicate her position as a working-class woman and most likely Indigenous, in direct contrast to the window display.

After considering what the visual image has to offer, we can also see the limitations of the visual resources available to students of the past. Are the people in the picture experiencing pleasure from the sensory experiences of that portion of the street? What is the emotional response to the actions of others using that space? Is the woman in the picture the owner of her home or a business, or do we assume (erroneously) she is not because her clothing tends toward the Indigenous and traditional? Because the photographer is anonymous, we do not know the reason for taking this particular picture at this particular angle, framed this way, taken at this time of day, or developed in this way.[3] How do any of those involved (photographer, subjects, onlookers) feel about the city or consider themselves as belonging to a wider community? How did they all feel about the smell or feel of the corner? Are they annoyed by the actions of those who share space with them and, if so, why? If not, why not? The photograph raises more questions than answers (as it should for historians)—answers provided in the preceding chapters via petitions and correspondence from the era in question.

Residents of Guadalajara from 1939 to 1947 experienced a city in transition. From being a regional commercial center, Guadalajara evolved into one of Mexico's national economic engines. Employment opportunities attracted migration from rural areas, from other cities in the republic, and (to a smaller extent) from around the world; these migrants all helped set the city on a path of population growth that outpaced the ability of city officials to cope. In this context, residents of Guadalajara took the efforts of city officials and retooled them to accomplish their own ends in subtle ways. This book is about the simple ways that city individuals and groups of residents created a sense of belonging and improvised new meanings for elite plans beyond powerful unions, cartels of business owners, or the blueprints of engineers and party bosses. As Guadalajara grew into a bulwark of the Mexican state and an iconic cultural representative of the nation's international image, average residents found ways to carve out their own sense of belonging in the city. Both long-term residents and newcomers alike found themselves in a city transformed around them or a city new to their living experience, respectively.

How did they attempt to avoid a feeling of alienation and disorientation in this transitionary moment? Beyond the limitations of identity and citizenship, residents of the city (both old and new) engaged in actions to help them find a sense of belonging. Such a sense might take one or both of two paths: individuals find belonging because they feel needed, and others find it because they understand that something about themselves "complements the system or environment" that they are in.[4] In each of the chapters in this book, we've seen women and men, the wealthy and the poor, renters and property owners, owners of businesses of all sizes, moralizers and partygoers, and many others from a wide range of urban residents who found a sense of belonging in Guadalajara. They did so not only by communicating their complementary position to city leaders but also by creating narratives of belonging. As sociologist Floya Anthias argues, people can establish a sense of being part of a wider community through telling stories about themselves and their place in their new society.[5] As such, I have adapted her concepts to see how Guadalajara's residents exercised agency to develop "coping strategies and negotiation of belonging" in a transitional space. These strategies helped them "assess their needs and life projects" in relation to their urban residency.[6]

Residents of the city who advocated for themselves and their neighbors and who mastered the space around them (or attempted to) became local experts in the navigation of and ways of belonging in the city by using their physical senses.[7] In chapter 1, petitions and letters to the city reveal the conflict found in the urban sensorium. In particular, sight, sound, scent, and touch served as avenues for *tapatíos* to interpret city life. Sensate belonging in Guadalajara gives readers a multilayered avenue to consider how the physical perception of an urban experience shaped the way that residents conceptualized their lives in a changing city. Residents did not just perceive the city with their senses, however, but also used them as a guide to justify conflict with (and regulation of) their neighbors. These conflicts then reveal the kind of city where the petitioners hoped to live and that others accepted, with either enthusiasm or resignation. As with chapter 2, the petitions in chapter 1 also reveal how those petitioned against lived (by either choice or circumstance). It also provides insight into a mid-twentieth-century urban population not yet completely subsumed by two centuries of liberals and revolutionaries constantly redefining modern urban life and working to shoehorn individuals into their ever-evolving definitions of what it meant to be modern.

Similarly, chapter 2 moved us into an exploration of how groups of neighbors used petitions to understand the city and their place in it but from a sense of morality or a craving for merriment. Whether they were true believers in the rhetoric of morality centered on families, bodily temperance, productivity, and regulated sexuality or not, they used that language to mobilize city inspectors on their behalf. Such attempts to regulate their neighbors, however, also refocus the historical imagination on the reader to consider the large number of *tapatíos* who were the objects of petitions. Though Guadalajara developed a public image as a bastion of traditional, conservative Mexican society and small industry productivity, petitions indicate an alternative view of city life. Social drinking, riotous drunkenness, sex, informal sports, public nudity, partying, gambling, and any number of other so-called offensive practices present a sociable and even therapeutic city populace who took the opportunity to reject the norms of the more vocal *gente decente*. In this regard, those being petitioned against communicated their own claims to city space through simply living in ways rejected by the moralistic slice of society.

For either petitioners or those petitioned against, their vision of the good life did not include nicely resolving differences without conflict. Conflict helped *tapatíos* find belonging in multiple ways: forming alliances with their neighbors, defining their own views of urban life, attempting to control others, or simply flaunting their rejection of official moralities all helped members find their place in urban life. Community is conflict. Much of the archival research used in this book focuses on divisions between parties, but these divisions are the stuff of city life. The battle itself is part of the community process, because engaging in the conflict of defining urban space is itself a ritual of belonging.

Conflict and community formed the heart of chapter 3, as well. When the global power of the Catholic Church and the Mexican state hammered out grand formal and informal accords that eased a century of tension, the religious Mexicans featured in chapter 3 found new ways to engage in religious conflict. Mexican Catholics and Protestants alike harnessed the anticlerical and public health language of the revolutionary state in attempts to undermine their ideological foes. Additionally, within congregations themselves, pastors and dissidents laid claim to ideological leadership and physical property from competing internal factions using the language and laws of a secular state. Petitions from religionists in Guadalajara reveal residents actively interpreting city regulations and adapting them to make a religious urban life not originally intended by the state. This act of improvisation, communicated through the ritual of correspondence, solidified for themselves their belonging to the city. But how else did people find belonging in the city under transformation?

In the first three chapters of the book, I introduced readers to a broad selection of characters with different lifestyles or social standing. One constant, however, is the presence of women throughout the sources, particularly in the petitions found in chapters 1 and 2, which showed how these women often served as leaders of neighborhood groups working to shape the space around them. In chapter 4, we come to a discussion of women actively shaping the city around them in the public sphere and in public space with property and business ownership and their active management of those resources. Construction permits, property transactions, water records, cemetery plot management—all these reveal women deeply involved in the construction, management, and sale of properties throughout Mexico's second-largest city.

During the crisis of urban growth in Guadalajara, women acted as real estate developers, rental property owners, and small-business entrepreneurs providing the infrastructure necessary to sustain the city. Women property owners accounted for a third of the new housing construction permits in the city, they provisioned the city's basic foodstuffs in new stores and stalls, and, as streams of sewage ran in the streets, elite women developed new water sources to help lessen a severe water crisis. Women participated in the majority of land transactions as well; their transactions constituted over 70 percent of the total number of property exchanges between 1939 and 1947 (many of those made between women, without any men involved). Guadalajara's women provided crucial services during a difficult period, becoming experts in the language of urban planning, which they used to engage city leaders. In an era before full suffrage, women provided neighborhood leadership and resources necessary to better the lives of their fellow residents and make Guadalajara their home. Still, it is important to avoid the trope of women sacrificing for the nation and instead draw attention to an additional and important element highlighted in chapter 4: women found ways to use city rules and regulations to build their own wealth and broaden their own commercial opportunities. Some women then took this wealth and used it either to support women in their immediate network of relatives or to benefit women in their profession as partners or employees. For these women, Guadalajara and the conflicts around property and property management allowed them to carve out their own sense of place and use of space in the city by literally claiming physical locations in the city and designing the aesthetic space through their property construction.

Residents of Guadalajara between 1939 and 1947 experienced a breather between the social storms of the era. The 1940s mark a transitionary period away from the nineteenth-century liberal city seized by revolutionary fervor after 1910 (both religious and secular). Populist revolutionaries and radical Catholics before 1939 not only spent their time clashing with one another in Guadalajara, but they also often fell outside the approval of national leadership in Mexico City.[8] Before 1939 a rotating door of governors and mayors did battle with both the presidents of Mexico and the Catholic Church. They did so while enduring a global economic crisis, clashes between factions of Catholic and socialist students, and the appearance of radical conservative oppositions such as the fascist Camisas Doradas (Gold Shirts).[9]

An increasingly bureaucratic city dominated by engineers of the ruling party emerged after the period covered in this book. The year 1947 marks a transitionary moment for the city of Guadalajara and its residents. I do not argue that it was a watershed, a seismic shift, a paradigmatic revolution, or any of the other phrases historians examining change over time are tempted to use. Churches continued to undermine one another, neighbors wagged their fingers in moral disapproval, people continued to defecate in the streets, nightclubs and public sex continued unabated, and women continued to fight for the resources they needed to maintain their property holdings. Instead, I argue that events of 1947 indicated that residents would be engaging in those activities in different contexts and therefore would respond in distinct ways that require future investigation.

According to scholar Irma Beatriz García Rojas, urbanization in Guadalajara remained rudimentary until 1947, when both the city and a more powerful Jalisco state governor became aggressive with systematized urban planning.[10] This planning included an expansion of the city footprint that outgoing governor Marcelino García Barragán (1943–47) termed an "economic conquest." This so-called conquest meant the purchase and colonization of large landed estates on the edge of the city and an explicit rejection of revolutionary communal lands known as *ejidos*.[11] After 1947 the economic conquest added roughly three thousand hectares to the city (about fifty thousand city lots) over the next decade. By contrast, between 1939 and 1947 Guadalajara officially added only an estimated eight hundred hectares (about seventeen thousand city lots) to areas open for urbanization.[12] This "economic conquest" emerged as part of a 1947 project carried out by the state's Comité de Planeación (Planning Commission, also created in 1947) to take control of the growth of the city. The state planners also hoped to add at least fifteen new public markets, which would help clear the streets of vendors and their stalls to make way for more automobiles and promote the look of a modern city.[13] Additionally, funding for this expansion came from increased taxes, borrowing, and the creation of the Patronato de la Habitación Popular (PHP, Popular Housing Authority) in a massive investment to create working-class and other residential housing.[14] The PHP is just one example of the explosion of state spending and borrowing for public growth and infrastructure that poured into Guadalajara in 1947.[15]

In discussing the changes that city leaders hoped to create after 1947, the *Gaceta de Guadalajara* heralded the election of Heliodoro Hernández Loza as municipal president (1947–48, the last two-year term for the office) as a sign of the city's rejuvenation. The magazine's page-one editorial extolled the city as the best place to "raise these structures and edifices that are called FAMILIES." The election of Hernández Loza would usher in an age in which what the newspaper called "The White City" was "pleased by virtue of having entered the path that allows it to return to its legendary privileges, to be reconquering its position as the second city of the Republic, unique in its kind and first in the order of *provincias*." Instead of alarmed concern and a call to action, the editorial suggested that the city was on the cusp of "reflecting the days of its distinguished majesties" in the coming years.[16]

Overseeing and directing the expansion, organization, and planning of the renewed city presented a mammoth task, and into that duty stepped members of the Centro de Ingenieros y Arquitectos de Guadalajara, A.C. (CIAG, Center for Engineers and Architects of Guadalajara). CIAG was formed in the summer and fall of 1947 with the aim to professionalize urban planning and offer technical assistance and guidance to the state and city.

The private organization claimed to represent the majority of professional engineers and architects in Guadalajara and had as its mission to help them network and to improve the lived environment.[17] Country club socialite and Universidad Autónoma de Guadalajara engineering professor Guillermo Blanco served as head of the organization. Other UAG faculty such as Joaquín Acevez provided leadership, as did engineers such as Porfirio Barba and Jorge Matute Remus (rector of the Universidad de Guadalajara from 1949 to 1953) who served as part of the governing board.[18] Some members of the board supervised major public works in the city, at times to their own benefit. For example, the building relocation discussed in chapter 4 and supervised by Jorge Matute Remus allowed the widening of avenida Juárez, at a cost of over 6 million pesos. This project permitted more automobile traffic into the center from the western half of the city, where Matute Remus built a large residential housing development. He later served as the municipal president of Guadalajara (1953–55) during the same period when Jalisco's state government began a herculean push to harness additional water sources for the city.[19]

As discussed in the introduction, the public/private initiative of the Consejo de Colaboración Municipal de Guadalajara (Council for Guadalajara Municipal Collaboration), first created in 1943 to little immediate result, moved with renewed vigor in 1947 to address planning coordination and funding concerns. With expansions and renewals of the group through the twentieth century, it accumulated a host of members representing city, state, business, labor, and agrarian concerns.[20] The new urban planning transformed the city from the late 1940s until Mexico's economic crash of the late 1970s. Over the next thirty years, Guadalajara entered into an aggressive modernization as defined by automobile advocates in the city center and outward, to the affluent western portions of the city. Broad, clean, tree-lined avenues carried *tapatíos* on buses and in automobiles to Latin America's first shopping mall (the Plaza del Sol) or to the gleaming airport that welcomed tourists and dignitaries from around the world. Secular revolutionary pretenses fell away as new streets like Juan Diego and Las Rosas (references to the appearance of the Virgin of Guadalupe in Mexico) sprang up in neighborhoods filled increasingly with U.S. and Canadian retirees. One observer of the city even described Guadalajara in

1971 as "practically rebuilt in the 1960's (including completely new water supply and drainage system)."[21]

Meanwhile, the working class and urban poor in peripheral neighborhoods to the east and south of the city experienced a different world. Economic struggles, the absence of consistent utility services, lack of transportation, violence, and much larger waves of rural migrants mired those areas in a gritty struggle for survival.[22] In these neighborhoods, religious leaders, labor unions, civic organizations, and youth gangs all assumed competing and overlapping layers of leadership that residents used in attempts to chase security and upward mobility. Urban planning and the ensuing changes to the city came with few benefits for the broader population, who fell outside the framing of Guadalajara that city leaders worked so hard to preserve. Guadalajara joined the nation as a whole in experiencing immense growth with little development in terms of quality housing. "Of the 5,200,000 homes visited in a 1950 census," notes one scholar, "60% were a single room and 25% had two rooms; 70% of all houses were made of adobe, brick, stakes and branches or rocks."[23] Despite the troubled condition of working-class housing, by the 1970s Guadalajara had only 1 percent of housing in illegal occupations (squatter settlements of the working class); the profit for building working-class housing by the private sector and the high cost to government for creating public housing meant that housing for the working class—in whatever condition—continued to be more readily available after 1947.[24]

Beyond urban planning, changes in the way that the city dealt with petitions and requests for aid and information emerged in 1947. The physical distance between *tapatíos* and their rulers represented by petitions became slightly more distant with the creation of the Sección de Información y Quejas (Information and Complaints Section). This new branch of city government received complaints, answered questions, and decided which letters and petitions would cross the desks of city leaders.[25] Enrique Chavero Ocampo, a young party functionary, served as the first person in the position, and he described it as a way to help provide "effective municipal services in cleaning, water, etc." and to inform the public of all administrative business in city government.[26] In addition to listing a telephone number for service from nine in the morning until eight in the evening, the office paid 200 pesos to the city to register and open a stall in the same archways where the storefront merchants referenced in chapter 1 had complained of *puestos* blocking their light.[27] Not only did the new complaint department direct correspondence and telephone calls away from the offices of other city officials, it also physically moved residents away from the municipal president and the city council by directing them to a street stall.

One might read the new strategy for dealing with complaints as a way to be more responsive to the city's residents if it had emerged as the only change to dealing with *tapatío* complaints. In addition to creating more distance between the city's leaders and its residents, the new system also altered the receptiveness of the city to petitions. Complaints that came from recognized bodies such as neighborhood associations or labor unions housed within the official structure of the ruling party received better attention. As one chronicle described it, those who began taking power in 1947 served as a generation that governed society "as an organized set of 'parties, sectors, unions, agrarian communities, confederations of business and industries, and banking associations.'"[28] For example, when a wave of complaints came in from the Colonia Fresno, the police gathered the residents of the area and required that they form an official neighborhood association to "bring an end to the overflowing difficulties" of the working-class neighborhood in the south of the city. This transition to official neighborhood associations created a situation of "decentralized public agencies" ripe for clientelism and patronage by members of city government who could "exercise an important control over urban space."[29] Additionally, a series of Jalisco state labor proclamations between 1943 and 1947 expanded union membership. However, they also allowed business owners to control the labor affiliation of their workers, allowing businesses to "organize and define the relationships with their workers."[30] By 1948 a consolidated bureaucracy had stifled labor activism in Guadalajara and placed unions firmly under the control of the ruling party and therefore the state as well.[31] Such a transition to party- or state-influenced (or controlled) organizations that attempted to channel dissent mirrored a movement afoot in other areas in Mexico.[32]

The larger political landscape of Guadalajara and Jalisco shifted in February 1947 when the state reformed Article 6 of the state's constitution and expanded governors' terms to six years. In their approval of the constitutional change, the *regidores* of Guadalajara cited various reasons for their support. First, they argued that states with six-year terms for governors exhibited "better social tranquility" and better progress for governors who had a freer hand to undertake public works. They also argued that lines of credit would be more available to governments with six-year terms than four years because of "the natural distrust that capital has" for the uncertainty that political change might offer. They also argued that Jalisco should align itself with the practices and norms of the national Constitution and other states that had already moved to six-year terms.[33] In short, the city endorsed increased political and economic power at the state level in the hands of the governor and alignment with the ideals of business and the federal government in Mexico City.

This political transformation came hand in hand with the selection of Jesús González Gallo (1947–53) as governor of Jalisco, though the election functioned as a formality to confirm him as President Manuel Ávila Camacho's (1940–46) choice for the job. From a family of local power brokers in northern Jalisco, González Gallo tightened the grip of the governor over municipal entities by giving rural bosses legitimacy in a redesigned court system. These regional power brokers, known as *caciques*, then extended their loyalty to his governorship.[34] Additionally, González Gallo deepened his relationship with Catholic politicians in the new Partido Acción Nacional (PAN, National Action Party) political movement, as well as with the middle class, industry leaders, and business organizations.[35] Serving first as the secretary to President Ávila Camacho and then as governor of Jalisco, Jesús González Gallo worked hard to construct "Mexico's and Jalisco's new image of progress and modernization" through means coercive, violent, conciliatory, and diplomatic.[36] This even played out in urban planning, in which he took a direct hand in gutting colonial buildings in Guadalajara to expand automobile access, modernize the look of the city, and demonstrate his commitment to the politics of developmentalism.[37] This program, sociologist John Walton has argued, created a totalizing bureaucratic urban culture of political developmentalism that "disadvantaged the working classes" and "threatened the civic culture that for so long had been a point of pride for *tapatíos*."[38] The transformation came hand in hand with a decrease in the number of developers building housing in the city. Gradually, "a new generation of various construction companies emerged [along with] new societies of developers that monopolized the subdivision of land in Guadalajara, consolidating land, capital, equipment, and socio-political relations and consequently consolidating their interests."[39]

González Gallo also demonstrated his devotion to more than a government program. The modifications carried out on the urban core transferred the traditional center of the city from the plaza (the Plaza de Armas) to the cathedral. From the cathedral a series of open plazas radiate outward, forming a giant cross referred to as the Cruz de Plazas. These acts of demolition, widening, and centering are referred to by Sálvador Díaz-Berrio Fernández as creating a "crucified city." He means this in multiple senses: engineers carved a giant cross in the center of the city and dedicated it to Christ and the Church, but the projects also worsened congestion and transportation problems, killing the livable center of the city.[40] The decades of demolition and replacement that followed the tenure of González Gallo prompted architect and historian Daniel Vázquez to complain of the trajectory of architectural preservation of the city: "What a shame that in this Guadalajara the *tapatíos*—if any are left in the city (are they all just *chilangos?*)—dedicate ourselves to erasing the past without building a future, we dedicate ourselves—or we rather, we let others dedicate themselves—to build an imitation of Mexico City but without actually capturing its being."[41]

The political developments at the state level in Jalisco signaled part of a larger transition creeping over Mexico. In January 1946 the ruling party—the Partido de la Revolución Mexicana (PRM, Mexican Revolutionary Party)—transitioned into a new entity called the Partido Revolucionario Institucional (PRI, Institutional Revolutionary Party). The party, however, served as an "adornment" for a more complex and coercive state apparatus.[42] Much like González Gallo, the emerging Mexican government used a carrot-and-stick approach it applied on a spectrum from seemingly random to Machiavellian genius that guaranteed Mexico would not slip into a renewed revolutionary struggle on the scale the nation faced from 1910 to 1920 and again from 1926 to 1929. Still untamed and actively involved in political matters, the military functioned as a key player in that stability, brutally crushing any overtly political resistance to the state but also acting as judge, jury, and executioner of criminals who brought violence or crime to Mexican

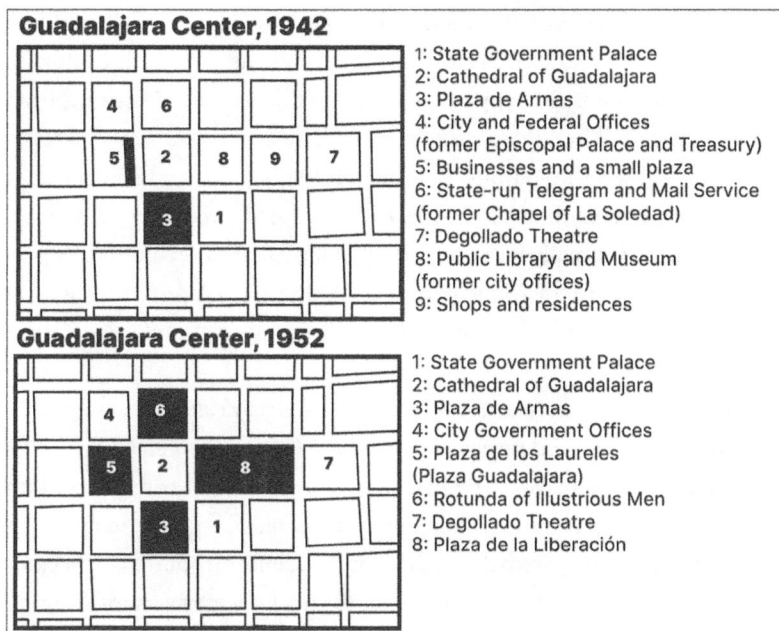

Guadalajara Center, 1942

1: State Government Palace
2: Cathedral of Guadalajara
3: Plaza de Armas
4: City and Federal Offices
(former Episcopal Palace and Treasury)
5: Businesses and a small plaza
6: State-run Telegram and Mail Service
(former Chapel of La Soledad)
7: Degollado Theatre
8: Public Library and Museum
(former city offices)
9: Shops and residences

Guadalajara Center, 1952

1: State Government Palace
2: Cathedral of Guadalajara
3: Plaza de Armas
4: City Government Offices
5: Plaza de los Laureles
(Plaza Guadalajara)
6: Rotunda of Illustrious Men
7: Degollado Theatre
8: Plaza de la Liberación

FIG. 14. This two-part diagram shows the major government and church buildings that formed the center of Guadalajara in the mid-twentieth century. The top shows the city center in 1942, and the bottom shows the same area in 1952, after Governor Jesús González Gallo executed a plan to raze buildings and thus make way for a series of new plazas that formed a giant cross around the cathedral. Map by the author.

communities.[43] Networks of municipal presidents, police, governors, rural bosses, labor organizers, business leaders, bureaucrats, media producers, clergy, educators, and elite families (to produce an incomplete list) worked together to preserve power, dish out favors, and guide the destiny of the nation.[44] By doing so, they managed to funnel a majority of the national income into their own coffers.[45]

At best, these informal and personalist strategies kept Mexico from exploding into renewed violence, pacified labor for industrial wealth, controlled regional power brokers, and maintained political stability. These results propelled the nation to an economic ascendancy that made Mexico a squarely middle-class and global economy—in theory. Recent scholarship argues that in the context of post–World War II economic growth around the world, Mexico's economic "miracle" had more the pattern of a boat lifted on a global economic tide, and the peace of the mid-twentieth century is more the successful cover-up of the deaths of thousands of Mexicans from state violence.[46] The *tapatíos* under study here expressed their desires to city leaders through petitions, but their children and grandchildren later responded to the authoritarian state with an armed, urban guerrilla insurgency and an eventually failed attempt to "implement a revolutionary government" to replace the ruling party.[47] By contrast, the *tapatíos* engaged in community building and conflict between 1939 and 1947, and their context seems now particularly tame.

Correspondence between residents of Guadalajara and the city government during this period reveals not only how *tapatíos* perceived the actual city around them but also the nature of the city they desired, based on their sense of place. Lauded for its beauty, Guadalajara lost its luster as population growth overwhelmed the city. Residents responded by becoming local experts on urban development to attack their adversaries, enrich themselves, establish the moral order of the city, and (for many women) take advantage of opportunities to develop properties and engage in commerce. In the context of water shortages, failing sewage systems, a tight housing market, and a dramatic aesthetic transition, *tapatíos* interacted with the city government to define urban space and attempt to harness city services to ends not intended by the authorities and to preserve (or create) a sense of place. Engaging in these conflicts helped residents find belonging in the city during an important transitionary time, no matter how they might define that belonging. The residents' rituals of correspondence also nurtured a sense of being heard through the constitutional process of petitioning. Beyond that, the process helped residents feel that the outcomes of the 1910 revolution (which at times they themselves defined) served them well.

Notes

Introduction

1. Muriá, *Breve historia*, 170. This growth is about twice what we see on average for Mexico between 1930 and 1960, according to Cross Morrison, "Population Change." Regarding private development versus state development, see Vázquez, *Guadalajara: Ensayos de interpretación*, 74–75; Ibáñez and Vázquez, *Guadalajara: Un análisis urbano*, 37; Walton, *Elites and Economic Development*, 154; and Morfín and Sánchez Van Dyck, "Controles jurídicos," 505.

2. Jiménez, *Making an Urban Public*, 34.

3. The term *tapatío* has various possible roots. Some argue that the term comes from the Nahuatl term *tlapatiotl*, which means "worth three" and references the hard work of people of the region (each is worth three laborers). Others argue the term comes from the word *tápalos*, a reference to embroidered mantillas and cloths made by Creole women in the region.

4. For more on the fragmented nature of urban life in Guadalajara, see Ramírez Sáiz and Safa Barraza, "Tendencias y retos recientes," 78–82.

5. Gomez, *Silver Veins, Dusty Lungs*, 160–61.

6. Dormady, *Primitive Revolution*, 1–2; Knight, *Mexican Revolution*, 1:239 (quote).

7. Benjamin, *La Revolución*, 165.

8. Salazar Cruz, *Espacio y vida cotidiana*, 6.

9. Hagerty et al., "Sense of Belonging," 173.

10. Anthias, "Where Do I Belong?," 498–99.

11. Pajnik and Anthias, "Migrant Work, Precarity and Agency," 2.

12. Anthias, "Where Do I Belong?," 499.

13. Napolitano, *Migration, Mujercitas, and Medicine Men*, 41–50.

14. Ruble, "Living Apart Together," 14.

15. For more on the issue of anonymity in Mexico's largest cities, see Ramírez Sáiz and Safa Barraza, "Tendencias y retos recientes."

16. Andelson, "Coming Together, Breaking Apart," 136, 141.

17. Hobsbawm, *Nations and Nationalism*, 12–13.

18. Gil, *Life in Provincial Mexico*, 2–3. By "imagine," I mean this in the sense used by Felipe Fernández Armesto, that "the only way to build up our picture of human societies and ecosystems of the past is to start with the evidence people have left. Then we assemble it bit by bit, with the help of imagination disciplined by sources." Fernández Armesto, *Oxford History of the World*, xxxiv. For other uses of the term, see French, "Imagining the Cultural History."

19. Van Young, *Hacienda and Market*.

20. Beezley, *Judas at the Jockey Club*, 108–24.

21. Dorantes González and Fortuny Loret de Mola, "El protestantismo histórico," 32–35; Dorantes, "Primeras etapas," 8–12.

22. While much has been written on secular and Protestant citizenship, Robert Curley is one of the few scholars to tackle a description of Catholic citizenship and civic life. See Curley, *Citizens and Believers*, 15–22.

23. For examples, see Ben Fallaw's *Religion and State Formation*, as well as his *Cárdenas Compromised*; see also Gillingham and Smith, *Dictablanda*; and Gillingham, *Cuauhtemoc's Bones*.

24. Kloppe-Santamaría, *In the Vortex of Violence*, 43, 58, 118.

25. Hélène Rivière d'Arc demonstrates that rural areas in Jalisco had contributed the majority of internal migration to Guadalajara by 1945. While the Cristero War served as one reason people left the outlying areas, economic and security reasons continued to spur migrations well after the war ended. See Rivière d'Arc, *Guadalajara y su región*, 90–93.

26. Kemmis, *Community and the Politics of Place*, 116–23.

27. Jiménez, *Making an Urban Public*, 34–40.

28. Campbell, *Campbell's New Revised Complete Guide*, 189.

29. Terry, *Terry's Guide to Mexico* (1910), 161.

30. This letter shows an address on the extension of calle José María Montenegro near the intersection with avenida Juan Álvarez, perhaps a thirty-minute walk from the center of Guadalajara.

31. Correspondencia, 1939, 1-08-19, Archivo Histórico Municipal de Guadalajara (AHMG). "Correspondencia" is the name of the collection, followed by the year of the item cited. The "1" is the numerical index designation for correspondence; the "08" is an indication of the kind of correspondence designated by the clerk. This number is conditional on the year it is used; for example, in 1939 it indicates *quejas* (complaints). At times the number is designated as two digits (08), and at times the clerk will have written it as just a single digit (8). Written as a single digit or double digit, the meaning is still the same. The "19" designates the order in which it was received. This piece of evidence is, then, a piece of correspondence (1) that registers a complaint (08), and it is the nineteenth piece of correspondence received in 1939.

32. Note that throughout this book I rarely refer to the people living in the city as "citizens" and instead use the term "residents," as women, children, and foreigners—the majority of residents—lacked full citizenship rights.

33. Czaplicka, "Urban History," 373.

34. Villa Pérez, "Participación y movilizaciones ciudadanas," 98–109.

35. Villa Pérez, "Participación y movilizaciones ciudadanas," 123–24.

36. Anthias, "Where Do I Belong?," 494–96 (quote, 495). See also Anthias, "Thinking through the Lens of Transnational Positionality," 6–8.

37. Gillingham, "Thoughts on Citizenship," 15.

38. On citizenship, see Leydet, "Citizenship." I chose to use Leydet because Gillingham draws substantively from that source for his essay on citizenship. On the concept of social integration, see the American Psychological Association Dictionary, s.v. "social integration," accessed April 19, 2018, https://dictionary.apa.org/social-integration.

39. Jiménez, *Making an Urban Public*, 34.

40. *El Occidental*, August 19, 1990.

41. *El Occidental*, August 19, 1990. Daniel Vázquez—who appears frequently in this work— was one of the city's most ardent supporters and fiercest critics.

42. Anthias, "Where Do I Belong?," 498–99. See also Anthias, *Translocational Belonging*, 4–5.

43. For an example of the colonial language of petitions, see Lockhart and Otte, *Letters and People of the Spanish Indies*.

44. Correspondencia, 1943, 1-08-11, AHMG.

45. Taxes in Mexico provided almost three-fourths of the money needed for development in the country during this time period, and people were governed by the Ley del Impuesto sobre la Renta de 1941. For more details on the Mexican income tax, see Urquidi, "El impuesto sobre la renta"; Valencia Islas, *El impuesto sobre la renta*; and Venegas Álvarez, *Presunciones y ficciones*.

46. Correspondencia, 1945, 1-3-29, AHMG.

47. Greer, "Analysis of Mexican Literacy," 468.

48. French, *Heart in the Glass Jar*, 44–46, 243–44; Mendiola, *Street Democracy*, 42–43.

49. Correspondencia, 1943, 1-06-40, AHMG.

50. Correspondencia, 1947, 4-37-31, AHMG.

51. Vázquez, *Guadalajara: Ensayos de interpretación*, 54–55.

52. French, *Heart in the Glass Jar*, 36.

53. Jacobs, *Death and Life of Great American Cities*, 50, 104–5.

54. Matute Remus, "La ciudad en el siglo XX," 441.

55. Bleynat, *Vendors' Capitalism*, 121.

56. Vaca et al., *Historia de Jalisco*, 609.

57. Sánchez Susarrey and Medina Sánchez, *Jalisco desde la Revolución*, 20–21; for a review of spending, see 280–81.

58. García, *Abandoning Their Beloved Land*, 30–32.

59. Gauss, *Made in Mexico*, 88–89.

60. "La nueva Guadalajara," *Gaceta Municipal*, June 1939, 3.

61. González de la Rocha, *Los recursos*, 39–41.

62. Arreguín González, "La planeación urbana," 307.

63. Arias, "La industria en perspectiva," 105.

64. Arroyo Alejandre, "Ires y venires," 21.

65. Hodos, *Second Cities*, 75.

66. Vázquez, *Guadalajara: Ensayos de interpretación*, 74–75. Vázquez states that from 1900 to 1943, the city opened eighteen new areas for housing. From 1943 to 1949 it opened thirty-two new areas. As Vázquez indicates, Margarita Sánchez Van Dyck argues in her PhD thesis from 1979 that no developer of any *fraccionamiento* for the working class—known as *fraccionamientos populares*—received punishment for code violations. See also *El Informador*, July 29, 2011.

67. The text of the original decree by Topete is included in H. Congreso del Estado de Jalisco, Decreto 15097, November 7, 2002, Ley de Desarrollo Urbano del Estado de Jalisco.

68. *Antología de la planeación*, 36.

69. Morfín and Sánchez Van Dyck, "Controles jurídicos," 490.

70. Correspondencia, 1939, 1-5-3, AHMG. This folder contains a series of reports from all over the city about the inability of the municipal government to maintain its properties—most notably schools.

71. Correspondencia sin Contestación, 1943, 1-00-0, AHMG (letter is dated December 15, 1942, and was misfiled in the 1943 folder).

72. Correspondencia sin Contestación, 1944, 1-00-0, AHMG.

73. Morfín and Sánchez Van Dyck, "Controles jurídicos," 501–2.

74. Correspondencia, 1939, 4-34-11, AHMG.

75. Correspondencia, 1939, 4-30-200, AHMG.

76. Vázquez, *Guadalajara: Ensayos de interpretación*, 37, 53; Decreto del H. Congreso del Estado de Jalisco 4882, December 21, 1943.

77. Ley de Desarrollo Urbano del Estado de Jalisco, Decreto 15097, H. Congreso del Estado de Jalisco, November 7, 2002.

78. Dormady, *Primitive Revolution*, 51.

79. Correspondencia, 1940, 4-36-27, AHMG.

80. Vázquez, *Guadalajara: Ensayos de interpretación*, 36–37.

81. This work aligns with that of Paul Gillingham, who has demonstrated that the late 1940s and 1950s featured the development of a powerful central state that used the

single-party structure as a façade of democracy. See Gillingham, *(Un)Revolutionary Mexico*.

82. Correspondencia, 1947, 2-11-12, AHMG.

83. Ley del Consejo de Colaboración, Decreto 5515, Congreso del Estado de Jalisco, December 31, 1949.

84. One can see this transition in small and large ways. For example, Daniel Vázquez argues that the removal of the train station from central Guadalajara and its new location to the south of the city indicated a new direction for the municipality, one that oriented it away from itself and more toward Mexico City and national concerns. See Vázquez, *Guadalajara: Ensayos de interpretación*, 54.

85. Vázquez, *Guadalajara: Ensayos de interpretación*, 77, 142–44.

86. For the complete discussion of the creation of the AMG (later also known as the Zona Metropolitano de Guadalajara, or ZMG) and its administration, see Arellano Ríos, "El área metropolitana."

87. Hélène Rivière d'Arc in her *Guadalajara y su región*, for example, provides an overview of the urban development of Guadalajara from its foundation until the late 1960s. Her narrative, however, covers the city in depth only until 1925, offers a brief discussion of population in the 1940s, and then moves on to cover the era after 1950 in depth. Architect Daniel Vázquez dedicates barely three pages to the era in his famed "La ciudad en perspectiva" essay, included in his book *Guadalajara: Ensayos de interpretación*. In the definitive edited collection of Muriá and Olveda, *Demografía y urbanismo*, the chapter by Juan Manuel Arreguín González names the era as the start of Guadalajara as metropolis, but nearly all of the major infrastructure developments he lists take place after 1947. On the two pages he dedicates to the era covered here, he lists no major physical developments in the city between 1935 and 1947, and he points to only three legal developments during the period. Arreguín González, "La planeación urbana," 309–11.

88. Razo Zaragoza, *Guadalajara*, 27.

89. Tenorio Trillo, *I Speak of the City*, xv.

90. M. Smith, *Sensing the Past*, 1–2. For an example of excellent research on the sense of sound and music in Mexico City, see Rasmussen, *Resistance Resounds*. For an earlier era, see Thomson, "Ceremonial and Political Roles of Village Bands." For the scent of death, see Weber, *Death Is All Around Us*; and Voekel, *Alone before God*.

91. Viquiera Albán, *Propriety and Permissiveness*, 215.

92. Hernández Chávez, *Mexico*, 232.

93. B. K. Smith, *Women in World History*, 52. In this regard, the present work finds creative agreement with Ageeth Sluis's view that urban growth after 1920 represented an incredible opportunity for women to expand their opportunities in the public sphere. Sluis, *Deco Body*, 1.

94. See works such as Arrom, *Women of Mexico City*; Lavrin, "In Search of the Colonial Woman in Mexico"; Gresores, "Mujeres de la colonia"; Jiménez Pelayo, "Las terratenientes de la Nueva Galicia." To some extent, Van Young, *Hacienda and Market*, explores the issue of dowries and property ownership, as does Voekel, *Alone before God*, which does so in an indirect manner by exploring the wills of women in the colonial era.

95. See Mendiola, *Street Democracy*; and B. Smith, *Pistoleros and Popular Movements*.

96. Castro, *Apostle of Progress*, 226–27.

97. Castro, *Apostle of Progress*, 233.

98. Ruiz Razura, *La Casa Cañedo*, 45.

99. Tuan, *Space and Place*, 4.

1. A Battle of the Senses

1. The Diccionario de la Real Academia Española includes the following as their definition of *provinciana*: "Natural o habitante de una provincia, en contraposición al de la capital." Real Academia Española, accessed April 4, 2025, https://dle.rae.es/provinciano?m=form.

2. Correspondencia, 1941, 1-02-50, AHMG.

3. Agostini, *Monuments of Progress*, 149.

4. Knight, *Mexican Revolution*, 1:41–42, 239–40.

5. French, *Peaceful and Working People*, 184.

6. Knight, *Mexican Revolution*, 1:9, 30–31.

7. A. López, "'Urgent Need for Hygiene,'" 89, 91–92.

8. Memorándum #38, July 16, 1942, Exp. 102-42, Libros 26, 1942, Fondo Salubridad, Sección Presidencia, Serie Acuerdos Presidenciales, Archivo Historico de la Secretaría de Salud (AHSS).

9. Hagerty et al., "Sense of Belonging," 173.

10. Bleynat, *Vendors' Capitalism*, 94.

11. Jacobs, *Death and Life of Great American Cities*, 29–30.

12. M. Smith, *Sensing the Past*, 119.

13. Montserrat Degen and Rose, "Sensory Experiencing of Urban Design," 3272.

14. Pizarro, "Teaching to Understand the Urban Sensorium," 274.

15. Merleau-Ponty, *Phenomenology of Perception*, 61.

16. Classen, *Deepest Sense*, xvi.

17. For more on narratives of belonging, see Anthias, "Where Do I Belong?"; and Ross, "Narratives of Belonging."

18. Terry, *Terry's Guide to Mexico* (1947), 459.

19. Terry, *Terry's Guide to Mexico* (1947), 462.

20. Van Pelt, *Old Architecture of Southern Mexico*, 5.

21. Strohmayer, "Engineering Vision," 75–76.

22. Cowan and Steward, introduction, 20–21.

23. Correspondencia, 1941, 4-36-30, AHMG.

24. Correspondencia, 1941, 4-36-30, AHMG.

25. Correspondencia, 1943, 4-34-48; 1947, 4-36-4, AHMG. The category of *albortante*, or light pole, became a category for organizing correspondence, mostly in reference to either the installation or replacement of lampposts after being destroyed by motor vehicles. The category appears alongside the older *alumbrado*, or "lighting," category that centered on correspondence mostly about requests for public lighting without reference to the pole itself.

26. Correspondencia, 1943, 1-08-16; 1947, 1-08-31, AHMG.

27. Correspondencia, 1942, 4-36-4, AHMG.

28. Correspondencia, 1944, 4-31-20, AHMG. The use of *ornato* in this case is interesting as a choice of words for the visual appearance of the city. Established in 1590, the Junta de Policía y Ornato Público in Spain had the distinction of policing cities for cleanliness, cleaning streets, and guaranteeing urban beauty. See Cámara Muñoz, "Modelo urbano y obras en Madrid," 41. Vendors at times would refer to their stand as "not constituting any damage to the aesthetic of the city" (*no constituya un demérito al ornato de la ciudad*).

29. Correspondencia, 1944, 4-38-6, AHMG.

30. Gillingham, *(Un)Revolutionary Mexico*, 222.

31. M. Smith, *Sensing the Past*, 35.

32. Correspondencia, 1939, 4-38-17, AHMG.

33. Referring to the area as a *barriada*, meaning either a peripheral or poor neighborhood, is an interesting choice. Situated as it was between the older working-class neighborhood of Mexicaltzingo and the Porfirian-era upper-class neighborhood of Colonia Americana, this *barriada*, at the time the petitioners wrote their letter in 1939, was hardly on the outer edges of the city, and it certainly was no shantytown, as the word implies in other areas of Latin America. While neither poor nor geographically peripheral, the neighborhood did lie outside the heart of the city, and the petition implies that the city is not extending services to such areas because they are peripheral. While the city has a sensory expectation of the darkness of a peripheral area, the neighbors demanded the same security and lighting experience the city center enjoyed.

34. Correspondencia, 1942, 4-38-11, AHMG.

35. Please note that I refer here to criminals who chose to commit their crimes in the dark. As the complaints of city residents attest, plenty of criminals—particularly police,

soldiers, bureaucrats, and politicians—were content to carry out their crimes in the light of day.

36. Weber, *Death Is All Around Us*, 74.

37. Correspondencia, 1941, 1-08-15, AHMG.

38. López, "Urgent Need for Hygiene," 94.

39. Removed bodies could be disposed of in a common grave, or they might be used by the medical school for dissection by anatomy students. See Correspondencia, 1944, 1-02-53; 1941, 1-08-15, AHMG. One historic cemetery—the Panteón Belén—is also where the medical school used to be housed, partially for ease of disposal of bodies and partially for ease of access to bodies for the students.

40. For Bourbon Reforms, see Will, *Death and Dying*; or Voekel, *Alone before God*. For the Porfirian era, see Weber, *Death Is All Around Us*. Much like Colignon, Porfirian elites worried about "repugnant spectacles" like a streetcar transporting bodies or funeral processions, as indicated in Weber, *Death Is All Around Us*, 67.

41. Zardini, *Sense of the City*, 179.

42. Fortuna, "La ciudad de los sonidos," 43.

43. Mirko Zardini quotes Canadian composer R. Murray Schafer in pointing out that "noise is just unwanted sound. . . . Noise is any undesired sound. Noise is the wrong sound in the wrong place. This makes noise, to be sure, a relative term." Schafer quoted in Zardini, *Sense of the City*, 163.

44. In an examination of sound as resistance and conflict in present-day Mexico City, Anthony William Rasmussen gives broad examples of sound in a variety of uses (daily life, business, sales, entertainment) and identifies a distinct continuity in cities regarding the competition between various groups and their use of sound. Rasmussen, "Resistance Resounds."

45. Not much is known about either cantina. La Alhambra appears to have been run by a foreign national from one of the Axis powers, as it was confiscated in 1943 and its contents auctioned off by the Junta de Administración y Vigilancia de la Propiedad Extranjera. *El Informador*, August 6, 1943.

46. Correspondencia, 1942, 1-08-21, AHMG.

47. Hernández Romero, "El jazz en México," 29–30.

48. Dormady, *Primitive Revolution*, 41.

49. Krauze, *Mexico: Biography of Power*, 614.

50. Ramírez, *Migrating Faith*, 186.

51. Correspondencia, 1942, 1-09-12, AHMG.

52. *El Informador*, June 6, 1930.

53. *El Informador*, October 19, 1932.

54. See *El Informador*, February 17, 1933, October 1, 1940.

55. *El Informador*, May 15, 1934.

56. *El Informador*, January 11, 1945.

57. Correspondencia, 1947, 1-00-103, AHMG.

58. *El Informador*, October 15, 1932, April 23, 1932, respectively.

59. *El Informador*, September 1, 1944.

60. Palacio Montiel, ". . . El vivir, mitad pueblerino, mitad ciudadano," 146; Castro, "Sounding the Mexican Nation." See also Hayes, "National Imaginings on the Air."

61. Correspondencia, 1947, 4-37-98, AHMG.

62. Thomson, "Ceremonial and Political Roles of Village Bands," 330–31, 337.

63. Correspondencia, 1947, 1-00-103, AHMG. In March of that year, temporary speakers were hung throughout the city to broadcast speeches from the visit of U.S. president Harry Truman.

64. Bender, Corpis, and Walkowitz, "Sound Politics," 1–2.

65. In Mexico City the recording of a scrap dealer's daughter, María del Mar Terrón Martínez, calling for "*colchones, tambores, refrigeradores, estufas*" and other items, has become a touchstone of working-class urban culture. It is even the subject of songs by various performers, such as Mexican Institute of Sound and a DJ club remix by Mike Fortu of Fortu & Mendoza.

66. Correspondencia, 1947, 1-08-1, AHMG.

67. Correspondencia, 1947, 1-08-24, AHMG.

68. Walton, "Cultura y economía," 381.

69. M. Smith, *Sensing the Past*, 48–49.

70. M. Smith, *Sensing the Past*, 52–53.

71. Correspondencia, 1947, 1-08-22, AHMG.

72. *El Informador*, June 8, 1943. When Zarkin took ill or attended parties, it made the society pages of *El Informador*, and when his son wed a Detroit socialite, it was reported in the *Detroit Jewish News* on March 3, 1950. At his passing in 1973, a Star of David appeared in the notice, and he was given the honorific "El Señor Don." Zarkin's workers brought him into the spotlight more than once, as he and his business were consistently featured in the 1940s in Departamento de Trabajo labor disputes with workers whom his business fired and had to rehire. *El Informador*, March 11, 1945, August 28, 1946, March 16, 1947.

73. *El Informador*, January 17, 1949.

74. Correspondencia, 1947, 1-08-37, AHMG.

75. Correspondencia, 1947, 1-06-64, AHMG. The list of small businesses with generators and boilers was solicited by the city and assembled by the Departamento del Trabajo y Previsión Social of Jalisco.

76. Gauss, *Made in Mexico*, 65, 86–87.

77. Correspondencia sin Contestación, 1945, 1-00-0, AHMG.

78. Classen, Howes, and Synnott, *Aroma*, 3.

79. Leonardo Frias, "La historia de México a través de sus olores," *Gaceta UNAM*, August 2, 2021, https://www.gaceta.unam.mx/a-que-huele-mexico.

80. Zardini, *Sense of the City*, 277.

81. M. Smith, *Sensing the Past*, 121.

82. Orwell, *Road to Wigan Pier*, 161, quoting Maugham's *On a Chinese Screen*.

83. Agostini, *Monuments of Progress*, 4, 34, 55; Miranda Pacheco, "Urbe inmunda," 178; Olivares, "¡A bañarse se ha dicho!," 221–24, 227–28.

84. Classen, Howes, and Synnott, *Aroma*, 161–65.

85. Classen, Howes, and Synnott, *Aroma*, 169–71.

86. Cited in Zardini, *Sense of the City*, 301.

87. Correspondencia, 1939, 4-30-200, AHMG.

88. Correspondencia, 1942, 1-08-55, AHMG.

89. Correspondencia, 1947, 1-08-60, AHMG.

90. Corbin, *Foul and the Fragrant*, 130.

91. Correspondencia, 1940, 1-08-20, AHMG.

92. Correspondencia, 1947, 4-37-44, AHMG.

93. Correspondencia sin Contestación, 1943, 1-00-0, AHMG.

94. Correspondencia, 1946, 1-07-7, AHMG.

95. Correspondencia, 1946, 1-07-7, AHMG.

96. Correspondencia, 1942, 1-08-14, AHMG.

97. *Excelsior*, February 4, 1937; *El Informador*, January 1, 1937, February 3, 1937, February 5, 1937.

98. Wheller, "Stench in Sixteenth-Century Venice," 25.

99. Correspondencia, 1940, 1-08-20, AHMG.

100. Correspondencia, 1939, 4-30-85, AHMG.

101. Correspondencia, 1946, 4-34-48, AHMG.

102. Correspondencia, 1942, 4-30-112, AHMG.

103. Correspondencia, 1940, 1-07-21, AHMG. In 1947 a federal agricultural school on the edge of the city (the Santa Ines School) used city sewer water to fertilize alfalfa and barley but insisted that none was used for the growth of vegetables and other directly consumed items. Correspondencia, 1947, 1-05-12, AHMG.

104. Correspondencia, 1944, 4-38-7, AHMG.

105. Cowan and Steward, introduction, 12–13; M. Smith, *Sensing History*, 90.

106. Sjölinder, "Spatial Cognition and Environmental Descriptions," 47–48.

107. Cowan and Steward, introduction, 12–13.

108. Classen, *Deepest Sense*, 178.

109. Arndt, "Touching London," 96–97, 104.

110. Palacio Montiel, "El vivir, mitad pueblerino, mitad ciudadano," 142.

111. Correspondencia, 1939, 4-30-37, AHMG.

112. "El censo muestra resaltante progreso del automóvil en 1922," *El Automóvil Americano*, February 1923. Palacio Montiel, "El vivir, mitad pueblerino, mitad ciudadano," 145, claims only 320 cars and bases her estimate on that of Francisco Javier Uribe Topete. See Uribe Topete, "Los transportes de los tapatíos."

113. Islas Rivera et al., *Urbanización y motorización en México*, 5, 18.

114. Sánchez Gómez, "Esbozo histórico del transporte," 394, 418–19.

115. Correspondencia, 1940, 4-30-186, AHMG.

116. Correspondencia, 1947, 4-37-34, 4-38-6, 4-38-38, 4-38-107, AHMG.

117. Correspondencia, 1940, 1-02-4, AHMG.

118. Correspondencia, 1940, 1-08-32, 1-08-33, AHMG.

119. Correspondencia, 1940, 1-02-20, 1-02-40, 4-38-23; 1941, 1-08-29; 1942, 4-36-2, 4-38-14, AHMG. The documents listed here all provide good examples of how people saw the violence of vehicles in city streets.

120. Correspondencia, 1941, 1-08-29, AHMG; *El Informador*, February 1, 1939.

121. Correspondencia, 1947, 1-00-9, AHMG.

122. *El Informador*, June 13, 1941.

123. Correspondencia, 1946, 1-08-53; 1947, 1-08-61, AHMG.

124. Correspondencia, 1947, 1-00-9, AHMG.

125. Correspondencia, 1944, 4-33-43, AHMG. While the city and bus driver unions extolled the virtues of bus transit, those same heavy, fast-moving buses were destroying the city streets put in place to accommodate them. Correspondencia, 1947, 4-38-59, AHMG.

126. Correspondencia, 1947, 4-37-34, AHMG.

127. Correspondencia, 1940, 1-02-16; 1944, 2-10-41; 1947, 4-37-74, 1-08-29, AHMG.

128. Correspondencia, 1947, 4-37-38, AHMG.

129. Correspondencia sin Contestación, 1947, 1-00-0, AHMG.

130. Arndt, *Touching London*, 104. Vázquez states that the Cámara de Comercio was established in 1888. Vázquez, *Guadalajara: Ensayos de interpretación*, 33.

131. Correspondencia, 1942, 4-36-2, AHMG.

132. For a selection of complaints, see Correspondencia, 1942, 1-02-5, 4-36-2, 4-36-3, 4-36-20; 1944, 4-34-36; and 1947, 4-37-69, AHMG.

133. Correspondencia, 1942, 4-07-21; 1943, 4-31-26, 4-31-13, AHMG.

134. Correspondencia, 1942, 4-36-4, AHMG.

135. Correspondencia, 1947, 4-37-64, AHMG.

136. Pallasmaa, *Eyes of the Skin*, 43.

137. "No más cantinas ni más facilidades," *Gaceta Municipal*, August 30, 1941.

138. Cowan and Steward, introduction, 11.

139. Kloppe-Santamaría, *In the Vortex of Violence*, 13, 17, 57–58, 67, 110. I do not mean to say that lynching or violence could not be carried out by urban residents against neighbors who departed from social norms. Instead, I only indicate that cities offered a measure

of opportunity, anonymity, and pleasure that departed from normalized village society or was not available in smaller towns.

2. Morality and Merriment

1. Correspondencia, 1942, 1-08-31, AHMG.
2. For more on *la sociedad culta*, see French, *Peaceful and Working People*, 63–107.
3. Escobar Hernández, "Los cabarets prohibidos," 107. Historian Bogar Escobar Hernández makes this argument about cabarets in 1960s and 1970s Guadalajara, and I am extending his ideas to a wider range of pleasure pursuits and to a period two decades further into the past.
4. French, *Peaceful and Working People*, 63–64.
5. Bauman, *Amor líquido*, 147–51.
6. Fiore, *Drama and Ethos*, 5–6.
7. Gutiérrez, "Mexican Masculinities," 264–65.
8. The petitioners indicated that they lived on calle Rayón, which lies about a half block west of Parque Revolución in an area expanded during the Porfiriato and called Colonia Americana. This area, however, was not one filled with the grand Porfirian homes on wide avenues found several blocks farther west. Calle Rayón is narrow and has family homes, apartment buildings, and small businesses.
9. Secretaría de la Economía Nacional, *Estados Unidos Mexicanos*, 13–27.
10. De la Torre, "Guadalajara vista desde la calzada," 45.
11. French, *Peaceful and Working People*, 4–7.
12. Vaughan, *Cultural Politics*, 100–105, 189–91.
13. Gomez, *Silver Veins, Dusty Lungs*, 161–64.
14. Masters, "Thousand Invisible Architects," 385–400.
15. Alonso, *Thread of Blood*, 85–90.
16. Alonso, *Thread of Blood*, 80–84.
17. Jaffary, "Sacred Defiance and Sexual Desecration," 50–55.
18. Tuñón, *Mujeres*, 114.
19. Toner, *Alcohol and Nationhood*, 237.
20. Altamirano, *La Navidad*, 58.
21. De la Garza Arregui, "El matrimonio según la epístola de Melchor Ocampo."
22. Alonso, *Thread of Blood*, 91.
23. Knight, *Bandits and Liberals*, chap. 2.
24. Buffington, *Criminal and Citizen*, 75.
25. Tuñón, *Mujeres*, 160. For more on the changes and contradictions for mothers and motherhood, see O'Connor, *Mothers Making Latin America*.

26. Porter, *Working Women*, xix.

27. Toxqui, "Taverns and Their Influence," 241.

28. Weiner, *Race, Nation, and Market*, 25–28.

29. Isais Contreras, "Alcoholismo, raza, y degeneración," 83.

30. Fallaw, *Religion and State Formation*, 220–21.

31. Fernández Aceves, "Guadalajaran Women," 306–8.

32. Dormady, *Primitive Revolution*.

33. Toner, *Alcohol and Nationhood*, 407–9, 419.

34. Ramos Escandón, "Challenging Legal and Gender Constraints," 65.

35. Bliss, "For the Health of the Nation," 205–7; Pierce and Toxqui, *Alcohol in Latin America*, 6–7.

36. Kloppe-Santamaría, *In the Vortex of Violence*, 61.

37. Jenks, "Becoming Vecinos"; Jiménez, *Making an Urban Public*, 21–23.

38. Panik and Anthias, "Migrant Work, Precarity and Agency," 2.

39. Correspondencia, 1943, 1-08-37, AHMG.

40. Correspondencia, 1943, 1-08-37, AHMG.

41. For an example of forged signatures, see Correspondencia, 1947, 1-08-09, AHMG, where a petition carrying multiple signatures demands an investigation of a household engaged in loud music and immoral behavior, only to have the inspector return a report that the residence was quiet with no sign of such activity and an additional comment that none of those who were reported to have signed the petition confirmed their signatures.

42. Fernández Aceves, "Struggle between the 'Metate' and the 'Molinos.'"

43. Cano, "Unconcealable Realities," 46–53.

44. Núñez Becerra, "Mujeres públicas," 274; Bliss, *Compromised Positions*, 44–48, 120–21; Buffington, *Criminal and Citizen*, 70–71.

45. Correspondencia, 1939, 3-22-8, AHMG.

46. Palacio Montiel, "El vivir, mitad pueblerino, mitad ciudadano," 148.

47. Correspondencia, 1947, 1-08-9, AHMG.

48. Schell, "Of the Sublime Mission of Mothers of Families," 111–12.

49. Bliss, *Compromised Positions*, 196–99.

50. Correspondencia, 1947, 1-08-9, AHMG.

51. Correspondencia, 1947, 1-08-9, AHMG.

52. Gillingham, *(Un)Revolutionary Mexico*, 208.

53. Fuentes, "Burdeles, prostitución y género," 240.

54. Correspondencia, 1942, 1-08-15, AHMG.

55. Correspondencia sin Contestación, 1944, 1-00-0, AHMG.

56. Correspondencia sin Contestación, 1944, 1-00-0 (Gallardo's letter is dated January 4, 1945, and is misfiled in the 1944 file).

57. Correspondencia sin Contestación, 1944, 1-00-0.

58. Joseph and Buchenau, *Mexico's Once and Future Revolution*, 16–17; McBride, *Land Systems of Mexico*, 155.

59. Hart, *Bitter Harvest*, 171–79; Dwyer, *Agrarian Dispute*, 17–19.

60. Dwyer, *Agrarian Dispute*, 20.

61. Regarding urban expropriations after the 1910 revolution, see Peña, "Eminent Domain and Expropriation Laws," 162–64.

62. Ibarra Ibarra, "Mercado de suelo," 7–12.

63. Correspondencia, 1941, 1-08-56, AHMG.

64. Morán Quiroz, "Percibir la ciudad," 170–71.

65. Correspondencia, 1941, 1-06-4, AHMG.

66. Correspondencia, 1943, 1-06-79, AHMG

67. Correspondencia, 1946, 1-06-90, AHMG. For more on the practice of pimps and madams luring young girls into sex work, see Bliss, *Compromised Positions*.

68. Maggi et al., "Rural-Urban Migration Patterns," 7.

69. Crossa, "Resisting the Entrepreneurial City," 53.

70. Toner, *Alcohol and Nationhood*, 126–29.

71. The phrase used in the source refers to *baños*, or baths—the term used for pools or bathhouses at the time.

72. As of this writing, it bears the name Hospital Salud de los Enfermos. Father Sánchez Araiza had established the original hospital to provide care for the city's most needy. *Semanario*, September 6, 2009.

73. *El Informador*, February 25, 1948.

74. Correspondencia, 1946, 1-08-33, AHMG.

75. For more on sexuality, health, and bathhouses, see Macías-González, "Bathhouse and Male Homosexuality," 35–36, 42–43.

76. Correspondencia, 1946, 1-08-29, AHMG.

77. Razo Zaragoza, *Guadalajara*, 113.

78. Correspondencia, 1947, 1-02-58; 1946, 1-08-31, AHMG.

79. Rodríguez Castillo, "Ver desde la calle," 36–42.

80. Correspondencia, 1946, 1-08-29, AHMG.

81. Correspondencia, 1946, 1-08-16, AHMG.

82. Ruiz Razura, "El convento de San Agustín," 43.

83. Correspondencia, 1939, 1-08-27, AHMG.

84. Correspondencia, 1946, 1-08-46, AHMG; Gillingham, *(Un)Revolutionary Mexico*, 208.

85. Correspondencia sin Contestación, 1943, 1-00-0, AHMG.

86. Nicoll, *Gambling*, chap. 2.

87. Correspondencia, 1945, 3-29-18, AHMG. As a side note, this is an additional example of a petition levied against a business attempting to use state regulation as a tool to dislodge competition. The petitioner had previously had business dealings with Severo Herrera that turned sour, and the petitioner was also a cantina owner. Had the city shut down Aguilar Preciado's business, Herrera would have suffered fines for allowing an unlicensed business on his property, and the petitioner would have also eliminated competition.

88. Galindo González et al., "Las academias municipales."

89. Anderson, "Sociability," 103.

90. Toxqui, "Taverns and Their Influence," 242.

91. "Consejos para combatir la criminalidad," El Informador, May 6, 1943.

92. Kennedy, "El complejo del tesgüino." 258.

93. Correspondencia, 1942, 1-08-21, AHMG.

94. El Informador, October 27, 1942.

95. Correspondencia, 1946, 3-29-59, AHMG.

96. Pulido Esteva, ";A su salud!," 185-90.

97. Correspondencia, 1942, 1-08-46, AHMG.

98. Correspondencia, 1941, 1-0-63; 1942, 1-08-1, AHMG.

99. El Informador, February 23, 1940.

100. El Informador, February 15, 1940.

101. Courtwright, Forces of Habit, 2, 173-74.

102. T. Mitchell, Intoxicated Identities, 5.

103. Haddu and Thornton, Legacies of the Past, 1-18.

104. T. Mitchell, Intoxicated Identities, 74, 79-82.

105. Courtwright, Forces of Habit, 98.

106. T. Mitchell, Intoxicated Identities, 48-50.

107. T. Mitchell, Intoxicated Identities, 10, 74.

108. Quintana, Maximino Ávila Camacho, 21, 124.

109. "Carta pastoral colectiva que el episcopado nacional dirige a Los Muy Ilustres Cabildos, al venerable clero secular y regular, y a todos los fieles, sobre la doctrina social de la Iglesia," August 30, 1935, Gobierno / Obispos / José Garibi Rivera / 1935-44, Exp. 19, Caja 2, Archivo Histórico del Arzobispado de Guadalajara (AHAG).

110. "Labrosidad y honradez será la norma de la comuna Tapatía," Gaceta Municipal, January 1939, 17-18.

111. French, Peaceful and Working People, 84-85.

112. Ege and Moser, introduction, 3-5.

113. Pierce, "Pulqueros, Cerveceros, and Mezcaleros," 162.

114. For more on cities moving toward recognizing nightlife as part of urban planning, see Cibin, "Forms of Night-Time Economy Governance."

3. Divine Hygiene

1. Hagerty et al., "Sense of Belonging," 173.
2. Gomez, *Silver Veins, Dusty Lungs*, 17.
3. Bowen, *Evangelism and Apostasy*, 83. Kurt Bowen is discussing his own disagreement with the "religious problem-solving perspective" proposed in Lofland and Stark, "Becoming a World-Saver."
4. Bantjes, "Regional Dynamics," 112.
5. Curley, "Anticlericalism and Public Space," 514.
6. Aldana Rendón, "Masonería y revolución," 25–26.
7. Joseph and Buchenau, *Mexico's Once and Future Revolution*, 16–17, 80–81, 88, 100–101, 128; Weis, *For Christ and Country*, 11–19.
8. Fernández Aceves, *Mujeres en el cambio social*, 96–97.
9. Aguirre Cristiani, "La jerarquía católica," 167.
10. Weis, *For Christ and Country*, 92, 117.
11. Inventario del Templos, 1918, Carpeta 2, Caja 9, Estadística de Iglesias, AHMG. For the concept of "unscripted anticlericalism," see Curley, *Citizens and Believers*, 204–12. See also the article from Curley and Omar, "Catolicismo cívico, reforma liberal y política moderna."
12. Bantjes, "Regional Dynamics," 113.
13. Curley, *Citizens and Believers*, 212.
14. Curley, "Political Catholicism," 48.
15. Fernández Aceves, "José Guadalupe Zuno," 98–99.
16. Buchenau, *Plutarco Elías Calles*, 127.
17. Reich, *Mexico's Hidden Revolution*, 13.
18. Wright-Rios, *Revolutions in Mexican Catholicism*, 20.
19. For a discussion of the various strains of anticlericalism in postrevolutionary Mexico, see Fallaw, "Varieties of Mexican Revolutionary Anticlericalism."
20. Dormady, *Primitive Revolution*, 32; Weis, "Revolution on Trial," 319.
21. Butler, *Mexico's Spiritual Reconquest*, 112–40. The Iglesia Católica Apostólica Mexicana was created by dissident Roman Catholic clergy in 1925 and backed by Mexican labor unions with the support of President Plutarco Elías Calles. It occupied churches confiscated from the Roman Catholic Church by the Mexican federal government. It used a similar liturgy to that of the Roman church, but as a Mexican national church it had no ties to the pope or the Vatican.

22. Tuck, *Holy War*, 31.

23. Meyer, *Cristero Rebellion*, 33–38.

24. Krauze, *Mexico: Biography of Power*, 424; Museo Nacional de Arte, *Arqueología del régimen*, 80, 96–102; Florescano, *Imágenes de la patria*, 366.

25. Bantjes, *As If Jesus Walked on Earth*, 7, 10.

26. Meyer, *Cristero Rebellion*, 48–49.

27. Weis, *For Christ and Country*, 121–26.

28. Reich, *Mexico's Hidden Revolution*, 28.

29. *El Informador*, June 21, 1934.

30. Jean Meyer and David Raby offer differing figures on the violence against schoolteachers, but both agree that it was significant. Raby's study examines violence against schoolteachers and says that at least 233 were targets of violence between 1931 and 1940—several years beyond the somewhat official end of antagonism toward religion by the Cárdenas administration. See Meyer, *Cristero Rebellion*, 203–6; and Raby, *Educación y revolución*. For the power of Catholics to force compromise on the local level, see Fallaw, *Religion and State Formation*.

31. Blancarte, "Intransigence, Anticommunism, and Reconciliation," 73–74.

32. Knight, *Mexican Revolution*, 2:499–500.

33. Pensado, *Love and Despair*, 5.

34. Meyer, "Catholic Resistance," 187; Fallaw, "'Anti-Priests,'" 216. For a case where the *juntas* were not an extension of clerical power, scholars can look to Morelos, where there are instances of the juntas serving as vigorous counters to the clergy. See Dormady, "'Disobedience, rebelliousness, . . . and discontent.'"

35. For more on the position of the Catholic leadership with respect to the post–Cristero War order, see Blancarte, "Intransigence, Anticommunism, and Reconciliation"; Blancarte, *El pensamiento social*; and Solis, "Secret Archives, Secret Societies."

36. Curley, *Citizens and Believers*, 255.

37. Curley, *Citizens and Believers*, 271.

38. Dorantes, "La llegada del evangelio Protestante," 60.

39. The full ban came just two years after the official arrival of Protestants in the city. Dorantes, "Primeras etapas," 9.

40. Dorantes, "Primeras etapas," 8–9.

41. McIntyre, *Protestantism and State Formation*, 18–19.

42. Hagerty et al., "Sense of Belonging," 173.

43. Dorantes, "Primeras etapas," 15–16.

44. Butler, "Revolution in Spirit," 8.

45. Bastian, "Protestants, Freemasons, and Spiritists," 77; Urías Horcasitas, "De moral y regeneración," 88.

46. Martínez Moctezuma, "La actividad física."

47. Dorantes, "Primeras etapas," 9; Fortuny Loret de Mola, *Los "otros" hermanos*, 213. According to Fortuny, by 2000 the average percentage of Protestants in Jalisco was 2.8 and in Guadalajara, 3.7. The Mexican census and data organization INEGI has shown that the proportion of Protestants had grown to about 5 percent by 2020—a fraction of a percent higher than the number of people who profess no religion in Guadalajara. Sistema Nacional de Información Estadística y Geografía, accessed February 21, 2025, https://cuentame.inegi.org.mx/descubre/conoce_tu_estado/tarjeta .html?estado=14.

48. "Bienvenidos a la Iglesia Anglicana de México," accessed October 4, 2017, http:// mexico-anglican.org/QuienesSomos.html (URL not functional after 2022); Voekel, "Liberal Religion," 84–94; Voekel, *For God and Liberty*, 226–37.

49. "Pablo González a Ayuntamiento," May 10, 1933, Carpeta 8, Caja 5, Templos Otros Credos, AHMG.

50. Pierce, "Pulqueros, Cerveceros, and Mezcaleros," 164, 173.

51. The petition's goal is in line with the confiscation and occupation of churches by the federal government, particularly in Mexico City. Most famously, the state tacitly supported the occupation of a church (also named La Soledad) in Mexico City by an independent Mexican Catholic Church (the Mexican Catholic Apostolic Church), and when that resulted in violence, the new church withdrew but the building remained in government hands as a library. See Reich, *Mexico's Hidden Revolution*, 12–13.

52. "Iglesia Episcopal Mexicana, Peticiones, Miguel Díaz a Presidente Municipal," December 11, 1936, Carpeta 25, Caja 9, Estadística de Iglesias, AHMG.

53. "José N. Robredo a Secretario de Gobernación," December 8, 1938, Carpeta 8, Caja 5, Templos Otros Credos, AHMG.

54. F-11-1950 / Fomento / Obras Publicas / No. de Inv. 12137 / Caja 453, Archivo Histórico del Estado de Jalisco (AHEJ); *El Informador*, August 26, 1952.

55. *El Informador*, September 27, 1939.

56. Zárate Weber, "Las vías sacras," 6, 11–16, 26.

57. See Fallaw, *Religion and State Formation*.

58. "Sr. Obispo José Garibi Rivera Datos y Su Bautismo," 1889, Gobierno / Obispos / José Garibi Rivera / 1935–44, Exp. 19, Caja 2, AHAG. Garibi Rivera served as Mexico's first cardinal, from 1958 to 1972. He was a pragmatic leader; for example, while decrying the pursuit of wealth as well as the pollution of Mexican society via films, the Archdiocese of Guadalajara maintained an active investment portfolio in at least one Mexican film company. "Cia. La Mexicana a Sr. Dr. José Garibi Rivera," March 11, 1937, Gobierno / Obispos / José Garibi Rivera / 1935–44, Exp. 19, Caja 2, AHAG; "Acción Católica ACJM Informes," 1938, Gobierno / Asociaciones / Acción Católica / 1936–40, Exp. 11, Caja 2, AHAG.

59. "Carta Pastoral Colectiva que el Episcopado Nacional Dirige a Los Muy II. Cabildos. Al VBLE. Clero Secular y Regular, y a Todos Los Fieles, Sobre La Doctrina Social de La Iglesia," August 30, 1935, Gobierno / Obispos / José Garibi Rivera / 1935-44, Exp. 19, Caja 2, AHAG.

60. José Garibi Rivera, "Circular: Sobre Facultades Extraordinarias," August 21, 1936, Gobierno / Obispos / José Garibi Rivera / 1935-44, Exp. 19, Caja 2, AHAG; ACJM [Asociación Católica de la Juventud Mexicana] Guadalajara, "ACJM Declaración," February 1944, Gobierno / Asociaciones / Acción Católica / 1936-40, Exp. 11, Caja 2, AHAG. Garibi Rivera's approach is an extension of earlier Catholic attempts to engage in the political public space of Jalisco as a "civic religion," one that encouraged Catholics to live their lives in ways that could shape society. See Curley, *Citizens and Believers*, 261. The Catholic Church in Mexico was engaged in a broad debate over controlling militant groups but also in promoting unity between Catholic groups. See Espinosa, *Jesuit Student Groups*. The Catholic leadership that sought to move Catholics toward the spiritual and the less overtly political issued pastoral documents on civic engagement because they had to deal with the ACM structure being engaged by political actors. See B. Smith, *Roots of Conservatism*, 201-3. Guadalajara was not immune to these entanglements; the Universidad Autónoma de Guadalajara, established in 1935 with the help of PAN co-founder Efraín González Luna, became a hotbed of activity for the Asociación Católica de la Juventud Mexicana and its less militant counterpart, Acción Católica. See Espinosa, *Jesuit Student Groups*, 51-52.

61. "Circular: Asociación Cristiana Femenina," December 21, 1938, Gobierno / Cartas Pastorales, Edictos y Circulares, Exp. 17, Caja 14, AHAG.

62. Serrano Álvarez, *La batalla del espíritu*, 47.

63. Garibi Rivera, "Circular: Ejercicio de la jurisdicción eclesiástica," March 4, 1938, Gobierno / Cartas Pastorales, Edictos y Circulares, Exp. 17, Caja 14, AHAG.

64. "Carta Pastoral Colectiva que el Episcopado Nacional Dirige a Los Muy II. Cabildos. Al VBLE. Clero Secular y Regular, y a Todos Los Fieles, sobre la Doctrina Social de la Iglesia," August 30, 1935.

65. IGJ [Inspección General de Justicia] / 1943-47, Exp. 0020, Memoria del Poder Ejecutivo, AHEJ.

66. Foment, "Selfhood and Nationhood in Latin America," 126.

67. Curley, "Political Catholicism," 48.

68. "No hacer reparaciones en tos templos," November 18, 1932, Carpeta 7, Caja 9, Estadística de Iglesias, AHMG.

69. "José N. Robredo a Secretario de Gobernación," December 8, 1938. Robredo, listed in the correspondence as a printer by profession, may have combined his professional skills to let his ecclesiastical zeal get ahead of his petition by printing his letterhead before his building was approved.

70. "José N. Robredo a Secretario de Gobernación," December 8, 1938.

71. "Al C. P. M. Manuel Y. Ochoa," June 23, 1938; and "Al Honorable C. P. M. Manuel Y. Ochoa," June 30, 1938, both in Carpeta 8, Caja 5, Templos Otros Credos, AHMG.

72. "Varios Vecinos," March 24, 1939, Carpeta 8, Caja 5, Templos Otros Credos, AHMG.

73. "Varios Vecinos," March 24, 1939.

74. "Varios Vecinos," March 24, 1939.

75. Correspondencia, 1939, 1-01-08, AHMG.

76. Correspondencia, 1939, 1-01-08.

77. Correspondencia, 1939, 1-01-08.

78. The word *agape* is part of both Christian literature and, by extension, Masonic symbolism. *El Informador*, January 6, 1940.

79. Attempts to locate members of the congregation in the municipal archive (AHMG) did not yield any conclusive evidence. The names of most signatories are incredibly common names, and in cases where more unique names matched, signatures did not match. The same results came from searching for the Templo de Cristo congregants in the digital repository of *El Informador*, as well as civil registry records. I conclude from these mostly unsuccessful attempts to locate the congregants that they were of little influence and had little power within the city.

80. B. Smith, "Anticlericalism, Politics, and Freemasonry," 561. For an example of Catholic antipathy toward Masons in Guadalajara early in the 1910 revolution, see Curley, "First Encounter," 142. For Masonic and Catholic clashes in Jalisco during the Cristero War, see González Navarro, *Masones y cristeros*.

81. B. Smith, "Anticlericalism, Politics, and Freemasonry," 574.

82. Boylan, "Gendering Faith," 209; Espinosa, *Jesuit Student Groups*, 35–36.

83. "'Principios Fundamentales de Acción Cívica' in Boletín de Acción Católica," October 1, 1935, Folletería / Publicaciones y Periódicas, Caja 9, ACM: Comité Diocesano, AHAG.

84. "Entrega de Templos," December 27, 1932, Carpeta 11, Caja 9, Estadística de Iglesias, AHMG; "Encargados de Templos," 1918, Carpeta 1; "Encargados de Templos," 1918, Carpeta 3; "Lista de Vecinos Aranzazú," 1926, Carpeta 3; and "Lista de Juntas de Vecinos," 1927, Carpeta 4, all in Caja 9, Estadísticas de Cultos, AHMG; "Lista de Templos," December 30, 1932; "Lista de Sacerdotes," 1932; and "Lista de Sacerdotes," 1935, August 19, 1935, all in Carpeta 6, Caja 9, Estadística de Iglesias, AHMG; "Asistentes de Comités y Subcomités de la Ciudad," 1937, Gobierno / Asociaciones / Acción Católica / 1936–40, Exp. 11, Caja 2, AHAG.

85. Certainly hygiene was an issue considered by Catholics in Mexico. During the 1909 Oaxaca Conference of Catholics that brought lay and clerical adherents together to discuss issues, the goal of improving the hygiene of "proletariat" homes and places of employment made the agenda. See Espinosa, *Jesuit Student Groups*, 22.

86. Boylan, "Gendering Faith," 210.

87. Muriá, *Breve historia*, 74.

88. Oliver, "Los servicios de salud," 70.

89. Oliver, "Los servicios de salud," 53–71.

90. Rivière d'Arc, *Guadalajara y su región*, 30–31; Orendain, "Salubridad e higiene," 83–84.

91. Oliver, "Los servicios de salud," 76.

92. Orendain, "Salubridad e higiene," 80–82.

93. Agostini, *Monuments of Progress*, 153; Soto Laveaga, "Science and Public Health," 564.

94. Orendain, "Salubridad e higiene," 84–85.

95. Weber, *Death Is All Around Us*, 187.

96. Weber, *Death Is All Around Us*, 25.

97. Mendoza López, "Causas más comunes de la mortalidad de los niños," 172–80.

98. Agostini, *Monuments of Progress*, 149.

99. Knight, *Mexican Revolution*, 1:41–42, 239–40.

100. French, *Peaceful and Working People*, 184.

101. Knight, *Mexican Revolution*, 1:9, 30–31; López, "'Urgent Need for Hygiene,'" 89, 91–92.

102. Walton, "Cultura y economía," 384–85.

103. Weber, *Death Is All Around Us*, 220.

104. Agostini, *Monuments of Progress*, 153.

105. See various documents from the Actas de Cabildo and Correspondencia from 1934 to 1940, AHMG.

106. Correspondencia, 1940, 1-02-17, AHMG, offers one example of the many hundreds of citations issued for having barbershops open on Sundays—a day when people would have time to take care of personal hygiene but also when no street sweepers would be working to remove the hair that barbers swept into the streets.

107. Much of the Cárdenas era's focus on social reform centered on anticlericalism, land, and temperance. For examples of how those social reforms worked together, see Pierce, "Sobering the Revolution."

108. "Labrosidad y honradez será la norma de la comuna Tapatía," *Gaceta Municipal*, January 1939, 17–18.

109. "El aseo público en Guadalajara solo puede ser ahora un problema en cuanto a la cooperación del público mismo," *Gaceta Municipal*, January 1940, 10–13.

110. Correspondencia, 1940, 1-07-18, AHMG.

111. *El Informador*, May 1, 1940.

112. Gomez, *Silver Veins, Dusty Lungs*, 161, 189.

113. For more on Luz del Mundo, see Dormady, *Primitive Revolution*, 19–62.

114. Ibarra Bellon and Lanczyner Reisel, "La Hermosa Provincia," 45.

115. Petitioners to Guadalajara municipal leaders, Exp. 5, Iglesias no Católicas, AHMG.

116. Petitioners to Guadalajara municipal leaders, Exp. 5, Iglesias no Católicas, AHMG; DGG [Dirección General de Gobierno], 2/340/(11)1 (7:25), Archivo General de la Nación (AGN).

117. *El Occidental*, November 30, 1942.

118. Fe en Cristo, Exp. 1, 17, 18, 20, Iglesias no Católicas, AHMG.

119. In the Correspondencia record, the name appears as Monclovio, but it very well could have been Moclovio, the name of a known Gaxiola brother and preacher.

120. Correspondencia, 1947, 1-00-21, AHMG.

121. Ramírez, *Migrating Faith*, 105–9.

122. For more on the transition from foreign leadership to domestic congregational leadership, see Baldwin, *Protestants and the Mexican Revolution*; and Pulido, "Solving Schism."

123. The Iglesia Anglicana is also listed as Episcopal Americana Protestante in the archive. "Permiso Sacerdote Frank W. Creighton," August 13, 1928, Carpeta 5, Caja 9, Estadística de Iglesias, AHMG.

124. "Permiso Sacerdote Frank W. Creighton," August 13, 1928.

125. "Secretaría de Hacienda y Crédito Público a Presidente Municipal," December 12, 1932, Carpeta 6, Caja 9, Estadística de Iglesias, AHMG. The Secretaría de Gobernación showed consistent flexibility in relation to the religious services provided for members of the foreign colonies; the office made a pronounced effort to accommodate those foreigners, probably because of their association with foreign consulates. When the German community sought to use San Francisco de Asís in 1933 as the meeting place for their congregation, the Secretaría de Gobernación made sure to guarantee that the cleric assigned spoke enough German to service the community, as certified by the German consulate official Eric Clemenz (whose wife had initiated the petition for the use of San Francisco). "Trans. of. Del. Srio. de Gobernación," May 3, 1933, Carpeta 34, Templo de San Francisco de Asís, Templos Católicos, AHMG.

126. Curley, *Citizens and Believers*, 271.

127. For more on earlier hygiene efforts dominated by the state, see Kapelusz-Poppi, "Rural Health," 262–63.

128. Voekel, *Alone before God*, 190–92. For the Catholic Church and science, see B. Smith, "Limits of Catholic Science."

129. Voekel, *Alone before God*, 190.

130. Hyde, *Concepts of Power*, 109–10, 116.

131. Weber, *Death Is All Around Us*, 182.

132. Kapelusz-Poppi, "Rural Health," 264.

133. See Pani, *Hygiene in Mexico*. For examples of state-centered historiography, see Kapelusz-Poppi, "Rural Health"; Agostini, *Monuments of Progress*; Bliss, *Compro-*

mised Positions; McLeod, "Public Health"; and Méndez Moreno, *El anticlericalismo en Tabasco*. Weber's *Death Is All Around Us* centers the work of reformers until the final chapter, where the author reveals the success of average citizens in frustrating the efforts of Porfirian elites.

134. Jiménez, *Making an Urban Public*, 93.
135. Jiménez, *Making an Urban Public*, 20.
136. Jiménez, *Making an Urban Public*, 18, 20.
137. Jiménez, *Making an Urban Public*, 337.
138. Van Young, *Other Rebellion*, 522.
139. Deans-Smith and Joseph, "Arena of Dispute," 205.
140. "Informe de Construcción y Reparaciones de Templos," January 5, 1940, Carpeta 34, Caja 9, Estadística de Iglesias, AHMG.
141. "Se pide informe y opinión," February 26, 1940; "Re: Pide Informe," April 4, 1940, both in Carpeta 8, Caja 5, Templos Otros Credos, AHMG.
142. "Informe sobre templo," June 6, 1940; "Le Informo sobre el templo," June 26, 1940; "Se suplica proporcionar informe sobre el Templo denominado de 'CRISTO' católico Episcopál Mexicana"; "Le informo sobre el Templo," November 27, 1940, all in Carpeta 8, Caja 5, Templos Otros Credos, AHMG.
143. "Informe sobre Apertura Iglesia Episcopal Mexicana," October 11, 1963, Carpeta 51, Caja 9, Estadística de Iglesias, AHMG. The Templo de Cristo church is still there today, tucked into a space between two warehouses in a neighborhood now dominated by bars, strip clubs, and hotels.
144. "Celebración de Cultos en Casas Particulares," January 29, 1942, Carpeta 37; "Lista de Templos," September 30, 1942, Carpeta 36; "Informes sobre Templos," June 15, 1957, Carpeta 45; "Asunto sobre Templos Evangélicos," February 27, 1954, Carpeta 44, all in Caja 9, Estadística de Iglesias, AHMG.
145. For example, Luz del Mundo had immense success in converting working-class members of Guadalajara society. The denomination's congregations grew, first to hundreds, then thousands, and then tens of thousands. That group received significant exemptions from urban planning regulations. See Dormady, *Primitive Revolution*, 52–62.

4. Concrete Requests

1. For some examples of women engaged in civic, political, labor, or educational leadership, see Fernández Aceves, *Mujeres en el cambio social*; Fregoso Centeno, *Siete historias de vida*; Zafra Oropeza, *La mujer en la historia de Jalisco*; and Jiménez Pelayo, "Las terratenientes de la Nueva Galicia."
2. Cosío Villegas, *Historia moderna de México*, 657.
3. Niblo, *Mexico in the 1940s*, 89–91.

4. Castro, *Apostle of Progress*, xviii–xix.

5. Matute Remus could not simply expropriate and evict the telephone company. After two years of appeals, the Telefónica Mexicana case had reached the Mexican Supreme Court. The court ruled in January 1950 that requesting that the company make room for the widening of the street was not a hardship, as the company would receive 290,000 pesos in compensation and they were already in the process of planning to expand their services in another location. However, because the original expropriation order had not specified that telephone services would be dramatically disrupted because of the demolition of the building, the court decided that it could not leave such a complicated matter in the hands of local officials, so it ordered the parties to find a way to modify the building without disrupting service. "Cia. Telefónica y Telegráfica Mexicana contra Acto de Ud. y de Otras Autoridades," F-11-1950 / Fomento / Obras Públicas / No. de Inv. 12138, Caja 453, AHEJ.

6. Juan Carlos Núñez Bustillos, "55 años de la hazaña," *Público-Milenio de Guadalajara*, October 23, 2005.

7. The names of the women do not appear in newspaper stories of the time nor in official documents regarding the move. While their property—at no. 80 calle Donato Guerra—appears numerous times, the women themselves are simply referred to as "*las señoras*." Additionally—probably because of the speed required for the move—the women did not receive an expropriation order (expropriation of urban properties could take months or years to conclude). Instead, Matute Remus negotiated with them directly from January to April 1950, convincing them to sell the property to the telephone company. F-11-1950 / Fomento / Obras Públicas / No. de Inv. 12138, Caja 453, AHEJ. As late as 1944 the property was listed in the classified section of *El Informador* as a "*lote*" for sale, with little other description of the property. At roughly the same time, somebody at the address was also selling used movie theater seats out of the property (also via the newspaper's classified section). It does not appear that the building could be considered a high-end property. *El Informador*, April 16, 1944, April 14, 1944, respectively.

8. *El Informador*, November 6, 1938, October 3, 1938, respectively.

9. *El Informador*, February 18, 1941.

10. Licencias para Construcción, 1939, plano 655, AHMG; *El Informador*, August 11, 1934, September 19, 1934; "México censo nacional, 1930," database with images, FamilySearch, December 4, 2019, https://familysearch.org/ark:/61903/1:1:M25V-H3W, Marina Ayala, in household of J. Félix Ayala, Chapala, Chapala, Jalisco, Mexico, FHL microfilm 1,507,522, citing p. 20, Distrito Federal, AGN.

11. Licencias para Construcción, 1939–47, AHMG. This total does not include about 1 percent of the documents where it was not possible to determine the gender of the property owner and 2 percent of licenses belonging to corporate bodies (such as unions or businesses) in which the role of women was not immediately obvious.

12. Hausermann, "Unintended Developments," 787–88; Villela Espinoza and Patiño Flota, "La equidad." Other scholars who focus on the twentieth-century ownership of land by women include Deere and León, *Empowering Women*.

13. For examples of work on women involved in owning haciendas, see Fregoso Centeno, "Dolores Palomar Arias"; and Jiménez Pelayo, "Las terratenientes de la Nueva Galicia." For work on Indigenous communities, see Cline, *Colonial Culhuacan*.

14. Tutino, "Breaking New Spain," 381–86; Tutino, *Mexico City, 1808*.

15. Carmen Diana Deere and Magdalena Léon make excellent comparisons of women's access to property in Latin America, with their work particularly centered on married women and rural settings. See Deere and León, *Empowering Women*. For an example of the focus on marriage and divorce, see Ramos Escandón, "Challenging Legal and Gender Constraints in Mexico"; and S. Mitchell, introduction. Vicente, "Singleness and the State," examines the social position of widows and single women in Porfirian Guadalajara using censuses but with a singular focus on the use of property for room rentals, a traditional business role for widowed or single women.

16. For some examples, see Porter, *Working Women*; Toxqui, "Breadwinners or Entrepreneurs"; and Mendiola, *Street Democracy*.

17. Licencias para Construcción, 1939, plano 198, AHMG.

18. *El Informador*, May 26, 1922, March 28, 1940; "México, Jalisco, Registro Civil, 1857–2000," database with images, FamilySearch, March 13, 2018, https://familysearch .org/ark:/61903/3:1:33S7-9PJM-FBX?cc=1918187&wc=MGD5-K6F%3A206555501 %2C215739401, Guadalajara > Matrimonios 1922 > image 454 of 878, Archivo del Registro Civil (Civil Registry State Archives), Jalisco.

19. Licencias para Construcción, 1939, plano 643, plano 644, AHMG.

20. Sluis, *Deco Body*, 7.

21. Vicente, "Singleness and the State," 46.

22. Percentages of applications are based on a random sampling of 63 percent. When compared to a complete calculation of marital status for applications in 1939, the variation is 0.5 percent.

23. The marital status of men among the permit applicants is more difficult to assess. Men simply identified themselves with the title "señor" or with professional titles such as "doctor," "licenciado," or other occupational terms. At times in petitions or letters they might indicate themselves honorable and married, though this was not consistent or even the norm in construction permit licenses.

24. Porter, *From Angel to Worker*, conclusion.

25. Huffaker, "Gendered Limitations of Women Property Owners."

26. Licencias para Construcción, 1940, plano 158; 1947, plano 184, AHMG.

27. *El Informador*, February 22, 1996; "México, Jalisco, Registro Civil, 1857–2000," database with images, FamilySearch, March 13, 2018, https://familysearch.org/ark:/61903

/3:1:33SQ-GPKZ-YGN?cc=1918187&wc=MG6J-N3F%3A207279601%2C208420401, Tamazula de Gordiano > Matrimonios 1924–1930 > image 512 of 923, Archivo del Registro Civil (Civil Registry State Archives), Jalisco.

28. *El Informador*, December 7, 1958, November 22, 1964, July 5, 1968.

29. Niblo, *Mexico in the 1940s*, 263–73.

30. The notary archive (Archivo de Instrumentos Públicos del Estado de Jalisco) consists of notary books cataloged under the name of each notary who kept the record. The sample of 1,840 is taken from the fourteen notarial collections in the archive. Of those fourteen, one was not available. Of the remaining thirteen, I consulted the seven largest sets of notary books, representing 367 of 403 notarial books. These seven were the collections of Enrique Arriola, Cenobio González, Felipe Vázquez Aldana, Francisco Medina Torre, José Pérez Verdía, Emiliano Robles León, and Gustavo R. Castro.

31. For the colonial period, Asunción Lavrin notes that in Tlaxcala, women controlled about 16 percent of property at 17.2 percent of property value. See Lavrin, "In Search of the Colonial Woman in Mexico," 44. For a comparison, consider that Silvia Arrom discovered that between 1803 and 1857, women signed about one-quarter of general notary documents in Mexico City—mostly wills and powers of attorney—but about half were dedicated to property transactions, guardianships, and other matters. See Arrom, *Women of Mexico City*, 172. In short, it appears that the amount of property owned by women in Mexico may have grown in the nineteenth and twentieth centuries. A project that looks at the growth of women's property ownership over time is needed.

32. Vázquez, *Guadalajara: Ensayos de interpretación*, 117.

33. Ibáñez and Vázquez, *Guadalajara: Un análisis urbano*, 37; Walton, *Elites and Economic Development*, 154.

34. John Walton in his book *Elites and Economic Development* mentions women only in their roles as workers in industrial settings like textiles or—as many do—in the sex industry.

35. I chose the term "archives of possession" in reference to Karen Roybal's work on U.S. property records that document the dispossession of Mexican and Native women in the U.S. Southwest after the U.S. invasion and annexation of Mexican territory. See Roybal, *Archives of Dispossession*.

36. From 1930, baptism record: "México, Jalisco, registros parroquiales, 1590–1979," Arandas, Santa María de Guadalupe, Bautismos de hijos legítimos, 1884–1886, FamilySearch, February 16, 2017, https://familysearch.org/ark:/61903/3:1:9392-GB37-VN ?cc=1874591&wc=3j61-BZS%3A171935401%2C171933202%2C172430401, image 317 of 370; Parroquias Católicas (Catholic parishes), Jalisco, Marriage certificate of Emilio—older brother of the sisters: "México, Jalisco, Registro Civil, 1857–2000," FamilySearch, March 13, 2018, https://familysearch.org/ark:/61903/1:1:QGQT-P7F5, Manuel Ascencio in entry for Emilio Ascencio Orozco and Amalia Orozco, 1900.

37. *El Informador*, September 30, 2018; "México censo nacional, 1930," database with images, FamilySearch, April 1, 2016, https://familysearch.org/ark:/61903/3:1:S3HT-62VW -51W?cc=1307314&wc=MG8T-SP8%3A287605701%2C292764401%2C287928101, Jalisco > Guadalajara > Hidalgo > image 1024 of 1446, Archivo General de la Nación, Distrito Federal (National Archives, Distrito Federal).

38. "México, Jalisco, Registro Civil, 1857–2000," database with images, FamilySearch, April 4, 2020, https://familysearch.org/ark:/61903/1:1:QG77-QSQP, Magdalena Orozco Orozco de Orozco, 1923.

39. Enrique Arriola: Exp. 4139, 4158, 4056, 4068, 4089, 4116, 4115, Libro 42; Exp. 4735, Libro 48; Exp. 4843, Libro 49; Exp. 5109, 5115, 5119, 5120, Libro 52; Francisco Medina de la Torre: Exp. 1036, Libro 9, all in Archivo de Instrumentos Públicos del Estado de Jalisco (AIPEJ).

40. Licencias para Construcción, 1942, plano 39; 1944, plano 454, AHMG.

41. Enrique Arriola, Exp. 4403, 1940 Libro 45, AIPEJ.

42. Enrique Arriola, Exp. 4725, 1941 Libro 47; Exp. 4972, 1942 Libro 50, both in AIPEJ.

43. Such phrasing appears in contract letters, applications, petitions, and many other documents submitted by women to the city or state. While this term represents only a minority of applications, it is pervasive. For just one example, see Francisco Medina de la Torre, Exp. 842, 1939 Libro 7, AIPEJ.

44. Cenobio González, Exp. 8508, 1944 Libro 32, AIPEJ.

45. *El Informador*, September 3, 1953; "México bautismos, 1560–1950," database, FamilySearch, April 10, 2020, https://familysearch.org/ark:/61903/1:1:NKTT-NY5, Ramon Calleros Moreno, 1870; "México, Jalisco, Registro Civil, 1857–2000," database with images, FamilySearch, February 22, 2021, https://www.familysearch.org/ark:/61903/1:1:QG77-Z3M5, Ramón Calleros Moreno Viuda de Calleros and María Concepción Iñigues, 1905.

46. Enrique Arriola, Exp. 4258, 1939 Libro 43, AIPEJ.

47. Huffaker, "Gendered Limitations of Women Property Owners," 127–31.

48. The property expropriation burden fell mostly on homeowners in the Barrera section of the Colonia Obrera neighborhood, formerly known as the Colonia Jalisciense.

49. Correspondencia, 1947, 4-38-29, AHMG. Micaéla and Isidro may have been close, as she traveled to visit him in the United States in 1924, when he lived in Oxnard, California. "Texas, Manifests of Permanent and Statistical Alien Arrivals at El Paso, 1924–1954," database, FamilySearch, August 5, 2020, https://www.familysearch.org/ark:/61903/1:1:C3S8-GT2M, Micaela Lareos De Arocha, 1924.

50. "United States World War II Draft Registration Cards, 1942," database with images, FamilySearch, November 24, 2020, https://familysearch.org/ark:/61903/1:1:V48G-1TQ, Isidoro Larios, 1942, citing NARA microfilm publication M1936, M1937, M1939, M1951, M1962, M1964, M1986, M2090, and M2097 (Washington DC: National Archives and

Records Administration, n.d.). When Micaéla entered the United States at El Paso in 1924 to visit her brother, she carried with her no more than 200 pesos. Isidro is listed in the 1940 U.S. Census as a farmworker who in the busy spring agricultural season of California worked no more than six hours. "United States Census, 1940," database with images, FamilySearch, January 6, 2021, https://www.familysearch.org/ark:/61903 /1:1:K9D5-SLQ, Isidoro Larios, Judicial Township 7, Santa Barbara, California, United States, citing enumeration district (ED) 42-60, sheet 1B, line 52, family 25, Sixteenth Census of the United States, 1940, NARA digital publication T627, Records of the Bureau of the Census, 1790–2007, RG 29 (Washington DC: National Archives and Records Administration, 2012), roll 334.

51. Vázquez, *Guadalajara: Ensayos de interpretación*, 171–72.

52. Correspondencia, 1943, 4-31-15, AHMG.

53. Correspondencia, 1943, 4-31-15, AHMG.

54. Goldsmit Brindis et al., *Contento y descontento*, 23, 66; Valerio Ulloa, "De Santander a Guadalajara," 44–59.

55. Jiménez Pelayo, "Las terratenientes de la Nueva Galicia," 25.

56. Correspondencia, 1946, 4-39-15, AHMG. The documents related to the Ciudad Universitaria are missing; the Indice de Correspondencia contains a description of the relevant documents.

57. Correspondencia, 1941, 4-36-28, AHMG.

58. Salvador Lanzaduri, "Y ya que del agua se habla, digámoslo todo de una vez," *Gaceta Municipal*, August 1941.

59. Correspondencia, 1947, 4-30-15, AHMG. Note the applicant's lack of water use for a toilet and bathtub or shower.

60. Correspondencia, 1947, 4-30-92, AHMG. I was unable to locate a record that indicates what type of doctor González Rodríguez was. She appears in the Diario Oficial of January 12, 1970, as a member of the electoral board (because she owned property) and also is listed in *El Informador* as being present at various social gatherings in the city.

61. Correspondencia, 1946, 2-10-3, AHMG.

62. Correspondencia, 1940, 4-30-8, AHMG.

63. Correspondencia, 1947, 1-05-51, AHMG.

64. Correspondencia, 1942, 1-05-7, AHMG.

65. The marriage record of María Refugio and Guillermo establishes the parental relationship with Francisca. "México, Jalisco, Registro Civil, 1857–2000," FamilySearch, March 11, 2025, https://www.familysearch.org/ark:/61903/1:1:QG77-3XPR, entry for Guillermo K. Tsubuku Tsukubu and Seikichi Tsubuku, 29 de agosto de 1919. For the age of her children, see the 1930 Mexican census: "México, Jalisco, Registro Civil, 1857–2000," database with images, FamilySearch, February 22, 2021, https://www.familysearch.org

/ark:/61903/1:1:QG77-Z67L, Seikichi Tsubuku in entry for Guillermo K. Tsubuku Tsukubu and María del Refugio Velázquez, 1919.

66. Correspondencia, 1946, 4-39-14, AHMG.

67. Licencias para Construcción, 1940, plano 732, AHMG.

68. Correspondencia, 1947, 2-10-47, AHMG.

69. Removed bodies could be disposed of in a common grave, or they might be used by the medical school for their students. See Correspondencia, 1944, 1-02-53; 1941, 1-08-15, AHMG. One historic cemetery—the Panteón Belén—is also where the medical school used to be located.

70. Correspondencia, 1941, 4-34-101, AHMG.

71. Correspondencia, 1941, 4-34-31, AHMG.

72. Correspondencia, 1945, 4-36-22, AHMG.

73. Correspondencia, 1941, 4-34-97, AHMG. Sofía Herrera's family published a large death notice in *El Informador* as well as the accompanying language that she died "in the bosom of our Holy Mother of the Apostolic Roman Catholic Church," thereby indicating her family's wealth and religious status.

74. "México, Jalisco, Registro Civil, 1857-2000," database with images, FamilySearch, February 22, 2021, https://www.familysearch.org/ark:/61903/1:1:QG73-9JCH, Sofia Herrera Silva, 1941. Sofia's husband had passed away in 1896 at the age of forty and is listed as a *comerciante*, or businessman. Her service to the revolutionary state appears to have come of her own connections. "México, Jalisco, Registro Civil, 1857-2000," database with images, FamilySearch, February 22, 2021, https://www.familysearch.org /ark:/61903/1:1:QGQ5-CRMQ, Juan Nepomuceno Gil, 1896.

75. Porter, *From Angel to Worker*, chap. 6.

76. Toxqui, "Breadwinners or Entrepreneurs," 113.

77. Fernández Aceves, "Mercado de trabajo," 250-62.

78. Hernández Galindo, "Migración japonesa a Jalisco," 127.

79. Nakasone and Yamaguchi Llanes, "Censo Nikkei de Guadalajara 2018," 156. México, Jalisco, Registros Parroquiales, 1590-1979, database with images, FamilySearch, August 16, 2021, https://www.familysearch.org/ark:/61903/1:1:68Z8-6B7P, M. Dolores Aoki in entry for Tomás Shiquematsu, julio de 1951, citing Christening, San José de Analco, Guadalajara, Jalisco, México, parroquias Católicas Jalisco (Catholic Church parishes, Jalisco), FHL (Family History Library) microfilm.

80. Smith, "Building a State."

81. Correspondencia, 1941, 1-04-32; 1939, 1-4-25; 1940, 1-4-19, AHMG. The file on the hunting rifles specifically refers to the business as the Armería Remington and gives permission to sell guns for hunting.

82. Correspondencia, 1939, 1-4-12, AHMG.

83. French, *Peaceful and Working People*, 99–100.

84. Porter, *From Angel to Worker*, chap. 7.

85. Correspondencia, 1939, 3-22-8, AHMG.

86. Pilcher, *¡Que vivan los tamales!*, 109.

87. Pilcher, *¡Que vivan los tamales!*, 108–9.

88. McIntyre, *Protestantism and State Formation*, 59.

89. Fernández Aceves, "Struggle between the 'Metate' and the 'Molinos,'" 157–59.

90. Gómez-Galvarriato, "Female Entrepreneurship," 91–94.

91. Olcott, *Revolutionary Women*, 7–16.

92. Olcott, *Revolutionary Women*, 17.

93. Olcott, *Revolutionary Women*, 7.

94. Deeds, Meyer, and Sherman, *Course of Mexican History*, 459.

95. S. Mitchell, introduction, 9, 13.

96. Gilly, *Mexican Revolution*, 10–12, 345n12; Russell, *History of Mexico*, 216–18; Weiner, *Race, Nation, and Market*, 56–57.

97. Kuznesof, "House, the Street, and the Brothel," 26. Liberalism and its focus on individual rights did not necessarily mean that women found full rights in society, however. As Christine Hunefeldt has argued, often liberalism simply changed the ways in which society made the lives of women difficult. See Hunefeldt, *Liberalism in the Bedroom*, 14–16.

98. Gilly, *Mexican Revolution*, 233.

99. Gilly, *Mexican Revolution*, 233, 237–38.

100. Díaz Soto y Gama, *La cuestión agraria en México*, 56–57.

101. Gilly, *Mexican Revolution*, 238; Knight, *Mexican Revolution*, 2:475–76.

102. Peña, "Eminent Domain and Expropriation Laws," 162.

103. Deere and León, *Empowering Women*, 43.

104. Lau Jaiven and Rodríguez Bravo, "El sufragio femenino," 80–81.

105. Bliss, *Compromised Positions*, 131.

106. Ramos Escandón, "Challenging Legal and Gender Constraints," 53–54, 60, 62–63, 65.

107. Deere and León, *Empowering Women*, 43.

108. S. Smith, *Gender and the Mexican Revolution*, 4–5.

109. Buck, "Meaning of the Women's Vote in Mexico," 73–74, 81–82.

110. Blumberg, "Income under Female versus Male Control," 29; Heron, *Desire for Development*, 96.

111. Secretaría de Gobernación, *Seis años de gobierno*.

112. Gillingham, *(Un)Revolutionary Mexico*, 190–92.

113. Chant, *Women and Survival in Mexican Cities*, 31.

114. Knight, *Mexican Revolution*, 2:527.

115. Saragoza, "Selling of Mexico," 102.

116. Gauss, *Made in Mexico*, 63.

117. Gauss, *Made in Mexico*, 91.

118. S. Mitchell, introduction, 10–12.

119. Schell, "Of the Sublime Mission of Mothers of Families," 111–12.

120. Perahia, "Las ciudades y su espacio público."

121. Morfín and Sánchez Van Dyck, "Controles jurídicos," 491–95.

122. Pateman, *Disorder of Women*, 121–22.

123. Ochoa, "Illicit Relations," chap. 4.

124. Arrom, *Women of Mexico City*, 260–62.

125. Tapia Tovar, "De gema a basura," 138–59.

126. Jackson Albarrán, "Medicalizing Modern Motherhood," 175.

127. French, *Peaceful and Working People*, 89–97.

128. Jiménez Pelayo, "Las terratenientes de la Nueva Galicia," 19.

129. Porter, *Working Women*, xviii, 191.

130. Porter, *Working Women*, 135.

131. Sluis, *Deco Body*, 13.

132. Zafra Oropeza, *La mujer en la historia de Jalisco*, 54–59.

133. Fernández Aceves, *Mujeres en el cambio social*, 11.

134. Tompkins and Foster, *Notable Twentieth-Century Latin American Women*, xx.

135. French, *Peaceful and Working People*, 90.

136. Adams, *Notable Latin American Women*, 165.

137. Solís Hernández and Gómez Olmos, "María Antonieta Pacheco Gaytán," 222.

138. Solís Hernández and Gómez Olmos, "María Antonieta Pacheco Gaytán," 216.

139. Honig, *Feminist Theory of Refusal*, 4–5.

140. Honig, *Feminist Theory of Refusal*, 19.

141. Ahmed, *Living a Feminist Life*, 239.

142. Sluis, *Deco Body*, 1, 68.

143. Fernández Aceves, *Mujeres en el cambio social*.

144. Lau Jaiven, "La participación de las mujeres"; McPhail Fanger and Lau Jaiven, *Rupturas y continuidades*; McPhail, *Juan Soriano y Lupe Marín*.

145. Fregoso Centeno, "Dolores Palomar Arias."

146. Lau Jaiven, "Todo tiene que ver con lo personal," 9–20.

147. Razo Zaragoza, *Guadalajara*, 19–20.

148. Carey, *Plaza of Sacrifices*, 13–22.

149. Arrom, *Women of Mexico City*, 61.

150. Arrom, *Women of Mexico City*, 57–58, 261.

151. Arrom, *Women of Mexico City*, 61.

152. Olcott, *Revolutionary Women*, 6.

153. Porter, *From Angel to Worker*, chap. 7.

154. Hutchison, *Labors Appropriate to Their Sex*, 5.

155. Tuñon, *Mujeres*, 247.

156. Benhabib, "Feminist Theory," 108–9.

157. In a brief visit to the Archivo Histórico Municipal de la Ciudad de Oaxaca, I found that their limited records on this period indicate that the smaller and more socially Indigenous Oaxaca City might follow a similar pattern. While the Oaxacan archive did not have a construction registration file, it did have in its collection two *censos y padrones de habitantes de la ciudad* available for near this period of study. Between one-quarter and one-half of registrants of property on streets in Oaxaca were identifiable as women and listed as the primary owners of the property. While this did not rise to the same level of property ownership as in Guadalajara, future and more expansive research in notarial records might offer additional insight to historians interested in comparative aspects of women in property ownership. For the Oaxaca example used here, see Censos y padrones de habitantes de la ciudad de Oaxaca, Exp. 61, Caja 1, Archivo Histórico Municipal de la Ciudad de Oaxaca (AHMCO).

158. Muriá, *Breve historia*, 170.

159. Coatsworth, *Growth against Development*.

160. Carey, *Plaza of Sacrifices*, 19.

Conclusion

1. Mraz, *History and Modern Media*, 61–63.

2. When the demolition of this area occurred in 1947, this shop moved elsewhere in the city. In 1977 it was bombed by urban guerrillas. Zamora García, *Ciudad en fuegos*, 30, 40; *El Informador*, September 14, 1977, January 23, 2002.

3. Mraz, "Mexican History in Photographs," 297–303.

4. Hagerty et al., "Sense of Belonging," 173.

5. Anthias, "Where Do I Belong?," 498–99.

6. Pajnik and Anthias, "Migrant Work, Precarity and Agency," 2.

7. Morán Quiroz, "Percibir la ciudad," 172–73.

8. Fernández Aceves, "Mercado de trabajo," 248.

9. Palacio Montiel, "El vivir, mitad pueblerino, mitad ciudadano," 141–42.

10. García Rojas, "Dos ciclos en la planeación," 167.

11. IGJ / 1943–47, Exp. 0020, Memoria del Poder Ejecutivo, AHEJ.

12. López Moreno, *La vivienda social*, 293.

13. Foja 11, Exp. 1, Acervo 2, Obras Públicas, Ampliaciones, Caja Javier Mina-Juárez, AHMG.

14. López Moreno, *La vivienda social*, 327–28, 506. For more on the borrowing to pay for development, see Foja 11, Exp. 2, Acervo 2, Obras Públicas, Ampliaciones, Caja Jávier Mina-Juárez, AHMG; and Correspondencia, 1947, 4-30-185, AHMG.

15. *Antología de la planeación*, 39.

16. "Guadalajara volverá a ser la Ciudad Blanca," *Gaceta de Guadalajara*, January 31, 1947.

17. Correspondencia, 1947, 1-09-84, AHMG.

18. Correspondencia, 1947, 1-09-84, AHMG; *El Informador*, September 18, 1948. UAG was Mexico's first private university, and it functioned as a foil for public socialist education, became a center of conservative Mexican political thought, and hosted part of a larger international network of anticommunist crusaders. See López Macedonio, "Historia de una colaboración"; and Dorantes, *El conflicto universitario en Guadalajara*.

19. Correspondencia, 1947, 4-38-59, AHMG. On the cost of the construction, see Foja 11, Exp. 1 and 2, Acervo 2, Obras Públicas, Ampliaciones, Caja Javier Mina-Juárez, AHMG; and Rivière d'Arc, *Guadalajara y su región*, 120.

20. Vázquez, *Guadalajara: Ensayos de interpretación*, 82–85.

21. Sable, *Latin American Urbanization*, xiv.

22. Calderón, "Books for Bullets," 114–15; Napolitano, *Migration, Mujercitas, and Medicine Men*, 17–22.

23. Greaves Lainé, "El México contemporáneo," 248.

24. Ibáñez and Vázquez, *Guadalajara: Un análisis urbano*, 37; Walton, *Elites and Economic Development*, 154. This figure does not take into account any illegal actions on the part of real estate developers to obtain and develop land, as referred to in Vázquez, *Guadalajara: Ensayos de interpretación*, 112.

25. *El Informador*, April 3, 1947; Correspondencia, 1947, 1-00-38; 1947, 4-36-33, AHMG.

26. *El Informador*, April 20, 1947.

27. Correspondencia, 1947, 4-37-71, AHMG.

28. Vaca et al., *Historia de Jalisco*, 608–9.

29. López Moreno, *La vivienda social*, 328.

30. Arias, "La industria en perspectiva," 109–10.

31. Tamayo, "Movimiento obrero," 154.

32. Bleynat, *Vendors' Capitalism*, 121–23.

33. Correspondencia, 1947, 4-30-37, AHMG.

34. Robles Ruvalcaba, "Emergence of the Rancho," 101, 117.

35. Gauss, *Made in Mexico*, 92.

36. Robles Ruvalcaba, "Emergence of the Rancho," 130.

37. García Espinosa, "Centros históricos," 5. For more on the politics of developmentalism, see Gutierrez González, "Intervenciones al paisaje urbano," where the author argues

that urban changes to Guadalajara came as part of a politics of industry that dominated the nation between 1940 and 1970.

38. Walton, "Cultura y economía," 375.

39. Morfín and Sánchez Van Dyck, "Controles jurídicos," 505.

40. Díaz-Berrio Fernández, "Espacios público," 121.

41. Vázquez, *Guadalajara: Ensayos de interpretación*, 99. *Chilangos* is a term used to denote people from Mexico City by those outside the city. In its true meaning, it refers to people from outside the city who have moved there, but as practiced by many people in cities around Mexico, they little differentiate its use.

42. Gillingham, *(Un)Revolutionary Mexico*, 3.

43. Rath, "Camouflaging the State," 98–103.

44. Camp, *Mexico's Mandarins*, 35–61, 122–51; Gillingham, *(Un)Revolutionary Mexico*, 3–5, 74, 112, 154, 222.

45. Cedillo and Calderón, *Challenging Authoritarianism*, 15n8.

46. Gillingham, *(Un)Revolutionary Mexico*, 5–6, 299n35; United Nations Office of the High Commissioner for Human Rights, press conference, November 26, 2021, https://www .ohchr.org/en/statements/2021/11/press-conference-following-visit-committee-enforced -disappearances-mexico.

47. Calderón, "From Books to Bullets," 105, 110–19.

Bibliography

Archives and Manuscript Materials

Archivo de Instrumentos Públicos del Estado de Jalisco (AIPEJ).
Archivo General de la Nación (AGN).
Archivo Histórico del Arzobispado de Guadalajara (AHAG).
Archivo Histórico de la Secretaría de Salud (AHSS).
Archivo Histórico del Estado de Jalisco (AHEJ).
Archivo Histórico Municipal de Guadalajara (AHMG).
Archivo Histórico Municipal de la Ciudad de Oaxaca (AHMCO).

Published Works

Adams, Jerome. *Notable Latin American Women: Twenty-Nine Leaders, Rebels, Poets, Battlers and Spies, 1500–1900.* Jefferson NC: McFarland, 1995.

Agostini, Claudia. *Monuments of Progress: Modernization and Public Health in Mexico City, 1876–1910.* Calgary AB: University of Calgary Press, 2003.

Aguirre Beltrán, Gonzalo. *La población negra de México.* Mexico City: Centro de Estudios Históricos del Agrarismo en México, 1946.

Aguirre Cristiani, María Gabriela. "La jerarquía católica en el exilio frente al nuevo marco jurídico revolucionario de 1917." *Política y cultura*, no. 48 (2017): 151–76.

Ahmed, Sara. *Living a Feminist Life.* Durham NC: Duke University Press, 2017.

Alcántara Ferrer, Sergio. "Cultura urbana y calidad de vida." In *Demografía y urbanismo: Lecturas históricas de Guadalajara III*, edited by José María Muriá and Jaime Olveda, 447–65. Guadalajara: INAH, Gobierno del Estado de Jalisco, Universidad de Guadalajara, 1992.

Aldana Rendón, Mario. "Masonería y revolución en Jalisco." *Estudios Jaliscienses* 58 (November 2004): 15–28.

Alonso, Ana Maria. *Thread of Blood: Colonialism, Revolution, and Gender on Mexico's Northern Frontier.* Tucson: University of Arizona Press, 1995.

Altamirano, Ignacio. *La Navidad en las montañas.* 5th ed. Paris: Biblioteca de la Europa y América, 1891.

Andelson, Jonathan G. "Coming Together, Breaking Apart: Sociogenesis and Schismogenesis in Intentional Communities." In *Intentional Community: An Anthropological Perspective*, edited by Susan Love Brown, 131–53. Albany: State University of New York Press, 2002.

Anderson, Sally. "Sociability: The Art of Form." In *Thinking through Sociality: An Anthropological Interrogation of Key Concepts*, edited by Vered Amit, 97–127. New York: Berghahn Books, 2015.

Anna, Timothy E. *Forging Mexico: 1821–1835*. Lincoln: University of Nebraska Press, 1998.

Anthias, Floya. "Thinking through the Lens of Translocational Positionality: An Intersectionality Frame for Understanding Identity and Belonging." *Translocations: Migrations and Social Change* 4, no. 1 (Winter 2008): 5–20.

———. *Translocational Belongings: Intersectional Dilemmas and Social Inequalities*. London: Routledge, 2020.

———. "Where Do I Belong? Narrating Collective Identity and Translocational Positionality." *Ethnicities* 2, no. 4 (2002): 491–514.

Antología de la planeación en México, 1917–1985: Tomo I—Los primeros intentos de planeación en México (1917–1946). Mexico City: Fondo de Cultura Económico, 1985.

Arellano Ríos, Alberto. "El área metropolitana de Guadalajara: Recorrido urbano y travesía político-institucional." *Revista Territorios y Regionalismos*, no. 6 (2022): 1–7.

Arias, Patricia. *Guadalajara, la gran ciudad de la pequeña industria*. Zamora: El Colegio de Michoacán, 1985.

———. "La industria en perspectiva." In *Guadalajara, la gran ciudad de la pequeña industria*, edited by Patricia Arias, 21–56. Zamora: El Colegio de Michoacán, 1985.

Arndt, Ava. "Touching London: Contact, Sensibility, and the City." In *The City and the Senses*, edited by Alexander Cowan and Jill Steward, 95–104. Aldershot, UK: Ashgate, 2007.

Arreguín González, Juan Manuel. "La planeación urbana." In *Demografía y urbanismo: Lecturas históricas de Guadalajara III*, edited by José María Muriá and Jaime Olveda, 307–18. Mexico City: INAH, 1992.

Arrom, Silvia. *The Women of Mexico City, 1790–1857*. Stanford CA: Stanford University Press, 1985.

Arroyo Alejandre, Jesús. "Ires y venires en el occidente." In *Guadalajara, la gran ciudad de la pequeña industria*, edited by Patricia Arias, 21–56. Zamora: El Colegio de Michoacán, 1985.

Ávila, Patricia, and Ana Rosa González García. "Agua para las ciudades en el porfiriato: El caso de Guadalajara, México." *Revista de El Colegio San Luis*, no. 4 (2012): 10–34.

Baldwin, Deborah. *Protestants and the Mexican Revolution: Missionaries, Ministers, and Social Change*. Urbana: University of Illinois Press, 1990.

Bantjes, Adrian. *As If Jesus Walked on Earth: Cardenismo, Sonora, and the Mexican Revolution*. Lanham MD: SR Books, 1998.

———. "The Regional Dynamics of Anticlericalism and Defanaticization in Revolutionary Mexico." In *Faith and Impiety in Revolutionary Mexico*, edited by Matthew Butler, 111–30. New York: Palgrave Macmillan, 2007.

Bastian, Jean-Pierre. "Protestants, Freemasons, and Spiritists." In *Faith and Impiety in Revolutionary Mexico*, edited by Matthew Butler, 75–92. New York: Palgrave, 2007.

Bauman, Zygmunt. *Amor líquido: Acerca de la fragilidad de los vínculos humanos*. Mexico City: Fonda de Cultura Económica, 2007.

Beezley, William H. *Judas at the Jockey Club and Other Episodes of Porfirian Mexico*. 2nd ed. Lincoln: University of Nebraska Press, 2004.

Bender, Daniel, Duane J. Corpis, and Daniel J. Walkowitz. "Sound Politics: Critically Listening to the Past." *Radical History Review*, no. 121 (January 2015): 1–7.

Benhabib, Seyla. "Feminist Theory and Hannah Arendt's Concept of Public Sphere." *History of the Human Sciences* 6, no. 2 (1993): 97–114.

Benjamin, Thomas. *La Revolución: Mexico's Great Revolution as Memory, Myth, and History*. Austin: University of Texas Press, 2000.

Berthe, Jean Pierre. "Introducción a la historia de Guadalajara y su región." In *Regiones y ciudades en América Latina: Trabajos realizados en el Institut des hautes études de l'Amérique latine*, edited by Jean Piel. Mexico City: Secretaría de Educación Pública, 1973.

Blancarte, Roberto. *El pensamiento social de los católicos mexicanos*. Mexico City: Fondo de Cultura Económica, 1996.

———. "Intransigence, Anticommunism, and Reconciliation: Church-State Relations in Transition." In *Dictablanda: Politics, Work, and Culture in Mexico, 1938–1968*, edited by Paul Gillingham and Benjamin T. Smith, 70–88. Durham NC: Duke University Press, 2014.

Bleynat, Ingrid. *Vendors' Capitalism: A Political Economy of Public Markets in Mexico City*. Stanford CA: Stanford University Press, 2021.

Bliss, Katherine Elaine. *Compromised Positions: Prostitution, Public Health, and Gender Politics in Revolutionary Mexico City*. University Park: Penn State University Press, 2001.

———. "For the Health of the Nation: Gender and Cultural Politics of Social Hygiene in Revolutionary Mexico." In *The Eagle and the Virgin: Nation and Cultural Revolution in Mexico, 1920–1940*, edited by Mary Kay Vaught and Stephen E. Lewis, 196–218. Durham NC: Duke University Press, 2006.

Blumberg, Rae Lesser. "Income under Female versus Male Control: Hypotheses from a Theory of Gender Stratification and Data from the Third World." *Journal of Family Issues* 9, no. 1 (March 1988): 51–84.

Bowen, Kurt. *Evangelism and Apostasy: The Evolution and Impact of Evangelicals in Modern Mexico*. Montreal: McGill-Queen's University Press, 1996.

Boylan, Kristina. "Gendering Faith, Altering the Nation: Mexican Catholic Women's Activism, 1917–1940." In *Sex in Revolution: Gender, Politics, and Power in Modern Mexico*, edited by Jocelyn Olcott, Mary Kay Vaughan, and Gabriela Cano, 199–222. Durham NC: Duke University Press, 2006.

Buchenau, Jurgen. *Plutarco Elías Calles and the Mexican Revolution*. Lanham MD: Rowman and Littlefield, 2007.

Buck, Sarah. "The Meaning of the Women's Vote in Mexico." In *The Women's Revolution in Mexico, 1910–1953*, edited by Stephanie Mitchell and Patience A. Schell, 73–98. Lanham MD: Rowman and Littlefield, 2007.

Buffington, Robert. *Criminal and Citizen in Modern Mexico*. Lincoln: University of Nebraska Press, 2000.

Butler, Matthew. *Mexico's Spiritual Reconquest: Indigenous Catholics and Father Perez's Revolutionary Church*. Albuquerque: University of New Mexico Press, 2023.

———. "A Revolution in Spirit." In *Faith and Impiety in Revolutionary Mexico*, edited by Matthew Butler, 1–20. New York: Palgrave, 2007.

Calderón, Fernando. "Books for Bullets: Youth Radicalism and Urban Guerrillas in Guadalajara." In *Challenging Authoritarianism in Mexico: Revolutionary Struggles and the Dirty War, 1964–1982*, edited by Fernando Herrera Calderón and Adela Cedillo, 105–28. New York: Routledge, 2012.

Calderón, Fernando, and Adela Cedillo, eds. *Challenging Authoritarianism in Mexico: Revolutionary Struggles and the Dirty War, 1964–1982*. New York: Routledge, 2012.

Cámara Muñoz, Alicia. "Modelo urbano y obras en Madrid en el reinado de Felipe II." In *Madrid en el contexto de lo Hispánico desde la época de los descubrimientos*, vol. 1, 31–48. Madrid: Departamento de Historia del Arte, 1994.

Camp, Roderic Ai. *Mexico's Mandarins: Crafting a Power Elite for the Twenty-First Century*. Berkeley: University of California Press, 2002.

Campbell, Reau. *Campbell's New Revised Complete Guide and Descriptive Book of Mexico*. Chicago: Rogers and Smith Company, 1899.

Cano, Gabriela. "Unconcealable Realities of Desire: Amelio Robles's (Transgender) Masculinity in the Mexican Revolution." In *Sex in Revolution: Gender, Politics, and Power in Modern Mexico*, edited by Jocelyn Olcott, Mary Kay Vaughan, and Gabriela Cano, 35–56. Durham NC: Duke University Press, 2006.

Carey, Elaine. *Plaza of Sacrifices: Gender, Power, and Terror in 1968 Mexico*. Albuquerque: University of New Mexico Press, 2005.

Castañeda, Carmen, ed. *Vivir en Guadalajara*. Guadalajara: Ayuntamiento de Guadalajara, 1992.

Castro, J. Justin. *Apostle of Progress: Modesto C. Rolland, Global Progressivism, and the Engineering of Revolutionary Mexico*. Lincoln: University of Nebraska Press, 2019.

———. "Sounding the Mexican Nation: Intellectuals, Radio Broadcasting, and the Revolutionary State in the 1920s." *Latin Americanist* 58, no. 3 (2014): 3–29.

Chant, Sylvia. *Women and Survival in Mexican Cities: Perspectives on Gender, Labour, Markets and Low-Income Households*. Manchester, UK: Manchester University Press, 1991.

Cibin, Alessia. "Forms of Night-Time Economy Governance: A Framework Towards Clarification." In *Transforming Urban Nightlife and the Development of Smart Public Spaces*, edited by Hisham Abusaada, Abeer Elshater, and Dennis Rodwell, 22–39. Beijing: IGI, 2021.

Classen, Constance. *The Deepest Sense: A Cultural History of Touch*. Urbana: University of Illinois Press, 2012.

Classen, Constance, David Howes, and Anthony Synnott. *Aroma: The Cultural History of Smell*. New York: Routledge, 1994.

Cline, Sarah L. *Colonial Culhuacan, 1580–1600: The Social History of an Aztec Town*. Albuquerque: University of New Mexico Press, 1986.

Coatsworth, John H. *Growth against Development: The Economic Impact of Railroads in Porfirian Mexico*. DeKalb: Northern Illinois University Press, 1981.

Connaughton, Brian F. *Clerical Ideology in a Revolutionary Age: The Guadalajara Church and the Idea of the Mexican Nation, 1788–1853*. Calgary AB: University of Calgary Press, 2003.

Corbin, Alain. *The Foul and the Fragrant: Odor and the French Social Imagination*. Cambridge MA: Harvard University Press, 1986.

Cosío Villegas, Daniel. *Historia moderna de México: La república restaurada—vida política*. Mexico City: Editorial Hermes, 1955.

Courtwright, David T. *Forces of Habit: Drugs and the Making of the Modern World*. Cambridge MA: Harvard University Press, 2002.

Covert, Lisa Pinley. *San Miguel de Allende: Mexicans, Foreigners, and the Making of a World Heritage Site*. Lincoln: University of Nebraska Press, 2017.

Cowan, Alexander, and Jill Steward. Introduction to *The City and the Senses*, edited by Alexander Cowan and Jill Steward, 1–24. Aldershot, UK: Ashgate, 2007.

Crossa, Veronica. "Resisting the Entrepreneurial City: Street Vendor's Struggle in the Mexico City's Historic Center." *International Journal of Urban and Regional Research* 33, no. 1 (2009): 43–63.

Cross Morrison, Paul. "Population Change in Mexico, 1950–1960." *Revista Geográfica* 32, no. 59 (1963): 79–92.

Curley, Robert. "Anticlericalism and Public Space in Revolutionary Jalisco." *The Americas* 65, no. 4 (April 2009): 511–33.

———. *Citizens and Believers: Religion and Politics in Revolutionary Jalisco, 1900–1930*. Albuquerque: University of New Mexico Press, 2018.

———. "The First Encounter: Catholic Politics in Revolutionary Jalisco, 1917–1919." In *Faith and Impiety in Revolutionary Mexico*, edited by Matthew Butler, 131–48. New York: Palgrave, 2007.

———. "Political Catholicism in Revolutionary Mexico, 1900–1926." Working Paper No. 349, Helen Kellogg Institute for International Studies, Bloomington, Indiana, May 2008. https://kellogg.nd.edu/sites/default/files/old_files/documents/349_0.pdf.

Curley Álvarez, Robert, and Jorge Omar. "Catolicismo cívico, reforma liberal y política moderna en el Jalisco rural, 1867–1890." *Historia Mexicana* 71, no. 2 (October 2021): 851–97.

Czaplicka, John J. "Urban History after a Return to Local Self-Determination—Local History and Civic Identity." In *Composing Urban History and the Constitution of Civic Identities*, edited by John J. Czaplicka and Blair A. Ruble, 372–410. Baltimore: Johns Hopkins University Press, 2003.

Deans-Smith, Susan, and Gilbert Joseph. "The Arena of Dispute." *Hispanic American Historical Review* 79, no. 2 (1999): 203–9.

Deeds, Susan M., Michael C. Meyer, and William L. Sherman. *The Course of Mexican History*. 11th ed. Oxford: University of Oxford Press, 2018.

Deere, Carmen Diana, and Magdalena León. *Empowering Women: Land and Property Rights in Latin America*. Pittsburgh: University of Pittsburgh Press, 2001.

De la Garza Arregui, Bernardina. "El matrimonio según la epístola de Melchor Ocampo." *MXC*, March 2017. https://mxc.com.mx/2017/03/02/matrimonio-segun-la-epistola-melchor-ocampo/.

De la Peña, Guillermo, and Renée de la Torre. "Religión y política en los barrios populares de Guadalajara." *Estudios Sociológicos* 7, no. 24 (1990): 571–602.

De la Torre, Renée. "Guadalajara vista desde la calzada: Fronteras culturales e imaginarios urbanos." *Alteridades* 8, no. 15 (1998): 45–55.

De la Torre Curiel, José Refugio, et al. *Evolución de la historiografía jalisciense, 1857–2010*. Zapopan: El Colegio de Jalisco, 2013.

Díaz-Berrio Fernández, Sálvador. "Espacios públicos: Necesarios, perdidos y recuperables." In *Espacio público en la ciudad contemporánea: Perspectivas críticas sobre su gestión, su patrimonialización y su proyecto*, edited by Mireia Viladevall i Guasch and María A. Castrillo Romón, 115–24. Valladolid: Universidad de Valladolid, 2010.

Díaz Soto y Gama, Antonio. *La cuestión agraria en México*. Mexico City: UNAM, 1959.

Dorantes, Alma. *El conflicto universitario en Guadalajara 1933–1937*. Mexico City: Secretaría de Cultura del Gobierno de Jalisco-INAH, 1993.

———. "La llegada del evangelio Protestante." In *Los "otros" hermanos: Minorías religiosas Protestantes en Jalisco*, edited by Patricia Fortuny Loret de Mola, 41–84. Guadalajara: Editorial Agata, 2005.

———. "Primeras etapas del protestantismo en Jalisco." *Estudios Jaliscienses*, no. 24 (May 1996): 5–18.

Dorantes González, Alma, and Patricia Fortuny Loret de Mola. "El protestantismo histórico frente a una encrucijada." *Estudios Jaliscienses*, no. 39 (February 2000): 30–42.

Dormady, Jason H. "'Disobedience, rebelliousness, . . . and discontent': Parishioner/Clerical Disputes in Tepalcingo, Morelos, 1937–1946." *SCOLAS Journal* 1, no. 1 (2014).

——. *Primitive Revolution: Restorationist Religion and the Idea of the Mexican Revolution, 1940–1968*. Albuquerque: University of New Mexico Press, 2011.

Durand, Jorge. "El movimiento inquilinario, 1922." In *Demografía y urbanismo: Lecturas históricas de Guadalajara III*, edited by José María Muriá and Jaime Olveda, 447–65. Guadalajara: INAH, Gobierno del Estado de Jalisco, Universidad de Guadalajara, 1992.

——. "Siglo y medio en el camino de la industrialización." In *Guadalajara, la gran ciudad de la pequeña industria*, edited by Patricia Arias, 21–56. Zamora: El Colegio de Michoacán, 1985.

Dwyer, John J. *The Agrarian Dispute: The Expropriation of American-Owned Rural Land in Postrevolutionary Mexico*. Durham NC: Duke University Press, 2008.

Ege, Moritz, and Johannes Moser. Introduction to *Urban Ethics: Conflicts over the Good and Proper Life in Cities*, edited by Moritz Ege and Johannes Moser, 3–27. London: Routledge, 2021.

"El censo muestra resaltante progreso del automóvil en 1922." *El Automóvil Americano*, February 1923.

Escobar Hernández, Bogar. "Los cabarets prohibidos y la autoridad en Guadalajara, Jalisco, México." *Dialogo Andina*, no. 42 (2013): 105–15.

Espinosa, David. *Jesuit Student Groups, the Universidad Iberoamericana, and Political Resistance in Mexico, 1913–1979*. Albuquerque: University of New Mexico Press, 2014.

Fallaw, Ben. "'Anti-Priests' versus Catholic-Socialists." In *Faith and Impiety in Revolutionary Mexico*, edited by Matthew Butler, 203–24. New York: Palgrave, 2007.

——. *Cárdenas Compromised: The Failure of Reform in Postrevolutionary Yucatán*. Durham NC: Duke University Press, 2001.

——. *Religion and State Formation in Postrevolutionary Mexico*. Durham NC: Duke University Press, 2013.

——. "Varieties of Mexican Revolutionary Anticlericalism: Radicalism, Iconoclasm, and Otherwise, 1914–1935." *The Americas* 65, no. 4 (2009): 481–509.

Fernández Aceves, María Teresa. "Guadalajaran Women and National Identity." In *The Eagle and the Virgin: Nation and Cultural Revolution in Mexico, 1920–1940*, edited by Mary Kay Vaught and Stephen E. Lewis, 297–313. Durham NC: Duke University Press, 2006.

——. "José Guadalupe Zuno Hernández and the Revolutionary Process in Jalisco." In *State Governors in the Mexican Revolution, 1910–1952: Portraits in Conflict, Courage and Corruption*, edited by Jürgen Buchenau and William H. Beezley, 95–108. Lanham MD: Rowman and Littlefield, 2009.

———. "Mercado de trabajo y condiciones de empleo femenino en Guadalajara (1920–1940)." In *Vivir en Guadalajara*, edited by Carmen Castañeda, 245–73. Guadalajara: Ayuntamiento de Guadalajara, 1992.

———. *Mujeres en el cambio social en el siglo XX mexicano*. Mexico City: Siglo XXI, 2014.

———. "The Struggle between the 'Metate' and the 'Molinos de Nixtamal' in Guadalajara, 1920–1940." In *Sex in Revolution: Gender, Politics, and Power in Modern Mexico*, edited by Jocelyn Olcott, Mary Kay Vaughan, and Gabriela Cano, 147–61. Durham NC: Duke University Press, 2006.

Fernández Armesto, Felipe, ed. *The Oxford History of the World*. Oxford: Oxford University Press, 2023.

Fiore, Robert L. *Drama and Ethos: Natural-Law Ethics in Spanish Golden Age Theater*. Lexington: University Press of Kentucky, 1975.

Florescano, Enrique. *Imágenes de la patria a través de los siglos*. Mexico City: Taurus, 2005.

Foment, Carlos. "Selfhood and Nationhood in Latin America: From Colonial Subject to Democratic Citizen." In *Empire to Nation: Historical Perspectives on the Making of the Modern World*, edited by Joseph W. Esherick, Hasan Kayali, and Eric Van Young, 106–33. Lanham MD: Rowman and Littlefield, 2006.

Fortuna, Carlos. "La ciudad de los sonidos: Una heurística de la sensibilidad en los paisajes urbanos contemporáneos." *Cuadernos de Antropología Social*, no. 30 (2009): 39–58.

Fortuny Loret de Mola, Patricia. *Los "otros" hermanos: Minorías religiosas Protestantes en Jalisco*. Guadalajara: Editorial Agata, 2005.

Fregoso Centeno, Anayanci. "Dolores Palomar Arias: 1898–1972, La familia y la religión en la construcción del sujeto." In *Siete historias de vida: Mujeres jaliscienses del siglo XX*, edited by Anayanci Fregoso Centeno, 41–66. Guadalajara: Editorial Universitaria–Universidad de Guadalajara, 2006.

———, ed. *Siete historias de vida: Mujeres jaliscienses del siglo XX*. Guadalajara: Editorial Universitaria–Universidad de Guadalajara, 2006.

French, William E. *The Heart in the Glass Jar: Love Letters, Bodies, and the Law in Mexico*. Lincoln: University of Nebraska Press, 2015.

———. "Imagining the Cultural History of Nineteenth-Century Mexico." *Hispanic American Historical Review* 79, no. 2 (May 1999): 249–67.

———. *A Peaceful and Working People: Manners, Morals, and Class Formation in Northern Mexico*. Albuquerque: University of New Mexico Press, 1996.

Fuentes, Pamela J. "Burdeles, prostitución y género a través de los procesos por lenocinio: Ciudad de México, década de 1940." In *Vicio, prostitución y delito: Mujeres transgresoras en los siglos XIX y XX*, edited by Elisa Speckman Guerra and Fabiola Bailón Vásquez, 227–56. Mexico City: Universidad Nacional Autónoma de México Instituto de Investigaciones Históricas, 2017.

Galindo González, Rosa María, Carlos Auner Medina Montejano, Cynthia Sarahi Martínez y Cota, and Martha Alicia Cortés Guzmán. "Las academias municipales: La formación técnica del siglo XXI para sobrevivir en México." Working paper distributed by the Organization of American States. Accessed April 7, 2025. https://recursos.educoas .org/publicaciones/las-academias-municipales-la-formaci-n-t-cnica-del-siglo-xxi-para -sobrevivir-en-m-xico.

García, Alberto. *Abandoning Their Beloved Land: The Politics of Bracero Migration in Mexico*. Oakland: University of California Press, 2023.

García, Jesús Zamora. *Ciudad en fuegos: La Unión del Pueblo en Guadalajara*. Guadalajara: Editorial Vavelia, 2007.

García Espinosa, Salvador. "Centros históricos ¿herencia del pasado o construcción del presente? Agentes detonadores de un nuevo esquema de ciudad." *Scripta Nova* 9, no. 194 (2005): 1–15.

García Rojas, Irma Beatriz. "Dos ciclos en la planeación urbana de Guadalajara." In *Vivir en Guadalajara*, edited by Carmen Castañeda, 161–76. Guadalajara: Ayuntamiento de Guadalajara, 1992.

Gauss, Susan M. *Made in Mexico: Regions, Nation, and the State in the Rise of Mexican Industrialism*. University Park: Penn State University Press, 2010.

Gil, Carlos B. *Life in Provincial Mexico: National and Regional History Seen from Mascota, Jalisco, 1867–1972*. Los Angeles: UCLA Latin American Centers Publications, 1983.

Gillingham, Paul. *Cuauhtémoc's Bones: Forging National Identity in Modern Mexico*. Albuquerque: University of New Mexico Press, 2011.

———. "Thoughts on Citizenship in Latin America, with Particular Reference to Mexico." *Mexican Studies/Estudios Mexicanos* 36, no. 1–2 (2020): 10–42.

———. *(Un)Revolutionary Mexico: The Birth of a Strange Dictatorship*. New Haven: Yale University Press, 2021.

Gillingham, Paul, and Benjamin T. Smith, eds. *Dictablanda: Politics, Work, and Culture in Mexico, 1938–1968*. Durham NC: Duke University Press, 2014.

Gilly, Adolfo. *The Mexican Revolution*. New York: New Press, 2005.

Goldsmit Brindis, Shulamit, et al. *Contento y descontento en Jalisco, Michoacán y Morelos, 1906–1911*. Mexico City: Universidad Iberoamericana, 1991.

Gomez, Rocio. *Silver Veins, Dusty Lungs: Mining, Water, and Public Health in Zacatecas, 1835–1946*. Lincoln: University of Nebraska Press, 2020.

Gómez-Galvarriato, Aurora. "Female Entrepreneurship as a Survival Strategy: Women during the Early Mechanisation of Corn Tortilla Production in Mexico City." *Continuity and Change* 35, no. 1 (2020): 75–103.

González de la Rocha, Mercedes. *Los recursos de la pobreza: Familias de bajos ingresos en Guadalajara*. Guadalajara: El Colegio de Jalisco, 1986.

González Navarro, Moisés. *Masones y cristeros en Jalisco*. Mexico City: El Colegio de México, 2000.

Greaves Lainé, Cecilia. "El México contemporáneo." In *La vida cotidiana en México*, edited by Pablo Escalante Gonzalbo et al., 241–78. Mexico City: El Colegio de México, 2010.

Greer, Thomas V. "An Analysis of Mexican Literacy." *Journal of Inter-American Studies* 11, no. 3 (July 1969): 466–76.

Gresores, Gabriela. "Mujeres de la colonia: Sostén invisible, principio ordenador e impulso dinámico." *Jornadas Interescuelas/Departamentos de Historia* (Universidad de Nacional Cuyo, Mendoza), 2013.

Gutiérrez, Ramón. "Mexican Masculinities." In *Masculinity and Sexuality in Modern Mexico*, edited by Victor Macías-Gonzáles and Anne Rubenstein, 262–72. Albuquerque: University of New Mexico Press, 2012.

Gutierrez González, Edmundo. "Intervenciones al paisaje urbano histórico de Guadalajara para el desarrollo económico." *Revista Gremium*, August 1, 2017. https://editorialrestauro.com.mx/.

Haddu, Miriam, and Niamh Thornton, eds. *Legacies of the Past: Memory and Trauma in Mexican Visual and Screen Cultures*. Edinburgh: Edinburgh University Press, 2020.

Hagerty, Bonnie M., J. Lynch-Sauer, K. L. Patusky, M. Bouwsema, and P. Collier. "Sense of Belonging: A Vital Mental Health Concept." *Archives of Psychiatric Nursing* 6, no. 3 (1992): 172–77.

Hart, Paul. *Bitter Harvest: The Social Transformation of Morelos, Mexico, and the Origins of the Zapatista Revolution, 1840–1910*. Albuquerque: University of New Mexico Press, 2005.

Hausermann, Heidi. "Unintended Developments: Gender, Environment, and Collective Governance in a Mexican Ejido." *Annals of the Association of American Geographers* 104, no. 4 (2014): 784–800.

Hayes, Joy Elizabeth. "National Imaginings on the Air: Radio in Mexico, 1920–1950." In *The Eagle and the Virgin: Nation and Cultural Revolution in Mexico, 1920–1940*, edited by Mary Kay Vaught and Stephen E. Lewis, 243–58. Durham NC: Duke University Press, 2006.

Hernández Chávez, Alicia. *Mexico: A Brief History*. Berkeley: University of California Press, 2006.

Hernández Galindo, Sergio. "Migración japonesa a Jalisco: De su ingreso a la concentración durante la Segunda Guerra Mundial." In *Presencia japonesa en Jalisco*, edited by Melba Falck Reyes, 107–36. Guadalajara: Universidad de Guadalajara, Centro de Estudios Japoneses, 2020.

Hernández Romero, Ramiro. "El jazz en México a mediados del siglo XX." *Revista Musical Chilena* 74, no. 233 (2020): 28–48.

Heron, Barbara. *Desire for Development: Whiteness, Gender, and the Helping Imperative*. Waterloo ON: Wilfrid Laurier University Press, 2007.

Hobsbawm, E. J. *Nations and Nationalism since 1780: Programme, Myth, Reality*. 2nd ed. Cambridge: Cambridge University Press, 1992.

Hodos, Jerome I. *Second Cities: Globalization and Local Politics in Manchester and Philadelphia*. Philadelphia: Temple University Press, 2011.

Honig, Bonnie. *A Feminist Theory of Refusal*. Cambridge MA: Harvard University Press, 2021.

Huffaker, Shauna. "Gendered Limitations of Women Property Owners: Three Women of Early Modern Cairo." *Hawwa* (Leiden) 10, no. 3 (2012): 127–50.

Hunefeldt, Christine. *Liberalism in the Bedroom: Quarreling Spouses in Nineteenth-Century Lima*. University Park: Penn State University Press, 2000.

Hutchison, Elizabeth Quay. *Labors Appropriate to Their Sex: Gender, Labor, and Politics in Urban Chile, 1900 to 1930*. Durham NC: Duke University Press, 2001.

Hyde, J. Keith. *Concepts of Power in Kierkegaard and Nietzsche*. Farnham, UK: Ashgate, 2010.

Ibáñez, Eduardo, and Daniel Vázquez. *Guadalajara: Un análisis urbano*. Guadalajara: Comisión de Coordinación Urbana del Valle de Guadalajara, 1970.

Ibarra Bellon, Araceli, and Alisa Lanczyner Reisel. "La Hermosa Provincia: Nacimiento y vida de una secta cristiana en Guadalajara." Master's thesis, Universidad de Guadalajara, 1972.

Ibarra Ibarra, Xóchitl, and Eduardo Moreno López. "Mercado de suelo y ciudad en el siglo XIX: La propiedad municipal en Guadalajara; El caso del cuartel V." In *Coloquio de historia urbana*, edited by Lucía González Torreros, 6–32. Guadalajara: Universidad de Guadalajara, 1996.

Isais Contreras, Miguel Ángel. "Alcoholismo, raza, y degeneración en Guadalajara a inicios de siglo XX." *Saberes* 3, no. 8 (July–December 2020): 75–98.

Islas Rivera, Víctor M., Eduardo Moctezuma Navarro, Salvador Hernández García, Martha Lelis Zaragoza, and Juan I. Ruvalcaba Martínez. *Urbanización y motorización en México*. Publicación técnica no. 362. Sanfandila: Instituto Mexicano de Transporte, 2011.

Jackson Albarrán, Elena. "Medicalizing Modern Motherhood in the Americas." *Journal of Women's History* 23, no. 2 (Summer 2021): 168–75.

Jacobs, Jane. *The Death and Life of Great American Cities*. New York: Vintage Books, 1992.

Jaffary, Nora E. "Sacred Defiance and Sexual Desecration: María Gertrudis Arévalo and the Holy Office in Eighteenth-Century Mexico." In *Sexuality and the Unnatural in Colonial Latin America*, edited by Zeb Tortorici, 43–57. Oakland: University of California Press, 2016.

Janz, Wes, and Bob Beckley. "Multivalence, Context, and Synthesis in Urban Design." *JAE* 36, no. 3 (Spring 1983): 7–13.

Jenks, Kelly L. "Becoming Vecinos: Civic Identities in Late Colonial New Mexico." In *New Mexico and the Pimería Alta: The Colonial Period in the American Southwest*, edited by John G. Douglass and William M. Graves, 213–38. Boulder: University Press of Colorado, 2017.

Jiménez, Christina M. *Making an Urban Public: Popular Claims to the City in Mexico, 1879–1932*. Pittsburgh: University of Pittsburgh Press, 2019.

Jiménez Pelayo, Agueda. "Las terratenientes de la Nueva Galicia en el siglo XVIII." In *La Mujer jalisciense: Clase, genero, y generación*, edited by Lucía Mantilla, 19–28. Guadalajara: Universidad de Guadalajara, 1989.

Joseph, Gilbert M., and Jürgen Buchenau. *Mexico's Once and Future Revolution: Social Upheaval and the Challenge of Rule since the Late Nineteenth Century*. Durham NC: Duke University Press, 2013.

Kapelusz-Poppi, Ana Maria. "Rural Health and State Construction in Post-Revolutionary Mexico: The Nicolaita Project for Rural Medical Services." *The Americas* 58, no. 2 (October 2001): 261–83.

Kemmis, Daniel. *Community and the Politics of Place*. Norman: University of Oklahoma Press.

Kennedy, John G. "El complejo del tesgüino: El rol de la bebida en la cultura tarahumara." In *Antropología del alcoholismo en México*, edited by E. Menéndez, 251–81. Mexico City: Centro de Investigaciones y Estudios Superiores en Antropología Social, 1991.

Kloppe-Santamaría, Gemma. *In the Vortex of Violence: Lynching, Extralegal Justice, and the State in Post-Revolutionary Mexico*. Oakland: University of California Press, 2020.

Knight, Alan. *Bandits and Liberals, Rebels and Saints: Latin America since Independence*. Lincoln: University of Nebraska Press, 2022. Kindle ed.

———. *The Mexican Revolution*. 2 vols. Lincoln: University of Nebraska Press, 1990.

Krauze, Enrique. *Mexico: Biography of Power; A History of Modern Mexico, 1810–1996*. New York: HarperCollins, 1997.

Kuznesof, Elizabeth. "The House, the Street and the Brothel: Gender in Latin American History." *History of Women in the Americas* 1, no. 1 (April 2013): 17–31.

Lau Jaiven, Ana. "Between These Boundaries: After Equal Rights for Women." *Política y Cultura*, no. 31 (2009): 235–55.

———. "La participación de las mujeres en la Revolución Mexicana: Juana Belén Gutiérrez de Mendoza (1875–1942)." *Diálogos* 5, no. 1–2 (2005).

———. "Todo tiene que ver con lo personal." In *Cada una desde su trinchera*, edited by Ana Lau Jaiven, 9–20. Mexico City: Programa Nacional de Las Mujeres, 2006.

Lau Jaiven, Ana, and Roxana Rodríguez Bravo. "El sufragio femenino y la Constitución de 1917: Una revisión." *Política y Cultura*, no. 48 (2017): 57–81.

Lavrin, Asunción. "In Search of the Colonial Woman in Mexico: The Seventeenth and Eighteenth Centuries." In *Latin American Women: Historical Perspectives*, edited by Asunción Lavrin, 23–59. Westport CT: Greenwood Press, 1978.

Leydet, Dominique. "Citizenship." In *The Stanford Encyclopedia of Philosophy*, Spring 2014 ed., edited by Edward N. Zalta. http://plato.stanford.edu/archives/spr2014/entries /citizenship.

Lockhart, James, and Enrique Otte. *Letters and People of the Spanish Indies: Sixteenth Century*. Cambridge: Cambridge University Press, 1976.

Lofland, John, and Rodney Stark. "Becoming a World-Saver: A Theory of Conversion to a Deviant Perspective." *American Sociological Review* 30, no. 6 (1965): 862–75.

López, Amanda M. "'An Urgent Need for Hygiene': Cremation, Class, and Public Health in Mexico City, 1879–1920." *Mexican Studies/Estudios Mexicanos* 31, no. 1 (Winter 2015): 88–124.

López Macedonio, Mónica Naymich. "Historia de una colaboración anticomunista transnacional." *Contemporánea: Historia y Problemas del Siglo XX* 1, no. 1 (2010): 133–58.

López Moreno, Eduardo. *La vivienda social: Una historia*. Puebla: Programa Editorial Red Nacional de Investigación Urbana, 1996.

Macías-González, Victor. "The Bathhouse and Male Homosexuality." In *Masculinity and Sexuality in Modern Mexico*, edited by Victor Macías-Gonzáles and Anne Rubenstein, 25–52. Albuquerque: University of New Mexico Press, 2012.

Maggi, Stefania, Aleck Ostry, Kristy Callaghan, Ruth Hershler, Lisa Chen, Amedeo D'Angiulli, and Clyde Hertzman. "Rural-Urban Migration Patterns and Mental Health Diagnoses of Adolescents and Young Adults in British Columbia, Canada: A Case-Control Study." *Child and Adolescent Psychiatry and Mental Health* 4, no. 1 (May 13, 2010).

Martínez Moctezuma, Lucia. "La actividad física de la comunidad rural: La YMCA en México durante la década de los años 20." *Revista Iberoamericana do Patrimônio Histórico-Educativo* 4, no. 1 (2018): 52–61.

Masters, Adrian. "A Thousand Invisible Architects: Vassals, the Petition and Response System, and the Creation of Spanish Imperial Caste Legislation." *Hispanic American Historical Review* 98, no. 3 (2018): 377–406.

Matute Remus, Jorge. "La ciudad en el siglo XX." In *Demografía y urbanismo: Lecturas históricas de Guadalajara III*, edited by José María Muriá and Jaime Olveda, 431–46. Mexico City: INAH, 1992.

McBride, George McCutchen. *The Land Systems of Mexico*. New York: American Geographical Society, 1923.

McIntyre, Kathleen. *Protestantism and State Formation in Postrevolutionary Oaxaca*. Albuquerque: University of New Mexico Press, 2019.

McLeod, James Angus. "Public Health, Social Assistance and the Consolidation of the Mexican State: 1888–1940." PhD diss., Tulane University, 1990.

McPhail, Elsie. *Juan Soriano y Lupe Marín: Retrato y/o autorretrato*. Mexico City: Siglo XXI, 2010.

McPhail Fanger, Elsie, and Ana Lau Jaiven. *Rupturas y continuidades: Historia y biografías de mujeres*. Mexico City: Universidad Autónoma Metropolitana, 2018.

Méndez Moreno, Carlos Domingo. *El anticlericalismo en Tabasco: Entre prácticas, símbolos y representaciones*. Morelia: Universidad Michoacana de San Nicolás de Hidalgo, 2016.

Mendiola, Sandra. *Street Democracy: Vendors, Violence, and Public Space in Late Twentieth-Century Mexico.* Lincoln: University of Nebraska Press, 2017.

Mendoza López, Miguel. "Causas más comunes de la mortalidad de los niños (1897)." In *Demografía y urbanismo: Lecturas históricas de Guadalajara III*, edited by José María Muriá and Jaime Olveda, 171–200. Mexico City: INAH, 1992.

Merleau-Ponty, Maurice. *The Phenomenology of Perception.* London: Routledge, 2005.

Meyer, Jean. "Catholic Resistance in 1930s Oaxaca." In *Faith and Impiety in Revolutionary Mexico*, edited by Matthew Butler, 185–202. New York: Palgrave, 2007.

———. *The Cristero Rebellion: The Mexican People between Church and State, 1926–1929.* Cambridge: Cambridge University Press, 1976.

Miranda Pacheco, Sergio. "Urbe inmunda: Poder y prejuicios socioambientales en la urbanización y desagüe de la ciudad y valle de México en el siglo XIX." In *De olfato: Aproximaciones a los olores den la historia de México*, edited by Élodie Dupuey García and Guadalupe Pinzón Ríos, 193–249. Mexico City: Fondo de Cultura Económica, 2020.

Mitchell, Stephanie. Introduction to *The Women's Revolution in Mexico, 1910–1953*, edited by Stephanie Mitchell and Patience A. Schell, 1–20. Lanham MD: Rowman and Littlefield, 2007.

Mitchell, Tim. *Intoxicated Identities: Alcohol's Power in Mexican History and Culture.* New York: Routledge, 2004.

Montserrat Degen, Monica, and Gillian Rose. "The Sensory Experiencing of Urban Design: The Role of Walking and Perceptual Memory." *Urban Studies* 49, no. 15 (November 1, 2012): 3271–87.

Morán Quiroz, Luis Rodolfo. "Percibir la ciudad en la vida cotidiana." In *La vida cotidiana: Prácticas, lugares y momentos*, edited by Genaro Zalpa and María Eugenia Patiño, 167–201. Aguascalientes: Universidad Autónoma de Aguascalientes, 2007.

Morfín, Guadalupe, and Margarita Sánchez Van Dyck. "Controles jurídicos y psicosociales en la producción de espacio urbano para sectores populares." In *Demografía y urbanismo: Lecturas históricas de Guadalajara III*, edited by José María Muriá and Jaime Olveda, 489–512. Mexico City: INAH, 1992.

Mraz, John. *History and Modern Media: A Personal Journey.* Nashville TN: Vanderbilt University Press, 2022.

———. "Mexican History in Photographs" In *The Mexico Reader*, edited by Gilbert M. Joseph and Timothy J. Henderson, 297–331. Durham NC: Duke University Press, 2002.

Muriá, José María. *Breve historia de Jalisco.* Mexico City: Fondo de Cultura Económica, 1995.

Muriá, José María, and Jaime Olveda, eds. *Demografía y urbanismo: Lecturas históricas de Guadalajara III*, Mexico City: INAH, 1992.

Museo Nacional de Arte. *Arqueología del régimen, 1919–1955.* Mexico City: Banamex, CONACULTA, INBA, 2003.

Nakasone, Takako, and Víctor Katsumi Yamaguchi Llanes. "Censo Nikkei de Guadalajara 2018." In *Presencia japonesa en Jalisco*, edited by Melba Falck Reyes, 137–70. Guadalajara: Universidad de Guadalajara, Centro de Estudios Japoneses, 2020.

Napolitano, Valentina. *Migration, Mujercitas, and Medicine Men: Living in Urban Guadalajara*. Berkeley: University of California Press, 2002.

Niblo, Stephen R. *Mexico in the 1940s: Modernity, Politics, and Corruption*. Wilmington DE: SR Books, 1999.

Nicoll, Fiona. *Gambling in Everyday Life: Spaces, Moments, and Products of Enjoyment*. New York: Routledge, 2019. Perlego ebook.

Núñez Becerra, Fernanda. "Mujeres públicas y consumidores privados, los clientes, esos desconocidos." In *Históricas Digital*, May 8, 2017. https://historicas.unam.mx/publicaciones /publicadigital/libros/vicio/671_04_07_Fernanda_Nunez_Becerra.pdf.

Ochoa, Margarita R. "Illicit Relations in a Multi-Ethnic City: Emotions, Fidelity, and Economic Obligations in Colonial Mexico." In *Courtship, Marriage, and Marriage Breakdown: Approaches from the History of Emotion*, edited by Andrea Thomson, Jeffrey Meek, and Katie Barclay. London: Taylor and Francis, 2019. Kindle ed.

O'Connor, Erin E. *Mothers Making Latin America: Gender, Households, and Politics since 1825*. Oxford: John Wiley & Sons, 2014.

Olcott, Jocelyn. *Revolutionary Women in Postrevolutionary Mexico*. Durham NC: Duke University Press, 2005.

Olivares, Omar. "¡A bañarse se ha dicho! Higienismo, olores y representaciones en la implantación de la ducha en el cambio del siglo XIX al XX en la Ciudad de México." In *De olfato: Aproximaciones a los olores den la historia de México*, edited by Élodie Dupuey García and Guadalupe Pinzón Ríos, 221–57. Mexico City: Fondo de Cultura Económica, 2020.

Oliver, Lilia V. "Los servicios de salud, el pensamiento ilustrado y la crisis agrícola de 1785– 1786." In *Demografía y urbanismo: Lecturas históricas de Guadalajara III*, edited by José María Muriá and Jaime Olveda, 53–78. Mexico City: INAH, 1992.

Orendain, Leopoldo I. "Salubridad e higiene." In *Demografía y urbanismo: Lecturas históricas de Guadalajara III*, edited by José María Muriá and Jaime Olveda, 79–88. Mexico City: INAH, 1992.

Orwell, George. *The Road to Wigan Pier*. New York: Harcourt and Brace, 1958.

Pajnik, Mojca, and Floya Anthias. "Migrant Work, Precarity and Agency." In *Work and the Challenges of Belonging: Migrants in Globalizing Economies*, edited by Mojca Pajnik and Floya Anthias, 1–8. Newcastle upon Tyne, UK: Cambridge Scholars, 2014.

Palacio Montiel, Celia. ". . . El vivir, mitad pueblerino, mitad ciudadano, en la urba luminosa y sonriente . . . La vida cotidiana en Guadalajara en la década de 1930." *Secuencia*, no. 80 (May–August 2011): 133–58.

Pallasmaa, Juhani. *The Eyes of the Skin*. Sussex, UK: Wiley & Sons, 2012.

Pani, Alberto J. *Hygiene in Mexico: A Study of Sanitary and Educational Problems*. New York: G. P. Putnam and Sons, 1916.

Pateman, Carol. *The Disorder of Women: Democracy, Feminism, and Political Theory*. Stanford CA: Stanford University Press, 1989.

Peña, Sergio. "Eminent Domain and Expropriation Laws: A Century of Urban and Regional Planning in Mexico." *Journal of Planning History* 20, no. 2 (2021): 157–75.

Pensado, Jaime M. *Love and Despair: How Catholic Activism Shaped Politics and the Counterculture in Modern Mexico*. Oakland: University of California Press, 2023.

Perahia, Raquel. "Las ciudades y su espacio público." Paper presented at the IX Coloquio Internacional de Geocrítica, Porto Alegre, Brazil, 2007. http://www.ub.edu/geocrit/9porto/perahia.htm.

Perez Verdía, Luís. *Historia particular del estado de Jalisco*. Guadalajara: Grafica Editorial, 1952.

Pierce, Gretchen. "Pulqueros, Cerveceros, and Mezcaleros: Small Alcohol Producers and Popular Resistance to Mexico's Anti-alcohol Campaigns, 1910–1940." In *Alcohol in Latin America: A Social and Cultural History*, edited by Gretchen Pierce and Áurea Toxqui, 161–84. Tucson: University of Arizona Press, 2014.

——. "Sobering the Revolution: Mexico's Anti-alcohol Campaigns and the Process of State Building, 1910–1940." PhD diss., University of Arizona, 2008.

Pierce, Gretchen, and Áurea Toxqui, eds. *Alcohol in Latin America: A Social and Cultural History*. Tucson: University of Arizona Press, 2014.

Pilcher, Jeffrey M. *¡Que vivan los tamales! Food and the Making of Mexican Identity*. Albuquerque: University of New Mexico Press, 1998.

Pizarro, Rafael. "Teaching to Understand the Urban Sensorium in the Digital Age: Lessons from the Studio." *Design Studies* 30, no. 3 (2009): 272–86.

Porter, Susie S. *From Angel to Worker: Middle-Class Identity and Female Consciousness in Mexico, 1890–1950*. Lincoln: University of Nebraska Press, 2018. Kindle ed.

——. *Working Women in Mexico City: Public Discourses and Material Conditions, 1879–1931*. Tucson: University of Arizona Press, 2003.

Pulido, Elisa. "Solving Schism in Nepantla: The Third Convention Returns to the LDS Fold." In *Just South of Zion: The Mormons in Mexico and Its Borderlands*, edited by Jason Dormady and Jared Tamez, 89–110. Albuquerque: University of New Mexico Press, 2015.

Pulido Esteva, Diego. "¡A su salud! Sociabilidades, libaciones y prácticas populares en la ciudad de México a principios del siglo XX." PhD thesis, El Colegio de México, 2012.

Quintana, Alejandro. *Maximino Ávila Camacho and the One-Party State: The Taming of Caudillismo and Caciquismo in Post-Revolutionary Mexico*. Lanham MD: Lexington Books, 2010.

Raby, David. *Educación y revolución social en México, 1921–1940*. Translated by Roberto Gómez Ciriza. Mexico City: SEP, 1974.

Ramírez, Daniel. *Migrating Faith: Pentecostalism in the United States and Mexico in the Twentieth Century.* Chapel Hill: University of North Carolina Press, 2015.

Ramírez Sáiz, Juan Manuel, and Patricia Safa Barraza. "Tendencias y retos recientes en tres metrópolis mexicanas: Ciudad de México, Guadalajara, y Monterrey." *Cuadernos de Antropología Social,* no. 30 (2009): 77–92.

Ramos Escandón, Carmen. "Challenging Legal and Gender Constraints in Mexico: Sofía Villa de Buentello's Criticism of Family Legislation, 1917–1927." In *The Women's Revolution in Mexico, 1910–1953,* edited by Stephanie Mitchell and Patience A. Schell, 56–72. Lanham MD: Rowman and Littlefield, 2007.

Rangel Silva, José Alfredo. "'Para reprimir a este difamador': Discursos públicos, valores y orden social en Guadalajara, México, 1885." *Hispanic American Historical Review* 97, no. 3 (August 2017): 457–84.

Rasmussen, Anthony William. "Resistance Resounds: Hearing Power in Mexico City." PhD diss., University of California, Riverside, 2017.

Rath, Thomas. "Camouflaging the State: The Army and the Limits of Hegemony in PRIísta Mexico, 1940–1960." In *Dictablanda: Politics, Work, and Culture in Mexico, 1938–1968,* edited by Paul Gillingham and Benjamin T. Smith, 89–107. Durham NC: Duke University Press, 2014.

Razo Zaragoza, José Luis. *Guadalajara.* Guadalajara: Secretaría General de Gobierno-Unidad Editorial, 1986.

Reich, Peter Lester. *Mexico's Hidden Revolution: The Catholic Church in Law and Politics since 1929.* Notre Dame IN: University of Notre Dame Press, 1995.

Rivière d'Arc, Hélène. *Guadalajara y su región: Influencias y dificultades de una metrópoli mexicana.* Translated by Carlos Montemayor and Josefina Anaya. Mexico City: Secretaría de Educación Pública, 1973.

Robles Ruvalcaba, Romina. "The Emergence of the Rancho and the Socioeconomic Transformation of the Caxcana, Jalisco, 1939–1959." PhD diss., University of Chicago, 2017.

Rodríguez Castillo, Luis. "Ver desde la calle: Trabajo infantil y vida cotidiana en la calle." *Estudios Jaliscienses,* no. 28 (May 1997): 35–52.

Ross, Karen. "Narratives of Belonging (and Not): Inter-Group Contact in Israel and the Formation of Ethno-National Identity Claims." *International Journal of Intercultural Relations* 42 (September 2014): 38–52.

Roybal, Karen R. *Archives of Dispossession: Recovering the Testimonios of Mexican American Herederas, 1848–1960.* Chapel Hill: University of North Carolina Press, 2017.

Rubenstein, Anne. *Bad Language, Naked Ladies, and Other Threats to the Nation: A Political History of Comic Books in Mexico.* Durham NC: Duke University Press, 2001.

Ruble, Blair A. "Living Apart Together: The City, Contested Identity, and Democratic Transitions." In *Composing Urban History and the Constitution of Civic Identities,* edited by John J. Czaplicka and Blair A. Ruble, 1–24. Baltimore: Johns Hopkins University Press, 2003.

Ruíz, María Teresa, Ricardo Ávila, and Bogar Escobar. "Una historiografía 'petrificada.'" *Estudios del Hombre*, no. 6 (1997): 61–77.

Ruiz Razura, Adriana. "El convento de San Agustín." *Estudios Jaliscienses*, no. 115 (February 2019): 27–44.

———. *La Casa Cañedo: Un palacio en Guadalajara*. Guadalajara: Universidad de Guadalajara, 2020.

Russell, Peter L. *The History of Mexico*. New York: Routledge, 2010.

Sable, Martin H. *Latin American Urbanization: A Guide to the Literature, Organizations and Personnel*. Metuchen NJ: Scarecrow Press, 1971.

Salazar Cruz, Clara Eugenia. *Espacio y vida cotidiana en la ciudad de México*. Mexico City: El Colegio de México, 1999.

Sánchez Gómez, Rodolfo. "Esbozo histórico del transporte." In *Demografía y urbanismo: Lecturas históricas de Guadalajara III*, edited by José María Muriá and Jaime Olveda, 389–419. Mexico City: INAH, 1992.

Sánchez Susarrey, Jaime, and Ignacio Medína Sánchez. *Jalisco desde la Revolución: Historia Política, 1940–1975*. Guadalajara: Universidad de Guadalajara, 1987.

Sánchez Van Dyck, Margarita. "Le phenomène du fractionnement populaire à Guadalajara." PhD thesis, Ecole des Hautes Etudes en Sciences Sociales, 1979.

Saragoza, Alex. "The Selling of Mexico: Tourism and the State, 1929–1952." In *Fragments of a Golden Age*, edited by Gilbert Joseph, Anne Rubenstein, and Eric Zolov, 91–115. Durham NC: Duke University Press, 2001.

Schell, Patience. "Of the Sublime Mission of Mothers of Families: The Union of Mexican Catholic Ladies in Revolutionary Mexico." In *The Women's Revolution in Mexico, 1910–1953*, edited by Stephanie Mitchel and Patience A. Schell, 99–124. Lanham MD: Rowman and Littlefield, 2007.

Secretaría de Gobernación. *Seis años de gobierno al servicio de México, 1934–1940*. Mexico City: La Nacional Impresora, S.A., 1940.

Secretaría de la Economía Nacional. *Estados Unidos Mexicanos, VI Censo de Población, 1940, Jalisco*. Mexico City: Dirección General de Estadística, 1943.

Serrano Álvarez, Pablo. *La batalla del espíritu: El movimiento sinarquista en el Bajío (1932–1951)*. Mexico City: CONACULTA, 1992.

Sjölinder, Marie. "Spatial Cognition and Environmental Descriptions." In *Exploring Navigation: Towards a Framework for Design and Evaluation of Navigation in Electronic Spaces*, edited by Nils Dahlbäck. Kista: Swedish Institute of Computer Science, 1998.

Sluis, Ageeth. *Deco Body, Deco City: Female Spectacle and Modernity in Mexico City, 1900–1939*. Lincoln: University of Nebraska Press, 2016.

Smith, Benjamin. "Anticlericalism, Politics, and Freemasonry in Mexico, 1920–1940." *The Americas* 65, no. 4 (2009).

———. "Building a State on the Cheap: Taxation, Social Movements, and Politics." In *Dictablanda: Politics, Work, and Culture in Mexico, 1938–1968*, edited by Paul Gillingham and Benjamin T. Smith, 255–71. Durham NC: Duke University Press, 2014.

———. "The Limits of Catholic Science and the Mexican Revolution." Paper presented at the Latin American Studies Association Conference, Toronto, Ontario, October 6–9, 2010.

———. *Pistoleros and Popular Movements: The Politics of State Formation in Postrevolutionary Oaxaca*. Lincoln: University of Nebraska Press, 2009.

———. *The Roots of Conservatism in Mexico: Catholicism, Society, and Politics in the Mixteca Baja, 1750–1962*. Albuquerque: University of New Mexico Press, 2012.

Smith, Bonnie K. *Women in World History, 1450 to Present*. London: Bloomsbury Academic Press, 2019.

Smith, Mark M. *Sensing the Past: Seeing, Hearing, Smelling, Tasting, and Touching in History*. Berkeley: University of California Press, 2007.

Smith, Stephanie J. *Gender and the Mexican Revolution: Yucatán Women and the Realities of Patriarchy*. Chapel Hill: University of North Carolina Press, 2009.

Solis, Yves. "Secret Archives, Secret Societies: New Perspectives on Mexico's Cristero Rebellion from the Vatican Secret Archive." In *Local Church, Global Church: Catholic Activism in Latin America from Rerum Novarum to Vatican II*, edited by Stephen J. C. Andes and Julia G. Young, 117–28. Washington DC: Catholic University of America Press, 2016.

Solís Hernández, Oliva, and Leticia Gómez Olmos. "María Antonieta Pacheco Gaytán: Una mujer empresaria en el mundo masculino." In *Seguir las huellas: Hacia el centenario del Primer Congreso Feminista 1916–2016*, edited by Gloria Tirado Villegas and Elva Vivera Gómez, 213–26. Puebla: Benemérita Universidad Autónoma de Puebla, 2015.

Soto Laveaga, Gabriela. "Science and Public Health in the Century of Revolution." In *Companion to Mexican History and Culture*, edited by William H. Beezley, 561–74. Hoboken NJ: Wiley, 2011.

Strohmayer, Ulf. "Engineering Vision in Early Modern Paris." In *The City and the Senses*, edited by Alexander Cowan and Jill Steward, 75–94. Aldershot, UK: Ashgate, 2007.

Tamayo, Jaime. "Movimiento obrero y lucha sindical." In *Guadalajara, la gran ciudad de la pequeña industria*, edited by Patricia Arias, 131–54. Zamora: El Colegio de Michoacán, 1985.

Tapia Tovar, Evangelina. "De gema a basura: Representaciones de la mujer en el bolero y sus implicaciones en la vida cotidiana." In *La vida cotidiana: Prácticas, lugares y momentos*, edited by Genaro Zalpa and María Eugenia Patiño, 133–65. Aguascalientes: Universidad Autónoma de Aguascalientes, 2007.

Tenorio Trillo, Mauricio. *I Speak of the City: Mexico City at the Turn of the Twentieth Century.* Chicago: University of Chicago Press, 2012.

Terry, T. Philip. *Terry's Guide to Mexico.* Boston: Rapid Service Press, 1947.

———. *Terry's Guide to Mexico: Handbook for Travelers.* Boston: Houghton Mifflin: 1910.

Thomson, Guy E. P. "The Ceremonial and Political Roles of Village Bands, 1846–1974." In *Rituals of Rule, Rituals of Resistance: Public Celebration and Popular Culture in Mexico,* edited by William Beezley, Cheryl English Martin, and William E. French, 307–42. Wilmington DE: SR Books, 1994.

Tompkins, Cynthia, and David William Foster. *Notable Twentieth-Century Latin American Women: A Biographical Dictionary.* Westport CT: Greenwood Press, 2001.

Toner, Deborah. *Alcohol and Nationhood in Nineteenth-Century Mexico.* Lincoln: University of Nebraska Press, 2015.

Torres Montes de Oca, J. Abelino. *Jalisco desde la Revolución: El comercio y su conformación, 1940–1987.* Guadalajara: Universidad de Guadalajara, 1987.

Toxqui, Áurea. "Breadwinners or Entrepreneurs: Women's Involvement in the *Pulquería* World of Mexico City, 1850–1910." In *Alcohol in Latin America: A Social and Cultural History,* edited by Gretchen Pierce and Áurea Toxqui, 104–30. Tucson: University of Arizona Press, 2014.

———. "Taverns and Their Influence in the Suburban Culture of Late-Nineteenth Century Mexico City." In *The Growth of Non-Western Cities: Primary and Secondary Urban Networking, c. 900–1900,* edited by Kenneth R. Hall. Latham MD: Rowman and Littlefield, 2011.

Tuan, Yi-Fu. *Space and Place: The Perspective of Experience.* Minneapolis: University of Minnesota Press, 1977.

Tuck, Jim. *The Holy War in Los Altos.* Tucson: University of Arizona Press, 1982.

Tuñon, Julia. *Mujeres: Entre la imagen y la acción.* Mexico City: CONACULTA, 2015.

Tutino, John. "Breaking New Spain, 1808–21: Remaking Power, Production, and Patriarchy before Iguala." *Mexican Studies/Estudios Mexicanos* 37, no. 3 (2021): 367–93.

———. *Mexico City, 1808: Power, Sovereignty, and Silver in an Age of War and Revolution.* Albuquerque: University of New Mexico Press, 2018.

Unikel, Luis. "Bibliografía sobre desarrollo urbano y regional en México." *Demografía y Economía* 6, no. 3 (1972): 377–408.

Urías Horcasitas, Beatriz. "De moral y regeneración: El programa de 'ingeniería social' posrevolucionario visto a trevés de las revistas masónicas mexicanas, 1930–1945." *Cuicuilco* 11, no. 32 (2004): 87–119.

Uribe Topete, Francisco Javier. "Los transportes de los tapatíos." In *Capítulos de historia de la ciudad de Guadalajara,* vol. 1, edited by Lina Rendón, 107–98. Guadalajara: Ayuntamiento de Guadalajara, 1992.

Urquidi, Víctor L. "El impuesto sobre la renta en el desarollo económico de México." In *El fracaso de la reforma fiscal de 1961*, edited by Víctor L. Urquidi, Luis Aboites Aguilar, and Mónica Unda Gutiérrez. Mexico City: El Colegio de México, 2011.

Vaca, Agustín, et al. *Historia de Jalisco: Tomo IV—Desde la consolidación del Porfiriato hasta mediados del siglo XX*. Guadalajara: UNED, 1982.

Valencia Islas, Arturo. "El impuesto sobre la renta en México, 1915–1941." Master's thesis, FCPyS-UNAM, 2011.

Valerio Ulloa, Sergio. "De Santander a Guadalajara: Los Somellera, empresarios del siglo XIX." *Estudios Jaliscienses*, no. 68 (May 2007): 44–59.

Van Pelt, Garrett. *Old Architecture of Southern Mexico*. Cleveland OH: J. H. Jansen, 1926.

Van Young, Eric. *Hacienda and Market in Eighteenth-Century Mexico: The Rural Economy of the Guadalajara Region, 1675–1820*. 2nd ed. Lanham MD: Rowman and Littlefield, 2006.

———. *The Other Rebellion: Popular Violence, Ideology, and the Mexican Struggle for Independence, 1810–1821*. Stanford CA: Stanford University Press, 2001.

———. "Urban Market and Hinterland: Guadalajara and Its Region in the Eighteenth Century." *Hispanic American Historical Review* 59, no. 4 (November 1979): 593–635.

Vaughan, Mary Kay. *Cultural Politics in Revolution: Teachers, Peasants, and Schools in Mexico, 1930–1940*. Tucson: University of Arizona Press, 1997.

Vázquez, Daniel. *Guadalajara: Ensayos de interpretación*. Guadalajara: El Colegio de Jalisco, 1989.

Venegas Álvarez, Sonia. *Presunciones y ficciones en el impuesto sobre la renta de las personas físicas en México*. Mexico City: Universidad Nacional Autónoma de México, 2007.

Vicente, Andrea. "Singleness and the State: Unmarried and Widowed Women in Guadalajara, Mexico, 1821–1910." PhD diss., University of Michigan, 2012.

Villa Pérez, Josefina Elizabeth. "Participación y movilizaciones ciudadanas como mecanismos de cohesión social en la frontera norte: Tijuana, 1942–1956." *Mexican Studies/Estudios Mexicanos* 36, no. 1–2 (2020): 97–126.

Villela Espinoza, María de Jesús, and Elena del Rosario Patiño Flota. "La equidad de género en el acceso a la propiedad de la tierra: Caso del ejido 'Benito Juárez,' municipio de Zacatecas." *Revista Iberoamericana de Producción Académica y Gestión Educativa*, no. 2 (July–December 2014): 1–12.

Viquiera Albán, Juan Pedro. *Propriety and Permissiveness in Bourbon Mexico*. Lanham MD: SR Books, 2004.

Voekel, Pamela. *Alone before God: The Religious Origins of Modernity in Mexico*. Durham NC: Duke University Press, 2002.

———. *For God and Liberty: Catholicism and Revolution in the Atlantic World, 1790–1861*. Oxford: Oxford University Press, 2022.

———. "Liberal Religion: The Schism of 1861." In *Religious Culture in Modern Mexico*, edited by Martin Austin Nesvig. Lanham MD: Rowman and Littlefield, 2007.

Walton, John. "Cultura y economía en la conformación de la vida urbana: Cuestiones generales y ejemplos latinoamericanos." In *Demografía y urbanismo: Lecturas históricas de Guadalajara III*, edited by José María Muriá and Jaime Olveda, 371–88. Mexico City: INAH, 1992.

———. *Elites and Economic Development: Comparative Studies on the Political Economy of Latin American Cities*. Austin: University of Texas Press, 1977.

———. "Guadalajara: Creating the Divided City." In *Metropolitan Latin America: The Challenge and the Response*, edited by Wayne A. Cornelius and Robert V. Kemper. New York: Sage, 1978.

Weber, Jonathan M. *Death Is All Around Us: Corpses, Chaos, and Public Health in Porfirian Mexico City*. Lincoln: University of Nebraska Press, 2019.

Weiner, Richard. *Race, Nation, and Market: Economic Culture in Porfirian Mexico*. Tucson: University of Arizona Press, 2004.

Weis, Robert. *For Christ and Country: Militant Catholic Youth in Post-Revolutionary Mexico*. Cambridge: Cambridge University Press, 2019.

———. "The Revolution on Trial: Assassination, Christianity, and the Rule of Law in 1920s Mexico." *Hispanic American Historical Review* 96, no. 2 (2016): 319–53.

Wheller, Jo. "Stench in Sixteenth-Century Venice." In *The City and the Senses*, edited by Alexander Cowan and Jill Steward, 25–38. Aldershot, UK: Ashgate, 2007.

Will, Martina. *Death and Dying in New Mexico*. Albuquerque: University of New Mexico Press, 2007.

Wright-Rios, Edward. *Revolutions in Mexican Catholicism*. Durham NC: Duke University Press, 2009.

Zafra Oropeza, Aurea. *La mujer en la historia de Jalisco*. Guadalajara: UNED, 1984.

Zárate Weber, David. "Las vías sacras de Guadalajara." *Estudios Jaliscienses*, no. 115 (February 2019): 6–26.

Zardini, Mirko, ed. *Sense of the City: An Alternate Approach to Urbanism*. Montreal: Canadian Centre for Architecture; Zurich: Lars Müller, 2005.

Index

Page numbers in italics refer to illustrations.

Hirata Aoki, María, 148–49

hospitals, 62, 100, 106, 146; Alcalde, 88–89; Belén, 116; Civil, 10

hygiene, 36–37, 94, 146, 157, 202n85, 203n106; celebrations, 119–20; for class and social control, 45, 55–57, 71; museum of, 37; and reducing human contact, 60–61; used to attack opponents, 31, 97–98, 104, 106, 109–10, 113–14, 115–21, 123, 125–26

identity, limitations of, 12–13

Iglesia Apostólica de Fe en Cristo, 121–22

Iglesia Católica Apostólica Mexicana (ICAM), 101

Iglesia Episcopal Mexicana, 105–13, 126, 204n123, 205n143

Iglesia Luz del Mundo (La Iglesia del Dios Vivo, Columna y Apoyo de la Verdad, La Luz del Mundo), 47, 120–22, 126, 205n145

illness, 8, 33, 56, 59, 72, 93, 116

import substitution industrialization (ISI), 156

improvisation in urban life, 19–20, 158, 170, 172

industry, 43–44, 53, 130, 138, 140, 165, 179, 214n37; groups in urban planning, 26; small, 39, 49–51, 54, 172; and women, 44

infrastructure: electricity, 21, 41, 46, 49, 151; paving and streets, 26, 29, 36, 57, 60–62, 64, 89, 117, 137, 143, 156; sewer and drainage, 21–23, 26, 55, 57–59, 66, 98, 144, 156, 173, 177, 182, 192n103; sidewalks, 10, 36, 38–39, 41, 61, 63–65, 80, 142, 167, 169; streets, widening, 32, 41, 60–61, 90, 130–32, 141, 176, 180, 206n5; water lines and access, 10, 21–23, 26, 36, 52–55, 57–59, 81, 98, 116–17, 119, 143,

144–45, 146–48, 152, 164, 173, 176–77, 182, 192n103, 210n59

Iñíguez de Parra, Virginia, 137–38

inspectors, 27, 57, 79, 121, 129, 143–44, 149, 151, 171; of drinking establishments, 18; and morality, 30, 95; and senses, 53–56; and sex work, 82–84

Jacobs, Jane, 19, 38

Jalisco: attorney general of, 86; courts of, 105, 122, 151, 179; Departamento de Trabajo y Previsión Social of, 191n72, 191n75; and disagreements with federal government, 20–21; governors of, 20–22, 26–27, 48–49, 90, 94–95, 99, 100, 105, 111–12, 117, 119, 146, 157, 174, 178, 179, 181; literacy rate of, 17; politicians of, and women, 137, 143, 146–47; state congress of, 23, 48, 105, 149; urban planning by, 22–25, 107, 126, 174, 178–79

Japanese immigrants, 146, 148–49

Jewish community, 50, 191n72

Jiménez, Maclovia, 146

Jiménez, María Guadalupe, 146

Jimenéz, María Guadalupe Vda. de, 46–47

Juárez, Benito, 99, 110, 160

juntas vecinales (juntas de vecinos), 26, 103, 110, 113, 115, 122, 199n34

Lake Chapala, 35

Landeros, J. Jesús, 15, 23

Lange, Hilda, 149–50

Lara, José, 84

Larios, Isidro, 141–42

Larios, Marcial, 141–42

Larios de Arocha, Micaéla, 141–42

La Soledad (Templo de Nuestra Señora de la Soledad) church, 105–7

M. Vda. de Ramírez, Concepción, 149

Printzen, Ernesto, 61–62
private property as public space, 157–58
private-public partnerships, 23
property networks, women's, 138–41
Protestants: alignment of, with liberalism, 103, 105–7; arrival of, in Guadalajara, 8, 31, 104, 200n47; belonging in society, 8, 31, 75, 97–98, 104–6, 122, 125; intra-congregational divisions of, 120–22; literature of, 102, 104; state regulation of, 122–23, 125–27; violence against, 8
Puebla, 13, 21, 28, 55

Quezada Vda. de González, Elvira, 65
Quijas, Marina, 147

Raquel, Mrs. 82–83
R. de Prado, Inés, 78–79
Refugio Barrera, María, 152
Refugio Barrera, Natalia, 152
regidores, 36–37, 119, 162, 178, 179
rental properties: for businesses, 91, 131, 133; *casas de departamentos* and *vecindades* as, 50, 69, 81, 120, *164*; houses as, 84, 139–40; ownership of, and women, 142–46, 158, 162, 164–65, 173, 207n15; for schools, 145–46, 186n70, 190n39, 192n103, 199n30, 211n69
Revolution of 1910: belonging and, 6, 8, 31, 182; consequences and influence of, 3–4, 19, 51, 56, 59, 65, 67, 82, 85, 93–94, 180; religion and, 97, 99, 101, 106, 109, 117, 125; shaping urban development, 3, 5, 14, 29–30, 36–37, 70, 73, 75, 84, 86, 91, 96, 129; and women, 134, 147, 154–55, 157, 163
Ríos, Modesta, 69–70, 72
rituals of belonging, 9, 13, 28, 38, 47, 127, 129, 153, 161, 172, 182

Rivas, Leonor, 43
Rivera, Felicitas, 69–70, 72
Robledo, Juan de Dios, 48
Robredo, José N., 110–15, 201n69
Rodrígues, Abel, 92
Rotonda de Hombres Ilustres (Rotonda de Jalisciences Ilustres), 107
Ruíz, Concepción, 69–70, 72
rural life, boredom of, 86–88
Ruvalcaba, Constanza, 86

sacred space, 3, 31, 98, 107–8, 121, 125
Saldaña Ruiz, Clotilde, 57
San Agustín church, 90
Sánches Araiza, Luis, 88
Sánchez, María Isabel, 54
Sánchez de Montaño, Fidela, 63–64
Sánchez Olea, Juan, 161
Sánchez Pareja, Eusebio, 116
San Francisco de Asís church, 107, *108*, 204n125
San José de Analco church, 85, 107, *108*, 148
San Juan de Dios church, 107, *108*
San Juan de Dios market, 42
San Miguel de Espiritu Santo church, 139
Santa Maria CA, 141
Santa María de Gracia church, 105
Santamaría de Nachtigal, Luz, 41
Santillán, Reynaldo, 120
schools, 82, 89, 90, 91, 94, 100, 101–2, 116, 118–19, 140; rental properties for, 145–46, 186n70, 190n39, 192n103, 199n30, 211n69
Sección de Información y Quejas, 177
Sector Hidalgo, 10, 11, 51, 55, 137, 149
Sector Juárez, 11, 81, 137, 152
Sector Libertad, 10, 11, 91, 137
Sector Reforma, 11, 50, 51, 83, 131, 137, 142
sexuality, 69–70, 79–80, 81

IN THE CONFLUENCIAS SERIES

To order or obtain more information on these or other University of Nebraska
Press titles, visit nebraskapress.unl.edu.

www.ingramcontent.com/pod-product-compliance
Lightning Source LLC
Chambersburg PA
CBHW020343270326
41926CB00007B/296